Labour and Christianity in the Mission

Series information:

RELIGION IN TRANSFORMING AFRICA
ISSN 2398-8673

Series Editors
Barbara Bompani, Joseph Hellweg, Ousmane Kane and **Emma Wild-Wood**

Editorial Reading Panel
Robert Baum (Dartmouth College)
Dianna Bell (University of Cape Town)
Ezra Chitando (University of Zimbabwe)
Martha Frederiks (Utrecht University)
Paul Gifford (SOAS)
David M. Gordon (Bowdoin College)
Jörg Haustein (University of Cambridge)
Paul Lubeck (Johns Hopkins University-SAIS)
Philomena Mwaura (Kenyatta University, Nairobi)
Hassan Ndzovu (Moi University)
Ebenezer Obadare (University of Kansas)
Abdulkader I. Tayob (University of Cape Town)
M. Sani Umar (Northwestern University)
Stephen Wooten (University of Oregon)

Series description
The series is open to submissions that examine local or regional realities on the complexities of religion and spirituality in Africa. Religion in Transforming Africa will showcase cutting-edge research into continent-wide issues on Christianity, Islam and other religions of Africa; Traditional beliefs and witchcraft; Religion, culture & society; History of religion, politics and power; Global networks and new missions; Religion in conflict and peace-building processes; Religion and development; Religious rituals and texts and their role in shaping religious ideologies and theologies. Innovative, and challenging current perspectives, the series provides an indispensable resource on this key area of African Studies for academics, students, international policy-makers and development practitioners.

Please contact the Series Editors with an outline or download the proposal form at www.jamescurrey.com.

Dr Barbara Bompani, Reader in Africa and International Development, University of Edinburgh: b.bompani@ed.ac.uk
Dr Joseph Hellweg, Associate Professor of Religion, Department of Religion, Florida State University: jhellweg@fsu.edu
Professor Ousmane Kane, Prince Alwaleed Bin Talal Professor of Contemporary Islamic Religion & Society, Harvard Divinity School: okane@hds.harvard.edu
Dr Emma Wild-Wood, Senior Lecturer, African Christianity and African Indigenous Religions, University of Edinburgh: emma.wildwood@ed.ac.uk

Previously published titles in the series are listed at the back of this volume.

Labour and Christianity in the Mission

African Workers in Tanganyika and Zanzibar, 1864–1926

MICHELLE LIEBST

JAMES CURREY

James Currey
is an imprint of
Boydell & Brewer Ltd
PO Box 9, Woodbridge
Suffolk IP12 3DF (GB)
www.jamescurrey.com
and of
Boydell & Brewer Inc.
668 Mt Hope Avenue
Rochester, NY 14620-2731 (US)
www.boydellandbrewer.com

© Michelle Liebst, 2021
First published in hardback 2021
Paperback edition 2024

All Rights Reserved. Except as permitted under current legislation no part of this work may be photocopied, stored in a retrieval system, published, performed in public, adapted, broadcast, transmitted, recorded or reproduced in any form or by any means, without the prior permission of the copyright owner

The right of Michelle Liebst to be identified as
the author of this work has been asserted in accordance with
sections 77 and 78 of the Copyright, Designs and Patents Act 1988

The publisher has no responsibility for the continued existence or accuracy of URLs for external or third-party internet websites referred to in this book, and does not guarantee that any content on such websites is, or will remain, accurate or appropriate

British Library Cataloguing in Publication Data
A catalogue record for this book is available from the British Library

ISBN 978-1-84701-275-3 (James Currey hardback)
ISBN 978-1-84701-371-2 (James Currey paperback)

Contents

	List of Illustrations	vii
	List of Abbreviations	ix
	Note on Language and Glossary	xi
	Acknowledgements	xiii
	Introduction: Rethinking Missions as Places of Work	1
1	Missionary Authority in Late Precolonial Magila, 1867–87	33
2	Building the Slave Market Church in Zanzibar, 1864–1900	75
3	Slave Status and the Mission Boys' School in Zanzibar, 1864–c.1930	101
4	Raising 'Mbweni Girls' in Zanzibar, 1864–c.1926	127
5	Domestic Service in Magila and Zanzibar, 1864–c.1930	147
	Conclusion	183
	Appendix 1: Chronology of UMCA Founding	191
	Appendix 2: General Chronology for Zanzibar and Magila	192
	Appendix 3: African Power-brokers and the Mission Elite	192
	Appendix 4: Bishops of the UMCA	193
	Appendix 5: Other Significant UMCA Missionaries	193
	Bibliography	195
	Index	219

Illustrations

Figure

1 Signpost near Korogwe, 18 August 2014   149

Tables

1 Adult ex-slave trajectories, Mbweni, 1874–77   87
2 Adult converts, Mbweni shamba, 1885–99   88
3 Students at Kiungani school, 1864–1901   110
4 Kiungani adults, 1890–99   110
5 Kiungani student life trajectories   121
6 Percentages indicate life trajectories of male ex-slave Kiungani students, 1890   122
7 Wages for cooks, c.1930   174

Abbreviations

CMS	Church Missionary Society. Founded in 1799.
MTD	Maria Theresa Dollar(s).
ZNA	Zanzibar National Archives.
SPG	Society for the Propagation of the Gospel in Foreign Parts. Established in 1701.
UMArch	Universities' Mission to Central Africa archive. These are held at the Bodleian in Oxford and usually referred to as the 'USPG archive'.
UMCA	Universities' Mission to Central Africa. Formed in 1858 as the 'Oxford and Cambridge Mission to Central Africa'.
USPG	United Society for the Propagation of the Gospel. Formed in 1965 to combine the UMCA and SPG.

Note on Language and Glossary

The majority of Swahili words have prefixes and suffixes. Four noun prefixes are common and used in this book. These signify:

Prefix	Meaning	Example 1	Example 2
Wa-	People	'*Wazigua*', meaning the Zigua people	'*Waungwana*', meaning people who are civilised
M-	A person	'*Mzigua*', meaning a person	'*Mwungwana*', meaning a person who is civilised
Ki-	A language or culture	'*Kizigua*', meaning the language of the Zigua people	n/a
U-	A place or abstraction of a noun	'*Uzigua*', which refers to the place in which the Zigua people live	'*Ungwana*', meaning 'civilisation'

These prefixes are not always consistent. For example, while '*Uzigua*' is a place, the place of the Bondei people is referred to without any prefix as Bonde, which also means 'valley'. The words listed below have been mentioned more than once in this book; other words are translated as and when they are mentioned.

Boi	Domestic servant
Dawa	Medicine
Desturi	Custom
Dhobi	Laundry work
Fingo, (pl. *mafingo*)	Charm(s) or amulets, worn on a person for protection against disease or witchcraft
Galo	Bondei version of jando
Heshima	Honour, respectability
Jando	Male youth initiation
Kanzu	A white or cream coloured ankle or floor length robe worn by men

Kibarua, (pl. *vibarua*)	Day labourer(s)
Kisibau, (pl. *visibau*)	Waitcoat(s)
Kungwi, (pl. *makungwi*)	Initiation leader(s), usually elder(s)
Mjoli, (pl. *wajoli*)	Fellow slave(s)
Mshenzi (pl. *washenzi*)	Uncivilised, primitive, pagan, upcountry person/people
Mswahili, (pl. *waswahili*)	'Swahili' had an ethnic connotation as it referred to non-Arab people, who were often slaves but elsewhere 'Swahili' implied high social status and a departure from slave status or '*ushenzi*'.
Mtumwa (pl. *watumwa*)	Slave(s), servant(s)
Mwenyeji, (pl. *wenyeji*)	Local, indigenous person
Mwungwana (pl. *waungwana*)	Civilised, urban, Muslim(s)
Mzee (pl. *wazee*)	Elder(s)
Mzungu, (pl. *wazungu*)	White person, European(s)
Nyika	Forest; uninhabited, uncultivated land
Pepo (pl. *mapepo*)	Wind, heaven, spirit, demon(s)
Shamba	Plantation, garden
Uboi	The state of being a domestic servant
Unyago	Female youth initiation
Ustaarabu	Culture, civilisation
Utumwa	Slavery
Wali, liwali	A governor. In the late precolonial era they were the Sultan's representatives. Later, German colonialists appointed *liwali* to work on the administration at district headquarters.

Acknowledgements

There are several historians who I owe for making this book possible. I would first like to express my sincerest appreciation to Felicitas Becker, who guided me intellectually through the research and writing process. Her insights, care and enthusiasm have made producing this book a stimulating and enjoyable experience. I am also indebted to Emma Hunter and David Maxwell for providing invaluable feedback. And it was Benedetta Rossi who not only implored me to submit a book proposal, but who also gave me the confidence to keep going. I may not have ever pursued an academic career in the first place, had it not been for the early encouragement of Richard Drayton, Toby Green, Anne Goldgar, Ludmilla Jordanova and Ian McBride at King's College London History Department.

I incurred an inordinate debt to my exceptional Swahili teachers: Yussuf Hamadi and Donavon McGrath. Their humour, energy and skilful teaching inspired and encouraged me to attempt to speak *Kiswahili sanifu*, much to the amusement of Tanzanian interlocutors. Swahili proficiency was crucial to my fieldwork, which challenged my assumptions and shaped the broader research questions with which I am still grappling. My gratitude for the patience and forbearance of my research assistants and hosts is impossible to adequately express. Zuhura Mohammed, who once had my only pair of shoes fixed without me even asking her to, was extremely kind to me. I must also thank Mohammed, my driver who occasionally doubled up as kitchen assistant and bought me barbequed *mahindi* from the side of the road because he knew it was my favourite local delicacy. Irene Mashasi, who welcomed me into her home and taught me how to make *chapatti*, was a wonderfully cheerful presence during my research in Zanzibar. Elias Mutani provided invaluable guidance, translations and even agreed to conduct some research by himself with old and new respondents.

In Tanzania, my hosts, Joel Makame in Msalabani, Baba Mbuji in Korogwe and Joyce Mbuji in Handeni, were beyond generous with their space, knowledge and sustenance. The people we interviewed were so giving with their time and memories and I thank them for welcoming us into their homes and patiently answering our questions and sharing their knowledge. In particular,

I would like to thank John Mhina, Antony Mabundo, John Selemani, Durham Kaleza, Vincent Semkuruto, Mayble Mzimba, Angelina Diwi, Josephine Mungayao and Sylvester Tayari for being such a pleasure to talk to and for their historical insights. Meanwhile, my wonderful father Mike and brother David would always lend me an ear and I could not have done this project without their help. Nicola Colangelo was a source of calm, fun and memorable life advice during the fieldwork.

I am immensely grateful to my step-father Alan Montgomery, who has always offered valuable critique and encouraged me to take breaks. Justine Willis and Sacha Hepburn also offered encouraging and constructive comments on portions of this work. I would also like to thank the countless people I have listened to and met at conferences and workshops. In particular, the following have given comments and contributions, either in person or via correspondence: James Brennan, Tom Cunningham, Christine Deslaurier, Shane Doyle, James Giblin, Sarah Longair, George Roberts, Dan Paget, Morgan Robinson, Stephen Rockel, Rachel Taylor, Justin Willis and Katharina Zöller to name a few. I must add a special thanks to Matthew Hopper and Emma Wild-Wood for their exceptionally kind encouragement and advice.

In addition, I would like to acknowledge the institutions that made my research and writing possible. Funding came from the following sources: Economic and Social Sciences Council (ESRC), Cambridge Home and EU Scholarship Scheme, ESRC Discretionary Fund, Holland Rose Studentship, Ellen McArthur Fund, Dr Lightfoot Fund, Royal Historical Society, Members' History Fund, Prince Consort Fund, Trinity Hall Travel Award, Fieldwork Funds, United Africa Company (UAC) of Nigeria and Smuts Memorial Fund (managed by the University of Cambridge in memory of Jan Christiaan Smuts).

This process would have been unimaginable without the Cambridge-born friendships of Pauline Kiesow, Ilesha Malhotra, Chris Wilson, David Lamoureux, Edoardo Andreoni, Ella Hollowood, Farhan Samanani, Gili Gurel, Jon Green, Josh Prichard and Rhys Jones. The friendship and laughter of Keli Hollidge and Valentina Kristensen were equally essential. There are other important members of my family not already mentioned who provided me with general emotional support. My mother Flo was always on the other end of the phone and I am grateful to her for taking such steadfast pride in me. My son Kasper has kept me smiling and entertained throughout the publishing process. Finally, my partner Luke has been a constant source of indispensable patience, love and support and it is to him that I dedicate this book.

Introduction: Rethinking Missions as Places of Work

In East Africa in the mid- to late-nineteenth century, missionaries demanded a range of skilled and unskilled workers, including builders, cooks, water-fetchers, porters and servants, in order to establish an ideal setting for their core aims: the conversion of souls and eventual establishment of an African ministry. As a result, Christian missionaries, who often arrived in Africa ahead of European colonisation, were some of the first Europeans to try and control African workers. The scarcely studied work of building churches, cleaning dishes and cooking meals is the basis of this labour history of Christian mission. By following the livelihood struggles of the African workers at the mission, many of whom had recently emerged from a background of slavery, this study explores the ways Africans made a living within the mission, as well as how they drew upon and adapted knowledge and networks from the mission to make a living elsewhere.

This study shows how joining the mission community meant gaining a patron, which could be a valuable asset for socially marginal people, such as slaves or former slaves. However, being in the mission community could feel oppressive, and did not necessarily secure an improved social or economic position. In fact, some found themselves re-marginalised as social hierarchies in the mission were challenging to negotiate. Moreover, becoming a mission employee, particularly a teacher, could mean a reduction in options as missionaries monopolised the recruitment of this occupation, especially in Tanganyika and Zanzibar, where government schools were rare until the 1930s. Missionaries offered very little in material terms and so the question is how African Christians and ex-slaves chose to negotiate their position, rather than if the mission was capable of transforming their wealth and status. Ultimately, it was up to the African convert or ex-slave to attempt to do this within the bounds of their available choices. In some cases, with the pursuit of status and that of wages at odds, conversion and the adoption of a mission-centred career was a high-risk life strategy.

The book investigates the variety of labour arrangements in the Anglican Universities' Mission to Central Africa (UMCA) in Tanzania and Zanzibar and reveals the interwoven strategies of missionary and African workers. In this context, it is striking that missionaries referred to themselves as 'workers' and to the African teachers and priests as 'helpers'. In contemporary developmentalism, a similar undervaluing of African workers is evident in the narrow conception of Africans as 'beneficiaries', rather than as workers who in fact make development possible.[1] This further underlines the importance of rethinking the way Africans engaged with mission, not as beneficiaries of humanitarian philanthropy, but as workers without whom there would be no Christian missions.

The African respondents to my research enquiries, most of whom were descendants of the African Christians I studied, had little recollection of Africans successfully making a living in the mission or from the missionaries. Their memories, strongly influenced by the experiences of the British colonial period, seemed hardly to consider teaching in mission schools as a way in which to make a livelihood. I quickly discovered that priests' donations and teachers' wages were never enough to fully support them and their families. Often, missionary employees supplemented their income with agriculture or, occasionally, commercial ventures, and sometimes used their association with the mission as leverage for other earning options. The written record corroborates this, as missionaries did not try to match other employers' wages, insisting that becoming a teacher should be a vocational choice demanding self-sacrifice.[2]

Historiographical context

In taking a labour history lens to the study of Christian mission, this study addresses two gaps in the literature. The first is in the field of Africa's labour history. From Frederick Cooper's analysis of the centrality of the political economy to the institution of slavery in Zanzibar, to Gareth Austin's finding that cash cropping was instrumental in facilitating the transition to wage labour in Ghana, significant bodies of research have focused on the history of slavery and wage labour.[3] However, more recently, scholars have pointed

---

[1] Benedetta Rossi, 'What "Development" Does to Work', *International Labor and Working-Class History,* 92 (ed 2017): 7–23.

[2] G. W. Broomfield, 'St Paul's High School, Kiungani', *Central Africa*, September 1926.

[3] Frederick Cooper, 'The Problem of Slavery in African Studies', *The Journal of African History,* 20, no. 1 (1 January 1979): 103–25; Gareth Austin, 'Cash Crops

out that labour history in Africa has neglected the forms of labour that lie between the extremes of chattel slavery and 'free' wage labour.[4] This greyer area encompasses most forms of labour in the world and is, therefore, greatly deserving of academic attention. Much headway has been made to this end. Research on 'voluntary' labour in the name of 'self-help' and/or civic duty is a case in point. Benedetta Rossi has shown how the so-called 'beneficiaries' of development projects in Niger accepted payment in food in return for their labour to avoid destitution.[5] Lacking the freedom to migrate for better labour conditions, these workers were usually women. Meanwhile, Emma Hunter has shown how the post-colonial Tanzanian state crafted the concept of 'virtuous citizenship' to legitimise 'voluntary' unpaid labour.[6] However, these studies all apply to the post-1930 period. Moreover, most of the labour history research has focused on commercial bodies and governments as employers, yet they were not the only European employers to attempt to control African labour.

The second gap relates to the scholarship on Christian missions, which usually presents missions as sites of religious conversion, education and healthcare. This narrow conception of a mission's activities reflects a broader problem in scholarship: that religion is thought of separately to socio-economic issues. Nonetheless, shifts are taking place to consider the role of missions more broadly. Scholars are increasingly connecting Christian missions to humanitarianism and developmentalism. In fact, NGOs, which are the institutions that most often come to mind when one thinks of 'development', were often built and dependent upon the ideological and logistical foundations of Christian missions. This observation raises an apparent paradox: that development, a symbol of science and this-worldly improvement, borrows heavily from other-worldly faith.[7] Equally, the thought of missions as places of work

---

and Freedom: Export Agriculture and the Decline of Slavery in Colonial West Africa', *International Review of Social History*, 54, no. 1 (April 2009): 1–37.

[4] Marcel van der van der Linden and Magaly Rodríguez García, 'Introduction', in *On Coerced Labor: Work and Compulsion after Chattel Slavery*, ed. Marcel van der Linden and Magaly Rodríguez García, Studies in Global Social History (Leiden, Netherlands; Boston, Massachusetts: Brill, 2016), 1–7.

[5] Benedetta Rossi, 'From Unfree Work to Working for Free: Labor, Aid, and Gender in the Nigerien Sahel, 1930–2000', *International Labor and Working-Class History*, 92 (ed 2017): 155–82.

[6] Emma Hunter, 'Voluntarism, Virtuous Citizenship, and Nation-Building in Late Colonial and Early Postcolonial Tanzania', *African Studies Review*, 58, no. 02 (September 2015): 43–61.

[7] This has been noted in Bertram Herbert Barnes and Janice Stein, 'Introduction: The Secularisation and Sanctification of Humanitarianism', in *Sacred Aid: Faith and Humanitarianism*, ed. Michael Barnett and Janice Stein (Oxford: Oxford University Press, 2012), 4; Manji and O'Coill.

and potential material gain sits uncomfortably with the stated other-worldly ideals that missionaries (both European and African) follow.

Much work has been carried out questioning the role of missions as sites of emancipation. For instance, the Church Missionary Society (CMS) scandals in Mombasa, in which punishments for 'immoral' behaviour were more greatly feared than slavery itself, have been widely commented upon.[8] Similar observations of less extreme cases can be found in studies of the UMCA and the Holy Ghost Fathers in Bagamoyo in Tanganyika.[9] However, little attention is paid to how ex-slaves attempted to leverage missions to alleviate their precarious living situations.

Some key works have explored the impact of mission education on livelihoods more generally. Notably, John Peel has shown how the Yoruba responded intellectually to the claims missionaries made about modernity and saw European knowledge as powerful.[10] Similarly, Derek Peterson emphasised how many Gikuyu eagerly appropriated Christian knowledge (in ways

---

[8] Robert W. Strayer, *Making of Mission Communities in East Africa: Anglicans and Africans in Colonial Kenya, 1875-1935* (London: Heinemann, 1978); Moses D. E. Nwulia, *Britain and Slavery in East Africa* (Washington, D.C., USA: Three Continents Press, 1975), 153; Jonathon Glassman, *Feasts and Riot: Revelry, Rebellion, and Popular Consciousness on the Swahili Coast, 1856-1888*, Social History of Africa (Portsmouth, NH; London; Nairobi; Dar es Salaam: Heinemann; James Currey; EAEP; Mkuki Na Nyota, 1995), 108–9; R. M. Githige, 'The Issue of Slavery: Relations between the CMS and the State on the East African Coast Prior to 1895', *Journal of Religion in Africa*, 16, no. 3 (1986): 209–25; Fred Morton, *Children of Ham: Freed Slaves and Fugitive Slaves on the Kenya Coast, 1873 to 1907*, African Modernization and Development Series, 1990, especially Chapter 3; Bennett comments specifically on the missionaries' difficulty in maintaining order. Norman R. Bennett, 'The Church Missionary Society at Mombasa', in *Boston University Papers in African History*, ed. Jeffrey Butler (Boston: Boston University Press, 1964), 192–94.

[9] John Iliffe, *A Modern History of Tanganyika* (Cambridge: Cambridge University Press, 1979), 84–85; Landeg White, *Magomero: Portrait of an African Village* (Cambridge: Cambridge University Press, 1987), 34–35, 37; Paul V. Kollman, *The Evangelization of Slaves and Catholic Origins in Eastern Africa* (Maryknoll, NY: Orbis Books, 2005), 76–83.

[10] John D. Y. Peel, *Religious Encounter and the Making of the Yoruba* (Bloomington, IN: Indiana University Press, 2000), 177; David Maxwell, 'Writing the History of African Christianity: Reflections of an Editor', *Journal of Religion in Africa*, 36, no. 3/4 (2006): 379–99. See also: Elizabeth Elbourne, 'Word Made Flesh: Christianity, Modernity, and Cultural Colonialism in the Work of Jean and John Comaroff', *The American Historical Review*, 108, no. 2 (2003): 435–59; Sally Engle Merry, 'Hegemony and Culture in Historical Anthropology: A Review Essay on Jean and John L. Comaroff's Of Revelation and Revolution', *The American Historical Review*, 108, no. 2 (1 April 2003): 460–70.

that were often far removed from the original intentions of missionaries), which is why so many Gikuyu parents insisted that their children learn English at school.[11] Yet in both the Gikuyu and Yoruba cases, missionary education was associated with elitism and the beginnings of an African middle class. Not necessarily in conflict with these accounts, other scholars have questioned the nature of the connection between missionary expansion and economic development, given that many missionaries claimed to be harbingers of prosperity as well as Christianity. As early as 1977, John McCracken argued that Scottish missions in southern Africa shouldered part of the responsibility for the region's economic 'underdevelopment'.[12] More recently and in contrast to McCracken, a research group including Remi Jedwab, Felix Meier zu Selhausen and Alexander Moradi asks whether there is a reason why the areas of greatest historical missionary activity also seem to be the areas with most promising economic development. This could be incidental. They argue that 'missionaries went to healthier, safer, and more accessible and developed areas, privileging the best locations first'. The research group suggest that these regions were more likely to be blessed with economic development, but this had little to do with the actual impact of the missions themselves.[13]

The problem is that missions have been understood as avenues to future livelihoods more often than they have been considered as sites of livelihoods in themselves. However, some research has shed light on connections between labour and Christian missions. For example, Andreana Pritchard's 2017 study of the UMCA between 1860 and 1970 takes into account labour practices and how they affected relationships within the mission. She uses personal stories, particularly of female lay evangelists, to argue that African Christian women harnessed daily performance of a certain set of 'civilized' Christian values and affective relationships to spread Christianity and develop cultural nationalisms. Her pioneering account is, however, not

---

[11] Derek R. Peterson, *Creative Writing: Translation, Bookkeeping, and the Work of Imagination in Colonial Kenya* (Porstmouth, NH: Heinemann, 2004). Similar findings were made in: Joseph E. Harris, *Repatriates and Refugees in Colonial Society: The Case of Kenya* (Washington, DC: Howard University Press, 1987); Strayer.
[12] John McCracken, 'Underdevelopment in Malawi: The Missionary Contribution', *African Affairs*, 76, no. 303 (1977): 197–98.
[13] Remi Jedwab, Felix Meier zu Selhausen and Alexander Moradi, 'The Economics of Missionary Expansion: Evidence from Africa and Implications for Development', Working Paper Series 1019, Department of Economics, University of Sussex Business School, 5 July 2018.

primarily about labour, but about how missions – or rather, the individuals within them – can make communities.[14]

Thomas Beidelman's 1982 monograph on the CMS in twentieth century Ukaguru, Tanzania, is another example. He showed how the variety of employment opportunities increased over time but also how many of their employees were discontented with the conditions of their labour, especially their wages. Some of the first paid roles were as catechists, evangelists, translators and servants but these wages remained stagnant while salaries for the more 'secular' employment of teachers, clerks, artisans and drivers increased. These 'secular' employees enjoyed more competitive salaries than African catechists and pastors.[15]

Barbara Cooper reveals similar findings in her account of the Sudan Interior Mission: workers were paid wages for domestic labour around the mission, but not for the 'higher work' of preaching. In other words, pay would only be given for work that the missionaries were not willing to do themselves.[16] Thus, clergy work was only paid for in food, which sits uneasily with the tendency for missionaries to offer moral guidance on labour conditions and expound the benefits of wage labour.[17] From the African perspective this seemed nonsensical, more so because Christians would often find themselves competing with Muslims for paid jobs.[18] Moreover, the men who decided they could no longer tolerate doing spiritual labour for free turned to Islam and often became prominent members of the Muslim community.[19] Cooper also showed that theft was often a way for mission workers to claim wages they felt they were owed, thus debunking the missionary interpretation that theft in missions happened because Africans were incapable of understanding the meaning of private property.[20] Most importantly, Cooper shows how the pursuit of social

---

[14] Andreana C. Prichard, *Sisters in Spirit: Christianity, Affect, and Community Building in East Africa, 1860–1970* (East Lansing, MI: Michigan State University Press, 2017).

[15] T. O. Beidelman, *Colonial Evangelism: A Socio-Historical Study of an East African Mission at the Grassroots* (Bloomington: Indiana University Press, 1982), 24; Bengt Sundkler, *Christian Ministry in Africa* (London: S. C. M. Press, 1960), 39–41, 116–17.

[16] Barbara MacGowan Cooper, *Evangelical Christians in the Muslim Sahel* (Bloomington, IN: Indiana University Press, 2006), 199.

[17] Cooper, 333. Remunerations for labour vary from mission to mission. Hunt found that African domestic workers in the Congo were often paid intermittently, not always with cash but with fruit, for example.

[18] Cooper, 183, 201.

[19] Cooper, 200.

[20] Cooper, 199.

status and of wealth were often at odds as converts would often choose unpaid religious work over paid domestic labour.

Nancy Rose Hunt also considered the labour and social mobility of Christian adherents. In her study of the British Baptist Missionary Society in the Yakusu region of today's Democratic Republic of the Congo, she argues that 'boy' or '*boi*' work (the employment of male students in the household) was essential to the domesticating processes in the mission and part of the performance of a 'tamed, domesticated harmony'.[21] It was a well-respected career until the 1950s, partly because the punishments for work-related failures were so severe.[22] Hunt examined how working as a domestic servant was necessary work experience for becoming a (male) nurse. Both roles necessitated physical and moral cleanliness to win the missionaries' trust.[23] This approach to medical training came to a head with a colonial regulation in 1954 introducing an upper age limit for students and a longer school day. This irritated one missionary who complained that, 'now knowledgeable lads are not even "kitchen-clean" when they come to the wards and operating theatre, and have to be "house-trained" at great cost of time and patience and energy'.[24] The career options Hunt describes for young women were quite different. Female domestic labour in the mission was generally work experience for becoming a wife, which would happen once the girl or woman became a 'Mama-girl' who worked in the Mademoiselle's bedroom. These workers accepted the debasing tasks (such as cleaning out chamber pots) but not without a sense of shame that oral history respondents expressed to Hunt.[25]

These insights into what it was like to make a living in a mission, though very useful, are centred on employer–servant relations and provide little context of the broader social networks that connected them to other Africans. Moreover, labour history is tangential to these authors' main aims. In contrast, this book is about livelihoods in the mission from the end of the precolonial period until the late 1920s; a time in which slave status was potent and dramatically shaped Africans' livelihood trajectories. Furthermore, there is still more to be done in terms of assessing the multiple forms of dependence that the mission offered.

The lack of research that treats missions as sites of livelihood struggles is a problem for several reasons. Firstly, the kinds of labour that existed in

---

[21] Nancy Rose Hunt, *Colonial Lexicon of Birth Ritual, Medicalization, and Mobility in the Congo* (Durham, NC: Duke University Press, 1999), 119–20, 122.
[22] Hunt, 136.
[23] Hunt, 128, 130.
[24] Of course, this also meant the end of cheap domestic labour. Hunt, 136.
[25] Hunt, 146.

mission settings, especially in the post-abolition period, usually lay somewhere between the extremes of coerced and free labour. This grey area is vastly underrepresented in the literature, as Marcel van der Linden and Magaly Rodríguez García rightly note.[26] Indeed, the abolition of slavery did not automatically bring about the freedom of so-called 'free' wage labour. Many transitional arrangements such as indentured labour, sharecropping, convict labour and debt peonage were introduced. Moreover, in many countries there were laws and institutions designed to 'rescue' or 'rehabilitate' displaced individuals, such as ex-slaves. [27] Missionaries often led these initiatives, not simply because they sympathised with the anti-slavery cause, but also because, especially at this relatively early stage of mission history, the mission could usually only convince socially and economically marginal people (e.g. slaves and ex-slaves) to become mission followers.

Missionaries did not only see ex-slaves as potential converts, they were also potential mission workers.[28] Equally, missionaries hoped that their workforces would also demonstrate the mission's religious tenets. These missions, the UMCA included, also tended to rely on 'voluntary' labour. For example, missionaries demanded that churches should be built without paying the builders' wages, and that teachers' wages should be paid from church alms that were collected from congregants.[29] This, the logic went, was to ensure that the work of developing the mission was not done out of financial gain but, rather, religious feeling. As already mentioned, there was much resistance to the missionaries' imposed culture of unpaid labour, but African employees of the mission still had to struggle to secure remuneration for this work.[30] African teachers started receiving wages before African clergymen. In 1899 Bishop Smythies made a case for introducing an 'adequate wage' for African deacons and priests. Wages in general were subject to a delicate negotiation when the employee, teacher or clergyman began a family. Missionaries considered

---

[26] van der Linden and Rodríguez García, 'Introduction'.
[27] van der Linden and Rodríguez García, 1.
[28] Matthew S. Hopper, *Slaves of One Master: Globalization and Slavery in Arabia in the Age of Empire* (New Haven, CT: Yale University Press, 2015), 171.
[29] The Lutheran Church had the same expectations for voluntary labour in the 1950s. Hunter, 'Voluntarism, Virtuous Citizenship, and Nation-Building in Late Colonial and Early Postcolonial Tanzania', *African Studies Review*, 58, no. 02 (September 2015), 48.
[30] Bishop Smythies of the UMCA was particularly concerned with the subject of wages for mission employees. In 1893 Smythies argued that teachers' salaries should not be fixed until they were approved by the principal of Kiungani boys' school – teachers received different salaries depending on their district. Bishop Charles Alan Smythies, 'The Bishop's Letter', *Central Africa*, June 1892.

wages as a temporary solution. Eventually, African Christians were meant to cover the cost of the teacher's living through charitable giving, but this rarely worked in practice and was the source of great conflict.[31] Africans and missionaries did not see the terms of the labour in the same light. For example, in the late nineteenth-century, children received food, wages and clothing for attending school. To the missionaries, these were gifts to help incentivise the children to learn. To the children and their guardians, the mission was paying the children a wage, or, more problematically, purchasing them as slaves. How these 'gifts' were received and what they may have been perceived to mean are of key interest in this study.

Procuring and managing African labour dominated everyday life for the missionaries. It follows that, if we do not pay attention to such a key part of the missionaries' daily activities, then we cannot fully understand the history of missions. It is well known that missionaries sought the labour of Africans to spread the word of God amongst other Africans, but historians have spent much less time on the missionaries' exploitation of labour in general; of the men, women and children who laboured as farmers, builders and servants. Given that the African ministry (which is the focus of much mission history research) was necessarily a male adult one, women and children have consequently been neglected from the narrative.

Missionaries tried to engineer new Christian communities and, in doing so, had to focus on gaining followers and workers. It was not that missionaries intentionally placed emphasis on the importance of employment, but rather that they struggled with the conundrum that other-worldly deeds required this-worldly economic and social transactions. Meanwhile, many Africans saw the opportunities the mission offered to create new livelihoods, networks and solidarities, which were potentially sustainable. Furthermore, missions are an interesting field of study in terms of labour and livelihood conditions as they turned existing hierarchies on their head.[32] It is critical that we understand how missions functioned as employers so we can understand their socio-economic role, and how this role contributed to their broader impact.

---

[31] Bishop Hine, 'The Conference at Likoma', *Central Africa*, December 1899.
[32] Fruitful studies have been carried out on labour organisation within armies, which, similarly to missions, defy or acquiesce to existing social hierarchies. For instance, hierarchy is central to this analysis of labour in the military context: Erik-Jan Zürcher, ed., *Fighting for a Living: A Comparative History of Military Labour 1500–2000* (Amsterdam: Amsterdam University Press, 2015).

The focus of study

This study centres on UMCA stations in Tanganyika and Zanzibar, which are considered as nodes in networks of exchange and spaces of economic activity. The missionaries constantly veered between submitting to local conditions and imposing their own ideals of what they felt to be the proper management and division of labour. A good example of this was their employment of slaves, a practice that was not always illegal for British subjects and was particularly widespread amongst explorers in need of porters. At the same time, the missionaries often felt they had to abandon their belief that they must not exercise formal authority outside of the main nucleus of the clergy as they managed their labour forces and attempted to reform freed slaves into (ideally skilled) free wageworkers. These issues bear on how historians understand the tensions between conversion, cultural adaption, industrialisation and capitalism but they also say something of the role of missionaries and Christian Africans as cultural brokers between the mission economies and the local economies with which they interacted.

Regarding periodisation, this book cuts across the divide of 'precolonial' and 'colonial'. I focus on the UMCA mission in its early stages, before and under German colonialism, prior to the more transformative British colonial presence. I begin with the UMCA's first settlement in Zanzibar in 1864 and end in 1926 when the diocese of Zanzibar was restructured, which increased African priests' authority and marked a new phase of mission history. I do not cover the early 1930s, a time of great change characterised by the dominance of the plantation industries in north-eastern Tanzania and the global economic depression of the early 1930s, which caused the UMCA to limit expenditure. The period does cover the end of slavery as a labour system, and so many of the mission workers were ex-slaves and (in the early years) slaves. The slave status, political allegiance and community memberships of the mission workers made their livelihood options complex and subject to change over time. [33] The workers' changeable conditions are a central interest of this study. The precise position and regional context of the mission are elaborated upon in the following section.

---

[33] Marcel van der Linden reminds us that workers could be subject to multiple and overlapping situations of coercion and autonomy. Marcel van der Linden, *Workers of the World: Essays toward a Global Labor History* (Leiden, Netherlands; Boston, MA: Brill, 2008), 32.

Regional contexts

The UMCA spread extensively in east and central Africa, but I focus on the majority-Muslim island of Zanzibar and the mainland region of Magila in north-eastern Tanzania, both of which require contextual explanation. Beginning with Zanzibar, it was of great economic importance as it dominated trade between Africa, India and the Middle East in the eighteenth and nineteenth centuries. In 1832 the Omani Sultanate began to establish itself in Zanzibar Town. Zanzibar was a slave trade hub, from which many slaves were subsequently transported to Oman. The most rapid growth of slave imports to Zanzibar, in the late 1840s, came at a time when increasing restrictions were being placed on the trade. In 1873 the slave trade was made illegal in Sultan Barghash of Zanzibar's dominions, although it continued clandestinely. In fact, the prohibition on the slave trade set off new slave trades on the mainland nearer to the coast. Barghash attempted to use his representatives to control the slave trade but he had limited authority over the mainland, which he had only recently begun to colonise, a fact that the missionaries seemed slow to recognise.[34]

The Sultan controlled Zanzibar's centralised government, though his power was limited. Meanwhile, slave-owners lacked class unity, as Frederick Cooper has noted. Plantations were major socio-political units in which the slaves themselves were politically important because slave masters could enlist them as followers. Slave owners had to be careful to create desirable ties of dependence with slaves to ensure that they accommodated their masters' demands. By fostering this kind of dependence, masters gained their slaves' attachment to the estate, while slaves had more personal control over the rhythm of their daily lives.[35]

In 1890 Zanzibar became a British protectorate.[36] The British retained the Sultanate, though the Sultan lost power and was only able to nominate successors. From 1890 to 1913, the Sultan's government, which was largely made up of European officers, worked alongside the British Consulate, administered through the British Foreign Office. The *maliwali* (district governors appointed by the Sultan) also retained much influence and authority.

---

[34] Mark R. Lipschutz and R. Kent Rasmussen, *Dictionary of African Historical Biography* (Berkeley, CA: University of California Press, 1989), 27; John Middleton, *World Monarchies and Dynasties* (London; New York: Routledge, 2015), 93.

[35] Cooper, 'The Problem of Slavery in African Studies'.

[36] Horace Waller, *Heligoland for Zanzibar, or, One Island Full of Free Men for Two Full of Slaves* (London: Edward Stanford, 26 & 27 Cockspur Street, Charing Cross, S.W., 1893); 'Annual Colonial Reports: Zanzibar, 1925', 1926, C2, UMArch.

Throughout the period this book covers, the Sultan played an important role, largely in terms of representation, in the Protectorate's governance.[37] Glassman used the term 'dual colonialism' to describe this system, whereby the British ruled over what remained an Arab imperial structure.[38] Currency reflected the dual system as the silver rupee and Maria Theresa Dollar (MTD), which originated from British India, and the copper pice, of the Sultanate, were the primary currencies.[39] In 1919 the British mandated Tanganyika, which caused Zanzibar's strategic role in the Empire to decline further as British control of the coastline became stronger.

As for the nature of the mission's presence on the island, Zanzibar was the first permanent UMCA settlement in Africa, dating from 1864, following several earlier failed attempts to settle on the mainland.[40] The missionaries had mixed feelings about Zanzibar. On the one hand, they believed it was essential to keep a presence there as a springboard for establishing themselves on the mainland and so it remained the logistical heart of the mission for the duration of this book's timeframe. On the other hand, missionaries also tended to see it as a place that made people, missionaries and Africans alike, susceptible to all kinds of sin, including arrogance, laziness, extravagance, alcoholism and carnal sin.[41] In Zanzibar, ex-slaves who came to the mission between 1864 and 1900, after escaping slave traders and owners, made up most of the converts. Many turned to Islam after living in the mission for a short period of time. In fact, the mission hardly encountered any friction with the Sultan because the missionaries had so little success converting Muslims.

Some 120km north-west of Zanzibar is the Magila region in north-eastern Tanzania, now more commonly referred to as Tanga. 'Magila' was the name of a village which was the site of the first permanent mainland mission settlement in the region in 1875. However, until the 1920s, the name was historically used to describe the diocese and region as a whole. In this book, I use the term 'Magila' to describe the diocese, rather than the village. I use the name Msalabani (which translates as 'at the cross' or 'on the cross') to refer to the village, though, confusingly, the sources often refer to Msalabani and Magila

---

[37] Sarah Longair, '"A Gracious Temple of Learning": The Museum and Colonial Culture in Zanzibar, 1900 – 1945' (PhD, London, Department of History, Classics and Archaeology Birkbeck College, University of London, 2012), 37–41.
[38] Jonathon Glassman, *War of Words, War of Stones: Racial Thought and Violence in Colonial Zanzibar* (Bloomington, IN: Indiana University Press, 2011), 78.
[39] 'Annual Colonial Reports: Zanzibar, 1925'.
[40] White, *Magomero: Portrait of an African Village*.
[41] Chapter 3 of this book; Michelle Liebst, 'Sin, Slave Status, and the "City": Zanzibar, 1865–c. 1930', *African Studies Review*, 60, no. 2 (September 2017): 139–60. doi.org/10.1017/asr.2017.81.

interchangeably. Magila diocese encompassed the key villages of Korogwe, Handeni, Muheza, Msalabani, Umba, Mkuzi and Misozwe. This region was close to the coast, but did not include any actual coastline. The people had long resorted to the coast for work, food, and trade in times of hardship.[42]

Early accounts suggest that in the nineteenth century Magila was mostly fertile and enjoyed considerable trade, profiting from exports of grain. It was also relatively free of disease despite continual migration. The more populated centre of the Magila region was surrounded by diverse landscapes. To the south-west, crops were relatively unreliable, though cattle and small stock were common. Going east, largely uninhabited, infertile scrubland filled the space between Magila and Tanga, making travel to the coast very difficult until the arrival of the Tanga railway in 1905. Finally, the north was also almost uninhabited, and boasted plentiful game.[43]

The Magila region was, and remains, home to three major ethnic identities, though the boundaries and meanings of ethnic affiliation have changed: firstly, the Shambaai, who lived in the fertile mountains; secondly, the Zigua, who lived further west around Handeni; and, finally, the Bondei, who lived in the region furthest to the east near Msalabani. The Bondei were the first people in the region to encounter the mission and so are mentioned in this book more often than other ethnicities. Some people of the region believe that the Bondei were a subset of the Zigua who came to Magila to flee war in the late nineteenth century.[44] Their ethnic identity in the nineteenth century was defined by the fact that they rebelled against the Shambaai Kingdom in the Kiva Rebellion of 1868. As a result, the Bondei's geographical boundaries also got smaller and were limited to the valley.[45]

---

[42] Justin Willis, '"And So They Called a Kiva": Histories of a War', *Azania: Journal of the British Institute in Eastern Africa*, 25, no. 1 (1990): 81.

[43] J. P. Farler, 'The Usambara Country in East Africa', *Proceedings of the Royal Geographical Society and Monthly Record of Geography*, 1, no. 2 (1 February 1879): 81–97. doi.org/10.2307/1800252; Justin Willis, 'The Makings of a Tribe: Bondei Identities and Histories', *The Journal of African History*, 33, no. 2 (1 January 1992): 194–95.

[44] Willis, 'The Makings of a Tribe: Bondei Identities and Histories', 206; Willis cites: Selemani Kiro, 'The History of the Zigua Tribe', *Tanganyika Notes and Records*, 1953.

[45] Willis, 'The Makings of a Tribe: Bondei Identities and Histories', 199–200; Godfrey Dale, 'An Account of the Principal Customs and Habits of the Natives Inhabiting the Bondei Country, Compiled Mainly for the Use of European Missionaries in the Country', *The Journal of the Anthropological Institute of Great Britain and Ireland*, 25 (1 January 1896): 182–83.

The Zigua encountered Christianity later than the Bondei, who were based to the east in Magila.[46] In fact, it is likely that the Zigua were particularly impacted by the fact that schooling diminished the pool of child labour.[47] Indeed, the oral history record suggested going to school posed a threat to the '*nguvu kazi*' (workforce) of the Zigua household, which depended on a pastoral livelihood. While the Bondei had diverse livestock, the Zigua were self-defined as cattle-keeping people and cattle must be watched all day, unlike goats that only require a half-day of grazing. It is for this reason that George Salim, a respondent, declared, 'the Bondeis are not cattle-keeping people'.[48] Whether Bondei people did not keep cattle because so many of them were Christian, or whether the Bondei were more easily proselytised because they did not keep cattle is debateable. The fact that Zigua people struggled more with their loss of child household labour, combined with the serious drought the Zigua region faced because of sisal plantations, was used by respondents to explain the relative poverty of Zigua people compared to Bondei people. Thus, typical livelihoods of certain ethnic groups are used to explain the extent to which Christianity was accepted by particular people.

Aided by the trade winds, the Tanzanian coast was an important region in the Indian Ocean commercial network in the nineteenth century, but the interior told a different story of interregional trade and limited contact with the coast.[49] In Magila, the separation from the coast was made possible by the aforementioned stretch of uncultivated land, which made journeys there treacherous. Even so, as Chapter 1 of this book shows, Magila's connections

---

[46] Keith Johnston, 'Notes of a Trip from Zanzibar to Usambara, in February and March, 1879', *Proceedings of the Royal Geographical Society and Monthly Record of Geography*, 1, no. 9 (1 September 1879): 545–58; Farler, 'The Usambara Country in East Africa'; Frank Weston, 'A Letter from the Bishop of Zanzibar', *Central Africa*, August 1909; Iliffe, *A Modern History of Tanganyika*, 43, 52, 65, 78.

[47] Canon Mwamazi, interview by Zuhura Mohammed, Mbezi-Kimara, Dar es Salaam, 29 October 2014, 00:30:00.

[48] This was said in English. George Salim, Part 1, interview by Zuhura Mohammed, 3 November 2014; Gerrard Michael Francis Kiongoa Yambi, interview by Zuhura Mohammed, Tanga, 25 October 2014, 00:37:00; Samuel Sepeku also suggested that the trend towards sending children to school changed diets. He argued that people stopped growing millet in the Misozwe region because it required child labour to scare away monkeys and other agricultural pests: Canon Samuel Sepeku, interview by Zuhura Mohammed, Mbezi, Kimara, Dar es Salaam, 29 October 2014, 00:20:30–00:22:02.

[49] Abdul Sheriff, *Slaves, Spices, & Ivory in Zanzibar: Integration of an East African Commercial Empire Into the World Economy, 1770–1873* (London: James Currey, 1987).

with the coast were increasingly important from the mid-nineteenth century. The Islamic presence in the Magila region, though obviously less strong than it was in Zanzibar, was nonetheless significant. Islam came to Magila many years before the missionaries. It was particularly strong among the Zigua, who had a trading history and were at that time (between the 1830s and 1850s) based to the west in Pangani and Saadani.[50]

The Shambaai civil war of 1868 caused the region much unrest and slaving in the second half of the nineteenth century (see Chapter 1), and famine in the early German period. It was the unsettled context that made mission patronage relevant, political and challenging for the missionaries to establish. The fact that the region was largely depopulated also helped make it easier for settlers to begin plantations there.[51]

Mainland Tanganyika was a German colony between 1889 and the First World War. It was not until the turn of the century that German plantations started to become profitable. This delay was due in part to some particularly damaging famines in 1894–96 and 1898–99. In these times of crisis, people travelled to Tanga and further afield for food and work, and it was mostly women and the elderly who went to the mission for help.[52]

In the 1900s German settlers' plantations, including their coffee-growing experiments, became more productive and investments increased. New economic opportunities started to develop, partly aided by the newly built railways.[53] German plantation development brought with it wage labour and monetisation.[54] Most workers were long-distance migrants. Meanwhile, people in the region generally sought to avoid plantation labour, even when sisal plantations boomed in the twentieth century. The Germans assumed that appropriating African land, combined with population growth, would eventually force Africans to work for European plantations. In the end, many benefitted from the European plantations without having to work for them, by selling plantation workers food. In the Usambaras, the workforce on

---

[50] Isaria N. Kimambo, 'Environmental Control and Hunger: In the Mountains and Plains of Nineteenth-Century Northeastern Tanzania', in *Custodians of the Land: Ecology & Culture in the History of Tanzania*, ed. G. Maddox, James L. Giblin, and Isaria N. Kimambo, Eastern African Studies (Athens: James Currey, 1996), 84–92.

[51] Iliffe, *A Modern History of Tanganyika*, 126, 287.

[52] Iliffe, 125; Justin Willis, 'The Nature of a Mission Community: The Universities' Mission to Central Africa in Bonde', *Past & Present*, no. 140 (1 August 1993): 151.

[53] Iliffe, *A Modern History of Tanganyika*, 125, 135.

[54] Jan-Georg Deutsch, *Emancipation without Abolition in German East Africa, c.1884–1914* (Oxford; Athens, OH: James Currey; Ohio University Press, 2006), 218–22.

European plantations was smaller, which meant less commercial opportunity for locals to sell food to the workers. Finally, the people of this region also came under more pressure to work on settlers' plantations than those in other regions.[55] For instance, in 1907 the District Officer gave every able-bodied, adult Shambaai male a card that forced him to work for a European for thirty days every four months or else be conscripted for public labour. Workers could choose their employers, but they worked for very low wages. This system spread to many other regions.[56]

In the German colonial period, missionaries were expected to help German officials ensure colonial law was followed and respected. This put missionaries in a difficult position. For example, one missionary named Christopher Fixsen working in the Zigua region resented being obliged by the government to urge people to pay taxes for their children going to school. The injustice of it seemed potent to him as he observed that 'the people don't want their children to learn'.[57] Or, at least, parents were less interested in the knowledge than the security education seemed to offer.[58] Missionaries generally did not try to correct the assumption that building schools would make villagers impervious to forced labour policies. Fixsen wrote regretfully that, 'we trade in their desire for schools, though we know its true motives'.[59] Though some missionaries did try to protect villagers by making a formality of signing children up to come to the mission school in order to make it harder for the government school teachers to interfere, there was very little missionaries could or did do to fight colonial forced labour policies.[60] The result was disappointing for missionaries, who were associated with the German regime that they considered coercive and despotic. For example, Fixsen recorded in 1914 that:

> The people round here have been ordered to have a dance of rejoicing tonight in celebration of the German emperor's birthday which was a day or two ago. They are beating a drum in a half-hearted way now. This proceeding has a spice of grim humour in it, for the people themselves would rejoice at nothing better than to drive the Germans into the sea and the missionaries after them.[61]

[55] Iliffe, *A Modern History of Tanganyika*, 152.
[56] Iliffe, 153.
[57] Rev. J. F. Christopher Fixsen to Mother, Kizara, 1 February 1914, A1 (22), 656, UMArch.
[58] Bishop Charles Alan Smythies, 'News from the Bondei Country', *Central Africa*, 1891.
[59] Rev. J. F. Christopher Fixsen to Mother, Kizara, 23 February 1912, A1 (22), 539, UMArch.
[60] Francis Eling Pearse to Duncan Travers, Kigongoi, Tanga, German East Africa, 23 January 1909, A1 (21), 123, UMArch.
[61] Rev. J. F. Christopher Fixsen to Mother, 1 February 1914.

Fixsen's observations do not appear to be representative of the north-eastern region where colonial authority was met with indifference, but his words are nonetheless striking.

The 1890s and early 1900s was a time in which the geographical economic, and social boundaries of villagers' lives were expanding. In 1904 the UMCA periodical *Central Africa* published Godfrey Dale's account of the changes he had witnessed since his arrival in 1892. Tanga town was bigger and had felt the greatest impact of colonial government. The swathes of *nyika* land that had dominated the journey between hinterland and coast had receded somewhat. People moved to towns and away from villages, partly as a consequence of famine but also as a result of increased security. In addition, people were moving between different rural regions, including the Usambara country. These migrants primarily included the Digo but also Manyema, Nyamwezi, and Masai people (who were as a rule said to be hostile to the mission except for the Nywamwezi). The demographic was younger than it had been, again, largely due to the disastrous effects of famine and disease. Meanwhile, networks within the mission itself had strengthened. 'Out-schools' in remote areas were more strictly supervised than the school in Msalabani, which was referred to as the 'central school'.[62]

The spread of the Swahili language also reflected the (gendered) broadening of villagers' networks. Even in the 1890s it was observed that it was only very old people who did not understand Swahili, though many did not speak it fluently and women rarely spoke it at all.[63] Speaking Swahili was a sign of one's gender and cultural advancement, in southern Tanzania as well as in Magila. Though he believed the honour attached to Swahili was inevitable, Dale was nonetheless troubled by the fact that, 'the teachers are very unwilling to use Bondei and the native clergy prefer to preach in Swahili'.[64] In fact, teachers insisted that they were unable to express themselves in anything but Swahili in their teaching.[65] Still, the memory of Swahili feeling foreign among elders, especially women, lives on in the oral history record. Respondents commonly

---

[62] Godfrey Dale, 'The Usambara Country: Changes during Ten Years', *Central Africa*, August 1904.
[63] J. H. Pearse to Duncan Travers, Magila, 6 March 1891, A1 (6) B, 1638, UMArch.
[64] Godfrey Dale, 'The Usambara Country: Changes during Ten Years'.
[65] W. E. Deerr, 'Our Boys at Work', *Central Africa*, October 1907; later on, Samuel Chiponde would express a preference for using Arabic, rather than Bantu, words in his work as a Swahili interpreter, believing that Bantu was inadequate in his efforts to translate complicated expressions such as 'Culpable homicide not amounting to murder.' 'Report of Education Conference 1925, Together with the Report of the Committee for the Standardisation of the Swahili Language', Tanganyika Territory (Dar es Salaam: Government printer, 1926), 102.

noted that, among their ancestors, if someone spoke good Swahili, he (it was usually a 'he') might be dubbed an outsider.[66] With the broadening of networks, the costs and benefits of missionary education were weighed differently.

The First World War disrupted the German forced labour system, and the war's end marked the beginning of British colonialism in mainland Tanzania. The First World War also marked a low ebb for the mission's status, as the Germans interned European and African clergy and teachers.[67] Finally, in July 1922, the British Mandate was agreed upon.[68] In the 1920s the boundaries of Tanganyika territory criss-crossed over the Magila diocese boundaries. Thus, from the 1920s the Magila diocese encompassed parts of the districts of Tanga, Pangani and Usambara. Later, the situation changed again. In 1926 Tanga district was redrawn to encompass Usambara and Pangani.[69] During the 1920s, there were estimated to be 22,000 to 29,000 followers of the UMCA in the whole of Tanganyika. Over half of these were claimed to be in Masasi, at least from 1926, when the Masasi diocese was formed.[70] With all this macro information in mind, it is important to remember that Magila was internally very diverse. The uneven change that Magila underwent meant great variation in life chances and options.

I deal with two very different locations: Magila, where a Christian community was established in a religiously plural environment, and Zanzibar, where Islam dominated. From a political perspective, as Glassman argued, Africans distinguished between the different European claims to power that

---

[66] The term many respondents used to describe these Swahili-speakers was '*mtu wa kuja*'.

[67] Willis, 'The Makings of a Tribe: Bondei Identities and Histories'; John Mhina, *Historia ya Magila Msalabani 1848-2012: Mlango wa Kuingia Kanisa la Anglikana Tanzania Bara*, 2012; Joel Sehoza, 'Samuel Sehoza' (Notes, Magila, 2012); Frank Weston, 'In Zigualand' (Diary, c 1921), A1 (18) B, UMArch.

[68] Iliffe, *A Modern History of Tanganyika*, 247.

[69] *Tanganyika Territory Blue Book for the year ended 31st December 1926* (Dar es Salaam: The Government Printer, 1930).

[70] *Tanganyika Territory Blue Book for the year ended 31st December 1921* (Dar es Salaam: The Government Printer, 1922); *Tanganyika Territory Blue Book for the year ended 31st December 1922* (Dar es Salaam: The Government Printer, 1923); *Tanganyika Territory Blue Book for the year ended 31st December 1923* (Dar es Salaam: The Government Printer, 1926); *Tanganyika Territory Blue Book for the year ended 31st December 1924* (Dar es Salaam: The Government Printer, 1926); *Tanganyika Territory Blue Book for the year ended 31st December 1925* (Dar es Salaam: The Government Printer, 1926); *Tanganyika Territory Blue Book for the year ended 31st December 1926*; *Tanganyika Territory Blue Book for the year ended 31st December 1927* (Dar es Salaam: The Government Printer, 1930).

were present on the mainland and coast. Namely, Germans were seen to be less influential than other European nationalities. This was partly because the commodities in which they traded were rarely manufactured in/by Germans, and seldom did they reach the mainland. Meanwhile, English prestige was derived from the fact that the British Consul-General in Zanzibar held so much influence over Indian merchants and the Omani throne.[71]

The mission's connections between mainland and coast were logistically and ideologically significant to the mission, and crucial to understanding network formation. Zanzibar Island, having long been a transnational space as part of the Omani Empire, remained a key stopping point for supplies, labour and education. Zanzibar and Magila were closely connected by educational networks. Kiungani boys' school and theological college in Zanzibar were crucial features of the UMCA's operations, because they produced most of the African teachers and clergy that operated on the mainland. Equally, ex-slave teachers in Zanzibar were required to work on the mainland as part of their careers.

Scholars rarely consider the Tanzanian hinterland and coast together. This is understandable as the historical experiences in these regions were so different, which makes comparison difficult. This is particularly the case with processes of Christianisation. Even so, by focusing on both regions, the fact that Magila was, like Zanzibar, a slave-society, becomes much clearer. Society in Magila was also facing a constant flow of 'aliens' (*watu wa kigeni*). Some were welcomed, some rejected; but all were suspected of having slave status. People with slave status attempted to create new identities and pursue emancipation. In both Zanzibar and Magila the mission was deeply tied into its dependants' struggles for status and livelihood, and the mission could not control the ways in which it was relevant to these struggles. The fact that the markers of status varied between Magila and Zanzibar, but also overlapped to some extent, highlights how these connections emerged.

The UMCA in context

The mission, formally established in 1865 as the 'Oxford and Cambridge Universities' Mission to Central Africa', was born out of the Anglo-Catholic tradition, which had a distinctive effect on missionary societies because it advocated episcopal autonomy from the home committee in the metropole. The idea was to allow the clergy to innovate ritual without having to constantly seek approval from the mission's organising body.[72] Another effect of

---

[71] Glassman, *Feasts and Riot*, 51.
[72] Steven S. Maughan, *Mighty England Do Good: Culture, Faith, Empire, and*

this position was to prioritise recruiting African clergy. The result was that the UMCA ordained African priests and deacons at a faster rate than the CMS.[73] Despite Steere's commitment to the UMCA, he criticised the Catholic approach to mission: 'The weakness of Roman missions with all their many excellencies lies in their artificiality and dependence upon foreign influences, the strength of Protestant mission with their innumerable defects lies in their putting a new power into native hands.'[74] Instead, Steere sought to learn from Africans and empower them. For instance, they found from their own experience that there was no market for English or European methods of agriculture or mechanics except among the very few Europeans on the island and some of this was taken in by the Special Envoy, Bartle Frere.[75] Yet in order to help the Christian boys and young men adopt African labour customs, the missionaries would have to allow them to the to be apprenticed by local masons, who were Muslim.[76]

The UMCA's emphasis on 'industrial work' might seem surprising as the UMCA missionaries were known for their elite social and economic backgrounds. In contrast to missionaries from other missionary societies, who were accustomed to manual labour, UMCA missionaries tended to be – though there were exceptions – upper class, financially self-sufficient, with Oxbridge university backgrounds. This is was palpable in their aversion to city life (see Chapter 3) and their inability to function without servants (see Chapter 5). Like most British missionaries, the booming self-assured world of Victorian industrialisation repulsed them. They wanted to seize the opportunity to escape from an industrial urban society because many of them had trained in urban slum parishes in England where they developed a sense that this destiny should be avoided at all costs.[77] The UMCA missionaries would often complain of the nature of two kinds of migrant labour . First was the

---

World in the Foreign Missions of the Church of England, 1850–1915 (Cambridge: Wm. B. Eerdmans Publishing, 2014), 117.

[73] Kevin Ward, *A History of Global Anglicanism* (Cambridge: Cambridge University Press, 2006), 159–60.

[74] Edward Steere to John Wogan Festing, Zanzibar, 24 February 1873, A1 (3) A, 85, UMArch.

[75] Sir Bartle Frere, 'Memorandum on Disposal of Liberated Slaves' (n.d.), 57, 84/1391, UKNA; Arthur Nugent West to St. Andrew's College, 1874, 7, A1 (3) A, 5-8, UMArch; Sir Henry Bartle Edward Frere, *Eastern Africa as a Field for Missionary Labour. Four Letters to the Archbishop of Canterbury, Etc.* (London, 1874), 23.

[76] J. P. Farler to Rev. W. H. Penney, 1883, A1 (IX), 126-8.

[77] Andrew N. Porter, 'The Universities' Mission to Central Africa', in *Missions, Nationalism and the End of Empire*, ed. Brian Stanley (Michigan and Cambridge: Wm. B. Eerdmans Publishing, 2003), 90–91.

precolonial agricultural migrant labour and second was the migrant labour to work in colonial industries. Missionaries protested partly because it made conversion more difficult as Christian teaching may have to be deferred and also because they believed it had a harmful effect on family life, inducing states of 'immorality'.[78] Thus, they did not wish to industrialise Africa but, rather, carefully supplant Christianity without disturbing the economy.[79] Equally, partly because missionaries were embedded in local dynamics of dependence, they did not always have the will or the ability to assist Africans wanting to engage with the world economy.[80]

Tensions between worldly and religious matters demonstrate how the UMCA missionaries defined themselves against other missionaries and other Europeans in general. They were, for instance, at least as sceptical about the moral impact of European culture and 'civilisation' on Africa – especially of European settler communities with their partiality to monetary excess and materialism – as they were of 'heathenism'. The missionaries' mistrust of what they saw as the materialism of both European and coastal cultures meant that they tried to live simply, even if their relative wealth compared to the people around them undermined the missionaries' efforts. As other historians have already pointed out, 'worldliness' (a term missionaries often used) by its very nature contradicted Christian principles, which valued humility and simplicity of life.[81] Objects of consumption and consumerism were, the missionaries thought, powerful agents of harmful aspects of European cultures. Some missionaries were much more tied to this principle than others because

---

[78] Weston vehemently critiqued migrant labour and forced labour in the colonial setting in controversial published pamphlets in 1917 and 1920, which were reprinted in many editions. Frank Weston, *The Black Slaves of Prussia : An Open Letter to General Smuts* (London: Universities' Mission to Central Africa, 1917); Frank Weston, *The Serfs of Great Britain: Being a Sequel to The Black Slaves of Prussia* (London, 1920).

[79] Andrew N. Porter, *Religion Versus Empire? British Protestant Missionaries and Overseas Expansion 1700–1914* (Manchester University Press, 2004), 330

[80] As Elbourne has noted more generally: Elbourne, 'Word Made Flesh: Christianity, Modernity, and Cultural Colonialism in the Work of Jean and John Comaroff', 438.

[81] Andrew Porter, *Religion Versus Empire? British Protestant Missionaries and Overseas Expansion, 1700–1914* (Manchester: Manchester University Press, 2004); David Maxwell, *Christians and Chiefs in Zimbabwe: A Social History of the Hwesa People C. 1870s–1990s* (Edinburgh: Edinburgh University Press, 1999), 2, 59; Peter Pels, *A Politics of Presence: Contacts between Missionaries and Waluguru in Late Colonial Tanganyika* (Amsterdam, Netherlands: Harwood Academic Publishers, 1999), 4; Peel, *Religious Encounter and the Making of the Yoruba*, 5.

they feared that Africans had already begun 'imitating'. 'It is wonderful how many men mistake Europeanization for real improvement,' remarked Bishop Steere in a report to the Home Committee in 1873. He continued, 'I don't see what we should gain by introducing a travesty of European dress and manners, the natives are going in that direction only too fast for themselves and the first result is moral degradation.'[82] Missionaries who shared these views would therefore boast about their lack of belongings and intentional state of poverty.[83] Yet at the same time, English luxuries such as afternoon tea and fine dining remained everyday practices for many missionaries and for the African convert, an invitation to such an event marked their status within the mission community.[84]

Compared to other missionary societies, the UMCA were particularly suspicious of what Frank Weston (UMCA bishop 1908–1924) referred to as 'patent leather shoes and other European sins'.[85] For the UMCA, education and employment were simply a way of spreading Christianity, and they generally had little interest in economic development. Although formal institutional education and wage labour were (especially in the early- to mid-twentieth century) some of the best means of escaping poverty and engaging with a capitalist economy, missionaries simultaneously limited access to those means. Despite all this, Africans worked around missionaries' attitudes and shaped the opportunities for social mobility that the mission provided to pursue their own ideas of modernity.

For many African Christians, the missionaries' attitudes towards materialism and the changing world did make a difference. But Africans in contact with the mission did not necessarily share missionaries' views. Just as Jean and John Comaroff suggested, missionaries had an unintentional or indirect impact on worldly lifestyles because they could rarely imagine how Christianity could succeed without material 'improvement'.[86] Unlike the Comaroffs, I do not argue that the adoption of certain European habits was a means of preparing Africans for subjection to a global capitalist order. The mission could

---

[82] Edward Steere to Festing, 24 February 1873.
[83] 84J. E Hine, *Days Gone by: Being Some Account of Past Years Chiefly in Central Africa* (London: J. Murray, 1924), 86, 95–96, 98.
[84] 'The Work at Likoma', *Central Africa*, July 1902.
[85] Frank Weston to H. M., St Mark's Theological College, Zanzibar, 23 March 1900, A1 (17) A, 60, UMArch. Weston took a particularly strong stance. As Andrew Porter has demonstrated, different missionaries had different objections to the colonial project. Porter, *Religion Versus Empire?*
[86] Jean Comaroff and John L. Comaroff, *Of Revelation and Revolution: The Dialectics of Modernity on a South African Frontier*, vol. 2 (Chicago; London: University of Chicago Press, 1997), 58.

not control the terms of reference whereby the mission-provided symbols of modernity were interpreted. Indeed, as John Peel argued, missionaries helped sustain colonialism and capitalism through mundane and material practices, rather than having a colonial quality inherent in their religious worldview, as the Comaroffs suggest.[87]

Part of the attraction of missions lay in the fact that, even if unintentionally, missionaries engaged Africans in modernity or, more specifically, the market economy and formal institutional education, and provided a connection to the colonial powers.[88] Moreover, as Peter Pels suggested, joining the mission school was one way of entering the cash economy, whether the missionaries approved of it or not.[89] Africans found ways of pursuing social mobility and having a stake in a coastal or European modernity, and were, thus, able and willing to circumvent the missionaries' attitudes. In short, UMCA missionaries were not able to shelter Africans from worldliness, but the remoteness of some parts of the mission, especially on the mainland, did some of that work for the missionaries.

The UMCA intended to help Africans develop 'their own country in the modern world', and sought to avoid what they saw as the threat of Africans becoming poor imitations of Europeans.[90] As Weston put it in 1905, 'if it is true that the African is going to wear a frock coat and a top hat some day, it is no part of the Mission's duty to teach him to do so'.[91] For these reasons, both African converts and missionaries were urged to live as simply as possible.[92] They were generally of the view that African participation in the global

---

[87] Peel, *Religious Encounter and the Making of the Yoruba*, 6.
[88] John D. Y. Peel, *Aladura: A Religious Movement among the Yoruba* (London: Oxford University Press, 1968); Terence O. Ranger, 'The Mwana Lesa Movement of 1925', in *Themes in the Christian History of Central Africa*, ed. Terence O. Ranger and John Weller (London: Heinemann, 1975), 67.
[89] Pels, *A Politics of Presence*, chap. 5.
[90] Diana K. Coldicott, *Two Zanzibar Missionaries: Canon and Mrs A.B. Hellier of the Universities' Mission to Central Africa* (Abingdon: Anton, Hearn & Scott, 2008), 41.
[91] H. Maynard Smith, *Frank, Bishop of Zanzibar: Life of Frank Weston, 1871-1924* (London: Society for Promoting Christian Knowledge, 1926), chap. 4 part 1.
[92] See for example: T., 'Bare Feet', *Central Africa: A Monthly Record of the Universities' Mission to Central Africa*, January 1920; Frank Weston to H. M., Kiungani, Zanzibar, 14 January 1899, A1 (17) A, 17, UMArch; Frank Weston to H. M., Kiungani, Zanzibar, 15 June 1901, A1 (17) A, 105, UMArch; Rev. J. K. Key to Rev. W. H. Penney, Mkuzi, 9 December 1888, A1 (6) A, 834, UMArch; Frank Weston, 'Some Remarks on Methods of Missionary Work, Being an Open Letter Addressed to the Rt. Rev. Lord Bishop of Zanzibar', St. Andrew's College, Kiungani, Zanzibar (private), December 1898, A1 (18) B, 138 and A1 (7), UMArch;

economy must take a slow and steady path and that it must be on African terms. This point of view partly explains why the missionaries had a difficult relationship with colonial authority. In the early twentieth century missionaries were increasingly critical of the government for their hard and fast changes to the country. Weston's brush with Lord Milner in 1920 helps to illustrate these tensions. Milner had issued a White Paper to make a case for labour policies that would further 'encourage' Africans to work for the colonial government. Weston promptly produced a pamphlet to criticise these proposed policies. For Weston, colonial authority had the responsibility to protect the 'weaker people' and Milner's policies were a 'new form of slavery'. Weston, and many other missionaries before him, were in favour of British colonialism over German colonialism from a very early period, but they had deep-set misgivings about British colonial policies.[93]

Reflecting the complexity of the mission itself, the UMCA sources pose several challenges for the historian of Africa. For instance, the missionaries rarely named any Africans whom they did not consider to be of high status, even if they had converted to Christianity. Thus, as Peel argued, the problem is not simply that missionary sources represent deep prejudices (though they often do), it is that missionaries had selective interests, and their records carry a host of assumptions, not only about Africans but also about Christianity, colonialism and themselves. Another problem is that when missionaries reported discussions with local people, African voices did not always appear coherent, as missionaries failed to fully understand them, or instrumentalised them in pursuit of their own agendas.[94] The published material, though rich and diverse, is often problematic as it was created in order to inspire support, donations and new missionary recruits. Moreover, there are risks involved with overly relying on mission sources that have found their way back to the metropole. Namely, sources damaging to the mission's reputation, or sources that were simply deemed irrelevant to missionaries, could have been destroyed in the process of bringing the collection together in the UK. Not all the letters in the UMCA archive were sent from Africa to the metropole, but many of the letters sent in the other direction or between mission stations would have been lost due to practical constraints. Because one is

---

'Wealth', *Central Africa*, August 1932; 'Intercessions and Thanksgivings' (Mkusi, 16 October 1922), A1 (22), 182, UMArch; Bishop Richardson, 'Letter to Members of UMCA', 1897, A1 (7), UMArch.

[93] Frank Weston, *The Black Slaves of Prussia: An Open Letter to General Smuts* (London: Universities Mission to Central Africa, 1917), 4.

[94] Peel, *Religious Encounter and the Making of the Yoruba*, 12–13.

often left reading one side of the conversation, it is sometimes quite difficult to detect what might be the subject matter.

Competing 'civilisations'

Beyond thinking of how Africans made a living at the mission, this study is also about the social ideals for which they strived. In other words, making a living is not only about economic survival; workers naturally have social ambitions, though, much of the time, social and economic ambitions are so closely intertwined that they are impossible to disconnect. In this sense, being civilised and expanding one's networks could help provide more and better livelihood opportunities. For most of the period this book explores, the mission was not hegemonic and it was not clear which identity (Christian/European or Muslim/Arabicate) led to a better life. In fact, these two cultural complexes were considered neither separate nor opposite to each other. The Swahili term, '*uungwana*', which roughly translates as 'civilisation' and relates closely – though not straightforwardly – to Swahili coastal cultures, is essential to this study.[95] '*Ustaarabu*', from the term 'Arab', also means 'civilization' and is often translated as meaning something like modernity. In 1873 Steere described the Swahili people as: 'a mixed race of Arabs and negroes. They hold only the villages or small towns on the sea, and the gardens and plantations adjoining. The Swahili are all Mohommedans, chiefly of the Shafi sect.' [96] Yet we should not take the common use of the term '*mwungwana*' as evidence of the hegemony of anyone who identified as such. As James de Vere Allen, a scholar of Swahili culture, explained:

> [T]he insistence of the *waungwana* upon certain privileges – upon their right to live in their own, stone-build sector of town, for instance, and upon certain forms of dress and rules of endogamy – should not necessarily be seen as a reflection of their lasting monopoly of real power. Rather it should be interpreted, in some contexts at least, as indicative of the tenuousness of their grasp upon it: by holding on to such relatively trivial points they were able to preserve the facade of their superiority over immigrant traders and others who often in fact controlled much of the wealth.[97]

---

[95] Felicitas Becker, *Becoming Muslim in Mainland Tanzania 1890–2000* (Oxford: Oxford University Press, 2008), 223; Felicitas Becker and P. Wenzel Geissler, eds., *Aids and Religious Practice in Africa* (Leiden: Brill, 2009), 122.
[96] Edward Steere, *Central African Mission, Its Present State and Prospects* (London: Rivingtons, 1873), 7–8.
[97] James de Vere Allen, 'Swahili Culture and the Nature of East Coast Settlement',

Thus, the *waungwana* had tenuous political hegemony. Less surprisingly, for those looking to achieve *uungwana*, and escape slavery and/or peasantry, a person had to seek patronage. Despite all this, they were nevertheless a positive symbol of socio-economic improvement. One respondent, Canon John Mwamazi, explained how terms such as '*waswahili*', '*waungwana*', '*wamrima*', and '*ustaarabu*' related to each other: 'Swahili people [*Waswahili*] were people of civilization [*wastaarabu*]; Swahili people were people who pray. And so to be Muslim was to be a gentleman [*muungwana*], to be a civilized person [*mstaarabu*], to be a person who was modern [*aliyestaarabika*]. So many entered and left behind their native cultures and customs to be Muslim.'[98] In this passage, Mwamazi demonstrates the overlap between being modern and being Muslim. Indeed, prayer and religion were central to the definition of '*mwungwana*'. Thus, becoming *mwungwana*, *mmrima* or *mswahili* meant converting to Islam as well as embracing coastal and urban identity.[99]

Especially in Zanzibar, the missionaries operated within a status economy in which a hegemonic Arabicate, Islamic coastal culture defined the markers of sophistication. They also depended on diplomatic contact to the Sultan (especially in the nineteenth century), and on good relations to other power-brokers who operated within this status economy. Moreover, missionaries used the same currencies and measures as the Muslim-dominated trade. At the same time, the meaning of Western/Christian progress was itself ambiguous for the missionaries, as they were so sceptical of the industrialising, profit-seeking, urban Victorian version of it. But how did the ideals of *uungwana* manifest themselves in everyday life? Various fashions and a commitment to education reflected the importance of Islamic cultures. Indeed, despite occasional disdain from educated Tanzanian Christians about uneducated Muslims, European influence was not the only drive for formal institutional education. As Anne Bang has observed, the importance of Islamic education was increasingly emphasised c. 1860–1940 in the western Indian

---

The International Journal of African Historical Studies, 14, no. 2 (1981): 317. doi.org/10.2307/218047.

[98] '*Waswahili ni watu ambao ni wastaarabu, waswahili watu wanaoswali. Watu wanaosali kwa hiyo kuwa mwislam ni kuwa muungwana, kuwa mstaarabu, kuwa mtu aliyestaarabika kama hivyo. Kwa hiyo wengi waliingia kuacha mila na desturi za kienyeji kuwa waislam.*' Canon Mwamazi, interview, 00:26:00.

[99] Glassman, *Feasts and Riot*, xvi.

Ocean world.[100] Moreover, speaking Swahili well was increasingly a prerequisite for becoming *mwungwana*.[101]

Missionaries utilised the vocabulary of Arabocentric modernity in their efforts to engineer Christian communities. In doing so, they fed into the existing cultural hegemony, rather than supplanting it. That language was Swahili, which the missionaries taught, partly in order to facilitate and unify mission education and communities. Another way to 'speak' this language was to distribute high status clothing among mission followers. For instance, mission school boarders and teachers wore *kanzu* (a white or cream coloured ankle or floor length robe worn by men), *kikoy* (a piece of cloth tied around the waist), and *kofia* (a brimless cylindrical cap with a flat crown, worn by men in East Africa, especially in Swahili-speaking cultures). These items were sought-after luxuries that may have been understood to be in exchange for their commitment as followers; a kind of payment.[102]

Missionaries also made use of the antonym of '*uungwana*': '*ushenzi*' ('uncivilised', 'heathen'). '*Shenzi*' had a broad meaning, though it was mainly an offensive term that townspeople would use to describe those they disapproved of, it also meant pagans, non-Muslims or converts who were criticised for their perceived lack of orthodoxy.[103] Joseph Thomson in 1881, and Edward Steere and Henry Bartle Frere in 1874 noted that coastal people used the term '*washenzi*' to denote something akin to 'wild folk'.[104] James Allen noted that

[100] Anne K. Bang, *Islamic Sufi Networks in the Western Indian Ocean (c.1880–1940)* (Leiden: Brill, 2014), 7, 108–42.

[101] Felicitas Becker, 'Obscuring and Revealing: Muslim Engagement with Volunteering and the Aid Sector in Tanzania', *African Studies Review*, 58, no. 02 (September 2015): 25.

[102] Semkuruto exclaimed, 'It was just a sheet, a *kikoi* and a jumper that's it, this was it was drawing them in, it drew people this to go to school. They were strategic about how they attracted people into school [...] they [the students] were really spoilt!' Vincent William Semkuruto, interview by Zuhura Mohammed, Dar es Salaam, 30 October 2014; similar views were presented in the interview of John Makange (pseudonym), interview by Zuhura Mohammed, Magila, 23 October 2014. Frewer explained that once students had invested a significant amount of time into the mission schools, they stood to gain materially. All money that the missionaries gave the male students was spent on clothing. Also, if they went to Kiungani, felt obliged to bring back gifts for their family members. C. C. Frewer, 'African Boys', *African Tidings*, May 1909.

[103] Glassman, *Feasts and Riot*, xvi, 241.

[104] Frere, *Eastern Africa as a Field for Missionary Labour. Four Letters to the Archbishop of Canterbury, Etc.*, 34; Steere, *Central African Mission, Its Present State and Prospects*, 8; Joseph Thomson, *To the Central African Lakes and Back* (London: Sampson, Low, Marston, Searle & Rivington, 1881), 72. Similarly, Burton defined '*washenzi*' as 'savages': Sir Richard Francis Burton, *Zanzibar;*

in the late nineteenth and early twentieth centuries, to be '*muungwana*' was to be 'civilised' and 'urbane'. Meanwhile, to be '*mshenzi*' was to be 'uncouth' and 'savage'.[105] Indeed, coastal people utilised '*shenzi*' and '*kafiri*' as terms of rebuke to describe upcountry people from the late nineteenth century onwards. As such, Glassman noted that '*mshenzi*' was 'a term of abuse used to refer to upcountry people, including newly imported slaves'.[106] Francis Eling Pearse, a UMCA missionary, made much the same observation in 1925, though he did not attribute it to slave status: '[A] young man from the hills [...] is openly derided as a *mshenzi* (heathen), which is practically a term of reproach, an insult, a fact which Europeans and especially missionaries should remember. [...] they [the Muslims] refuse him [the youth] to eat with them. As the African of the wilds is above all things hospitable to the passing stranger, this cuts him to the quick.'[107]

Despite this missionary's concern about causing offense, the term '*shenzi*' was used in Swahili church literature that was distributed in the mission to describe practices the missionaries had outlawed.[108] The other major chasm between what it was to be '*mwunwgana*' and '*mshenzi*' revolved around slave status.[109] In much the same way that missionaries did not trust that ex-slaves could be genuine converts, Tanganyikans felt they could trust *wauungwana* because they had kin.[110] As explained in the previous section, it was not the missionaries' intention to enhance the social mobility of the grassroots to build

---

city, island and coast, vol. 2 (London: Tinsley Brothers, 1872), 338. The term '*shenzi*' also had a history as an ethnonym in Bonde. The Bondei were referred to as '*washenzi*' prior to the breakup of the Shambaa kingdom. Burton, 2:161; Steere, *Central African Mission, Its Present State and Prospects*, 8; Lawrence Kombo to J. P. Farler, Magila, Tanga, 15 May 1879, A1 (6) A, 425, UMArch; Willis, 'The Makings of a Tribe: Bondei Identities and Histories', 196. As Glassman, who cites German sources, has suggested, the pejorative sense of '*shenzi*' may partly be explained by the fact that most of Bondei were ruled by the Kilindi. Glassman, *Feasts and Riot*, 241.

[105] Allen, 'Swahili Culture and the Nature of East Coast Settlement', 316.
[106] Glassman, *Feasts and Riot*, 62.
[107] Francis Eling Pearse, *Africa on the Hilltops* (London: Universities' Mission to Central Africa, 1926), 27.
[108] *Habari za Mwezi: Bonde na Zigua*, vol. 2, 12 (Kanisa la Msalaba Mtakatifu, Magila, 1896); *Kitabu cha Ibada za Kanuni na kuhudumu sakramenti pamoja na kawaida za kanisa ilivyo desturi ya kanisa la unguja [The Book of Principle Services and Ministering the Sacraments of the Zanzibar Church]* (Society of SS. Peter & Paul, 1928).
[109] Glassman, *Feasts and Riot*, xvi, 62.
[110] This saying collected by Krapf illustrates this point well: '*Kua kalima, kua kulla neno, laken wtuma (hawana kalima) hawafanii hivi.*' ('Free men hold together, assist each other in word and in everything, but slaves do not and cannot, because they are dependent on their master and cannot join others.') Johann Ludwig

up a Christian community. Nonetheless, struggles over competing claims to civilised status were central to the experiences of mission workers and, even, to the missionaries themselves.

Case studies and research findings

The book consists of five case studies in a loosely chronological sequence. Chapter 1 is about the UMCA's founding work in Magila in north-eastern Tanzania from 1867 to 1887 as I explore the mission's first mainland project to build in stone. At this stage, education and employment were highly politicised and had very little to do with respectability and social mobility. If anything, the mission presented a serious obstacle to people's livelihoods as the missionaries' activities threatened the provision of sustenance by burning lime in the forests. Rather, the mission provided – albeit limited – opportunities for political advancement and security. Indeed, this chapter reveals how the mission competed with other local power-brokers for labour, natural resources and political authority. Conflicts regarding labour were at the centre of these interactions as missionaries were trying to build the mission stations out of stone. The chapter untangles fragmented historical accounts to demonstrate what I call an example of 'extraversion', that is, African leaders relying on resources brought in from the outside to maintain patronage relations. In this case, it was the headmen who exploited missionary wealth for their own ends.

Chapter 2 turns our attention to the mission in Zanzibar and takes the building of the UMCA cathedral in Zanzibar, known as the Slave Market Church, as a case study of mission labour management. The fact that most of the labour in Zanzibar at the time was slave labour put missionaries in a difficult position. On the one hand, they believed in ending slavery and their abolitionist activity won them significant funding. On the other hand, missionaries wanted to build and establish themselves. That required labour. Thus, missionaries – apparently unwittingly – hired slaves to carry out their ambitious building projects, notably the Slave Market Church. This chapter is about how this affected the reputation of missionaries in Zanzibar and the extent to which missionaries altered their opinions on slavery though the building process.

Chapter 3 turns our attention to the boys' school in Kiungani, Zanzibar and examines the value of the mission to those attempting to mitigate their slave or ex-slave status. This school was initially built for ex-slave children but, from the 1890s, missionaries increasingly aimed to use it as a space in which to teach mainland students who were thought of as 'voluntary', in stark contrast to the ex-slaves who did not chose to be at the mission of their own free will.

Krapf, *A Dictionary of the Swahili Language* (London: Trübner and Co., 1882), 269.

Throughout this time, missionaries derided the school's relative proximity to the 'city' of Zanzibar, which apparently radiated immoral behaviour. I argue that the education and work the mission offered to ex-slaves, and descendants of slaves, was of little value to all but a small, mission-educated elite. It was to this small group that mission education and work had the capacity to provide a degree of emancipation. Yet even for those who resisted Christianity, the personal networks they made among African Christians were highly valuable but not sufficient by themselves because networking with Muslims and being part of the coastal modernity was so essential. Moreover, a 'coastal', implicitly Muslim notion of modernity was hegemonic in Zanzibar, and networking with Muslims was required to establish a place in the status economy derived from this notion. Thus, the mission had only a limited utility to those seeking to make the most of a Swahili coastal modernity.

Chapter 4 turns to the counterpart female experience. Because the sexes were so starkly separated in the Zanzibar mission, it is essential to consider the history of the girls and women separately, too. I also analyse the situations of male and female students separately because the mission intensified the already gendered trajectories for moving on from slave status. The UMCA's Zanzibar girls' school was further from the city in an area called Mbweni. This was intentional to the missionaries' design to protect women and girls, above all, from the immoralities of urban life. Equally, this was a site in which women and girls were to be aligned with 'traditional' mainland values and household labour. 'Mbweni girls', that is, students of the eponymous UMCA girls' school, were unique among women associated with the mission for their high level of education, but this did not necessarily ease their troubles when finding marriage suitors or work. Although the mission did not necessarily help these women find livelihoods, it did serve as a crucial safety net and networking environment for many.

Chapter 5 sets out the history of domestic service, from its beginnings as a constituent of the mission school curriculum to its emergence in the twentieth century as a respectable form of skilled employment. The relationship between domestic service and the mission reveals just how closely education and work were intertwined. Domestic service also had roots in the cultures of slaves seeking to emerge as *waungwana*. Thus, the chapter untangles the associations between domestic service, European domesticity, and the status contests of coastal cultures.

In contrast to a body of literature that links converting to Christianity and/or working for a mission society to positive social mobility, I argue that the valuing of mission education was a later development, which began after the period this book covers, from the 1930s onwards. Prior to that point, the mission was not culturally hegemonic and status struggles were pursued in multiple idioms, drawing from the Islamic cultures of coastal East Africa as much as from the cultures of Anglican Christianity. Although the mission might not have provided a route to prosperity, it did offer partial livelihoods through the work that the missions required. Access to education in the earlier years of mission did not necessarily equate with desirable socio-economic conditions. Many socially marginal students were, concurrently, workers who depended on the mission in order to make a living. This aspect of the relation between European missionaries and Africans integrated in missions deserves closer attention and scrutiny.

Before the British altered the political economy, education had only limited appeal, while the teaching profession was not highly esteemed by Africans, although it offered some teachers the security and status of a regular income. However, after the First World War and with British colonialism in Tanzania, things changed. Missionaries were no longer major employers, but the mission did rise to prominence as a place of education. From the 1920s, school children, or their families, willingly paid school fees. Conversely, in the nineteenth century, school children received gifts for going to school. By the end of the period covered, Christians were at a social and economic advantage by virtue of their access to formal institutional education. This was a major shift and schooling became an obvious path towards future employment and economic mobility. From this point, people carried knowledge and experience away with them from the mission to make a living elsewhere. The pre-1914 period is a relatively understudied phase of mission history because it is obscured by the phase that followed it, in which the mission's role as a provider of a valuable education was obvious. Reading the entire move towards Christian-educated elites gaining influence and taking a place in the colonial system as a process that culminated at the time of independence is to do history backwards.[111]

Converts, many of whom came from marginal social backgrounds, sought to overcome a heritage of exploitative social relations and to redraw the field for the negotiation of dependency to their advantage. But, as I will show, the mission also contributed to new sets of exploitative social relations in a hierarchy of work and education. The mission did not (during the period this book covers) create unified and progressive 'communities'.[112] Rather, the UMCA provided resources for status struggles. The definitions of status in these struggles continued to draw on a variety of sources, not all of them English, European or Christian.

---

[111] Much as Cooper suggests: Frederick Cooper, *Africa since 1940: The Past of the Present* (Cambridge: Cambridge University Press, 2002), 20.

[112] Later on in the British colonial and early postcolonial periods a more unified Christian community emerged, as explained in Prichard, *Sisters in Spirit*.

CHAPTER 1

Missionary Authority in Late Precolonial Magila, 1867–87

In May 1881 a headman and slave-dealer named Segao claimed the ancestors had visited him in the night with a message about the UMCA missionaries.[1] Segao, who was hostile to the mission, was based in Mkuzi village in the Magila[2] region near the *nyika* (uncultivated land, forest) where the missionaries had been burning lime to produce the mortar for building a stone church and other stone buildings at their main site in Msalabani a few miles away. Segao's vision suggested that this lime-burning disturbed and angered the ancestors, so much so that they were rendering healers' medicine ineffective against the attacks of raiders and slave-traders, who were identified as Wadigo. This incident was part of a longer story of conflict. Between 1880 and 1881 a range of people, from the grassroots up to one of the greatest powerbrokers of the region, known as Kibanga, were all in a dispute with the mission over the lime-burning.

The conflict over lime-burning was the culmination, and a particularly striking example, of on-going varied and complex tensions that developed from the UMCA's first visit to Magila in 1867. This lime-burning conflict is a lens into the multiple and ambivalent ways in which local people felt about the mission. At this time, missionaries were extremely vulnerable due to their lack of local knowledge. Yet, simultaneously, missionaries had the potential to be extremely powerful because they were perceived to hold valuable connections with the coast and, thus, access to gunpowder and arms.

Relationships between local powerholders and missionaries were often fraught, but strong – if relatively short-lived – alliances did emerge.

---

[1] J. P. Farler, 'Other Troubles at Magila', *Central Africa*, September 1884.
[2] I refer to 'Magila' as Msalabani (a name that was later ascribed to it) to avoid confusion between Magila the village and Magila the region.

Missionaries saw these relationships as foundational to their conversion strategy. Anne Marie Stoner-Eby, working on Masasi in southern Tanzania, suggested that the UMCA only began to gain converts once they responded positively to the chiefs and made alliances with them.[3] The findings here suggest a different story because, in the UMCA stations of Magila, missionaries only began securing a steady flow of converts once they had abandoned their top-down conversion strategy around the time German colonialism began. This is explained at least in part by how Masasi and Magila had different strategies regarding the deployment of ex-slaves. Masasi's development began with a failed experiment to import ex-slaves from Zanzibar, which was abandoned in 1882. In contrast, only a few dozen ex-slaves were sent to Magila when missionaries were attempting to address labour shortages. Therefore, unlike Masasi, the Magila mission was immediately designed to establish alliances with chiefs, rather than focusing on ex-slaves. However, again apparently unlike Masasi, allying with chiefs in Magila brought few advantages. The fact that chiefs sent their dependants (often slaves or orphans of deceased chiefs) to the mission school may have done more to attach slave status to the mission than bolster its legitimacy, as these dependants were usually displaced children.[4] In this period, it was truer than ever that 'mission communities' and 'Christian communities' were not synonymous. As such, the people of the mission should be considered as followers rather than converts. These followers included a range of individuals, including child pawns, slaves fleeing their masters, as well as non-slaves grasping at opportunities to supplement their livelihoods.

To better understand the wider social, political and economic context of the time, it is essential that we explore how missionaries and local powerholders both worked together and against each other. These interactions also help explain how the missionaries' labour demands had a significant impact on the way they were perceived. This chapter will explore the case of the lime-burning conflict in detail, as well as the missionaries' top-down conversion strategy. It will also assess the role of slave trading and human pawnship in terms of the political relationships between missionaries and Africans. But first, it is essential to set out the political context.

---

[3] Anne Marie Stoner-Eby, 'African Leaders Engage Mission Christianity: Anglicans in Tanzania, 1876–1926' (PhD, Pennsylvania, University of Pennsylvania, 2003), xii, xiv, 402.

[4] As Willis suggested. Justin Willis, 'The Makings of a Tribe: Bondei Identities and Histories', *The Journal of African History* 33, no. 2 (1 January 1992): 191–208; Stoner-Eby, 'African Leaders Engage Mission Christianity: Anglicans in Tanzania, 1876-1926', xiv.

The political context

Kimweri ya Nyumbai, the King of the Kilindi clan, based in Vuga, ruled the Shambaai kingdom from 1815 to 1862. The zenith of his power, which was based on his rain medicine, came in the 1850s.[5] Steven Feierman's oral history record suggests people in Shambaai remembered this being a peaceful and prosperous time. However, Kimweri's 'golden age' faced significant resistance as the Bondei, a very loosely defined group made up of multiple clans who had long-standing grievances, saw very limited benefits in being part of the Kilindi state, especially considering the violent enforcement of tribute payments.[6] Crucially, Kimweri failed to recognise the necessity of firearms in order to secure power.[7] All levels of people, including petty local headmen, were able to buy firearms with slaves and multiply the number of slaves they owned by using the firearms to procure more slaves. This economic free-for-all rendered the Shambaai kingdom vulnerable. [8]

Kimweri's death in 1862 compounded the Shambaai Kingdom's vulnerability, which in turn prompted the kingdom's split. Semboja, one of Kimweri's younger sons, swiftly seized the throne.[9] The Bondei did not tolerate the authority of Semboja, partly because he was Kilindi, and thus represented the Bondei's oppressors. Semboja also lacked the central quality of a Kilindi chief in that he did not possess rain magic, but he made up for that in his trading power.[10] This led to the Kiva rebellion of 1868, causing the breakup of the

---

[5] J. P. Farler, 'The Usambara Country in East Africa', *Proceedings of the Royal Geographical Society and Monthly Record of Geography* 1, no. 2 (1 February 1879): 81. doi.org/10.2307/1800252; John Iliffe, *A Modern History of Tanganyika* (Cambridge: Cambridge University Press, 1979), 22; Steven Feierman, *Peasant Intellectuals: Anthropology and History in Tanzania* (Madison, WI: University of Wisconsin Press, 1990), 88–89.

[6] Iliffe, *A Modern History of Tanganyika*, 65–66; Willis, 'The Makings of a Tribe: Bondei Identities and Histories'; Feierman, *Peasant Intellectuals: Anthropology and History in Tanzania*, 49–50.

[7] Iliffe, *A Modern History of Tanganyika*, 65–66; Feierman put less emphasis on the demanding nature of Shambaai rule. He suggested that conflict over tribute labour was fairly minimal. Though, he did add that conflict over livestock tribute was far more contentious. Feierman, *Peasant Intellectuals: Anthropology and History in Tanzania*, 52.

[8] Willis, 'The Makings of a Tribe: Bondei Identities and Histories', 195–97; Iliffe, *A Modern History of Tanganyika*, 66; Feierman, *Peasant Intellectuals: Anthropology and History in Tanzania*, 69.

[9] Iliffe, *A Modern History of Tanganyika*, 65–66; Feierman, *Peasant Intellectuals: Anthropology and History in Tanzania*, 69, 89.

[10] Which is why he demanded 'money, hunting weapons and medicine' from the German colonialists he negotiated with c. 1894. Jonathon Glassman, *Feasts*

Shambaai state and expulsion of Kilindi governors from Bonde.[11] This did not put a complete stop to Semboja's authority, which was revolutionary because it marked a point at which the political power that claimed to ensure security and sustenance of the peasantry was less important than it once had been.[12] Even so, Kibanga, who was one of Kimweri's sons, based at Handei, was the most powerful individual in the Bondei region. Unlike Semboja, Kibanga ingratiated the Bondei.[13]

By the time the missionaries became established in the Magila region, Kilindi rule was already in decline. In 1867, Charles Argentine Alington tried (and failed) to plant a UMCA mission station in the Kilindi royal capital of Vuga.[14] From 1868 onwards, there had been a sustained period of unrest, creating the many but weak power-brokers that Farler encountered. This was a period known locally as '*pato*' ('rapacity'). The Magila region was highly unstable, and there were frequent small-scale grassroots attacks in the north-east against slave-traders and exploitative chiefs.[15] The disorder persisted into the 1880s. The Wadigo, who had spread south from the Shimba hills, were associated with much of the raiding for women and children to trade as slaves.[16] The Bondei and the mission consequently had tense relations with the Wabondei.[17]

---

and Riot: Revelry, Rebellion, and Popular Consciousness on the Swahili Coast, 1856–1888, Social History of Africa (Portsmouth, NH; London; Nairobi; Dar es Salaam: Heinemann; James Currey; EAEP; Mkuki Na Nyota, 1995), 51; Johann Ludwig Krapf and Ernst Georg Ravenstein, *Travels, Researches, and Missionary Labours, during an Eighteen Years' Residence in Eastern Africa* (London: Trübner and Co., 1860), 384.

[11] According to Farler the Bondei were assisted by Maliko, Wali of Fort Tongwe (a slave of Seyyid Majid, the late Sultan of Zanzibar), and called themselves Wakiva. Farler, 'The Usambara Country in East Africa', 85.

[12] Feierman, *Peasant Intellectuals: Anthropology and History in Tanzania*, 115.

[13] Iliffe, *A Modern History of Tanganyika*, 65–66; Feierman, *Peasant Intellectuals: Anthropology and History in Tanzania*, 89.

[14] Similarly, in 1876, Farler tried to establish a mission station at a town called Pambili, which had a history of being a dominant political centre A. E. M. Anderson-Morshead, *The History of the Universities' Mission to Central Africa 1859–1896* (London: Universities Mission to Central Africa, 1897).

[15] Iliffe, *A Modern History of Tanganyika*, 65.

[16] Charles Yorke, Pambili, Tanga, c 1881, A1 (6) A, 248, UMArch; Edward Steere to Rev. W. H. Penney, Zanzibar, June 1881, A1 (3) A, 348, UMArch; J. P. Farler to Rev. W. H. Penney, Kiungani, Zanzibar, August 1884, A1 (6) A, 441, UMArch; J. P. Farler to Rev. W. H. Penney, Zanzibar, 24 August 1881, A1 (6) A, 403, 408, UMArch.

[17] Even in 1925, the Wadigo had retained their commitment to Islam despite their proximity to eager missionaries. Although this article is by Hellier, the comments

In May 1881, the UMCA missionary John Farler reported that 'The whole Usambara and Bondei country is in a state of anarchy. There is no head chief, and all are jealous one of another, while the Wadigo in the north and the Wakilindi in the south-west are constantly making raids upon them.'[18] Eventually, as part of a wider trend in coastal regions, each chiefdom became almost independent and narrowly attached to villages rather than whole regions.[19] Despite the fact that the glory of Vuga was a thing of the past, UMCA missionaries stubbornly clung to the idea that the Shambaai kingdom was where the power rightfully lay. As late as 1886, a missionary proclaimed that Vuga was 'the real capital of this country'.[20]

At this time of crisis, the missionaries were able to offer limited protection to insecure commoners.[21] For instance, they seem to have made trading less dangerous. The market near Msalabani in Magila, named Mambo Sasa, had previously been a site of violence, triggered by the frequent raids organised by the headman and slave-trader, Maliko of Tongwe, who demanded tributes from the people using his status as *wali* (governor).[22] Moreover, slave-captives

---

about the Wadigo were lifted from a letter from Athanasio Semkiwa, a Bondei mission teacher. Rev. A. B. Hellier, 'How We Begin', *Central Africa*, August 1925.

[18] J. P. Farler to Rev. W. H. Penney, HMS London, Zanzibar, 30 May 1881, A1 (6) A, 422, UMArch.

[19] Anderson-Morshead, *The History of the Universities' Mission to Central Africa 1859–1896*, 233; Iliffe, *A Modern History of Tanganyika*, 66; J. P. Farler, 'A Letter from Archdeacon Farler', *Central Africa*, July 1887; Willis' account corroborates this observation: Justin Willis, 'The Administration of Bonde, 1920–60: A Study of the Implementation of Indirect Rule in Tanganyika', *African Affairs*, 92, no. 366 (1 January 1993): 53–67. doi.org/10.2307/723096.

[20] J. P. Farler to Bishop Edward Steere, Magila, Tanga, 30 September 1876, A1 (6) A, 398, UMArch; Anderson-Morshead, *The History of the Universities' Mission to Central Africa 1859-1896*; Farler, 'The Usambara Country in East Africa'; 'Our Post Bag', *Central Africa*, February 1886.

[21] 'Our African Postbag', *Central Africa*, May 1885; Yorke, c 1881; Bishop Edward Steere to Robins, Zanzibar, October 1879, A1 (3) B, 501, UMArch. An example of the missionaries' limited capacity to protect mission people from danger is this invasion from 1884, in which Wallis' 'cook and right-hand man' named Nguruwe (nicknamed by the missionaries, 'Piggy') was killed with a poinsoned arrow. Other examples revolve around slave raiders capturing Christians, which will be explored later in this chapter. Mr Wallis, 'The Boondei and Digo War: Fighting at Mkuzi', *Central Africa*, April 1884.

[22] Farler, 'The Usambara Country in East Africa', 87; J. P. Farler, 'Mission Work in Africa' July 1887; J. P. Farler, 'Dr Lenz and the Missionaries', *Central Africa*, September 1887; J. P. Farler, 'The Power of the Gospel', *Central Africa*, September 1887; J. P. Farler to Rev. W. H. Penney, Magila, Zanzibar, (October 1887), A1 (6) A, 531, UMArch; Godfrey Dale, 'An Account of the Principal Customs and Habits of the Natives Inhabiting the Bondei Country, Compiled Mainly for

and famine victims would turn to the mission to seek protection and nourishment. Missionaries offered food in return for labour, smallpox vaccines, and legal protection to slave-captives or slaves looking to challenge their masters.[23]

In the very early days of mission, the missionaries were also – at least in theory – to provide Christian villages. It was not up to the missionary to challenge local authority, but to modify it by teaching chiefs how to govern on Christian principles and their subjects to obey.[24] Shortly after MacKenzie (UMCA bishop, 1861–62) outlined these ideas at a meeting in Manchester in 1860, the first group of UMCA missionaries were at war with the Ajawa in Magomero. Not without controversy, Mackenzie was said to have walked with his pastoral staff in one hand, and his rifle in the other. [25]

From at least the early 1870s, UMCA missionaries agreed that the strategy of setting up Christian villages, made up largely of displaced peoples, should be abandoned. They frequently cited the failed ex-slave settlements at Magomero, Masasi and Zanzibar to illustrate this point. According to missionaries, there was a danger they would attract dependants to the mission who were socially marginal or rejected. In addition, establishing Christian villages usually involved establishing polities headed by missionary-chiefs, who would have to compromise on their morals to maintain power.[26] The missionaries concluded that this strategy was troublesome and likely to result in disingenuous

---

the Use of European Missionaries in the Country', *The Journal of the Anthropological Institute of Great Britain and Ireland*, 25 (January 1, 1896): 204–5, doi:10.2307/2842244; Ven. J. P. Farler, 'Native Routes in East Africa from Pangani to the Masai Country and the Victoria Nyanza', *Proceedings of the Royal Geographical Society and Monthly Record of Geography*, 4, no. 12 (December 1, 1882): 84, doi:10.2307/1800695.

[23] J. P. Farler to Rev. W. H. Penney, Kiungani, Zanzibar, 17 June 1884, 201, A1 (6) A, 434, UMArch.

[24] 'Report of the Meeting at Manchester', 23 May 1860, A1 (3) C, 812, UMArch.

[25] Anderson-Morshead, *The History of the Universities' Mission to Central Africa 1859–1896*, 21–25; Landeg White, *Magomero: Portrait of an African Village* (Cambridge: Cambridge University Press, 1987). Comparable problems arose out of the Masasi ex-slave settlement established in 1872, which showed missionaries that they could not detach themselves from politics. 'Synod' (Zanzibar: Universities' Mission to Central Africa, 5 May 1886), D4, 1, UMArch; Chauncy Maples , 'A Village Community in East Africa', *Mission Life*, 8, no. March (1882): 98; *William Carmichael Porter: Missionary* (Westminster: Universities' Mission to Central Africa, 1910), 11–15; T. O. Ranger, 'Missionary Adaptation of African Religious Institutions: The Masasi Case', in *The Historical Study of African Religion: With Special Reference to East and Central Africa*, ed. Isaria N. Kimambo and T. O. Ranger (Berkeley: University of California Press, 1972), 227.

[26] Bishop Smythies, 'The Church Congress', *Central Africa*, 1890.

conversion. The missionaries' dilemma was that they did not wish to rule, but, because they still wanted to advise, they could not avoid engaging in politics.

Edward Steere, a UMCA bishop (1873–82), played an important role in the mission's revaluation of missionary policies. Steere was particularly committed to the UMCA's non-interventionist doctrine towards political power, violence, war, law and order. As he succinctly put it, 'A king must tolerate many things which a bishop is bound to denounce.'[27] For instance, in 1882 Steere advised that: 'Politically, we have no rights at all, and can only live in the country by the permission or sufferance of the people we find there. There can therefore be no formal administration of justice, or claim to independence, or anything like making war.'[28] A grey area emerged when it came to the question of how much authority a missionary should have over his congregation because Steere believed a missionary should have absolute authority over his African congregation when it came to their religious discipline. Thus, Steere offered this advice to a missionary: 'Of course you will do your best to defend yourself and them against criminals of all kinds, and will try to keep the peace, and preserve order and propriety among your own people. [...] your power is practically unlimited, only it must be exercised with great coolness and discretion, and kept as clear as possible in your religious work.'[29]

Missionaries were also not meant to execute corporal punishment according to Steere. The most extreme discipline a missionary could give was, Steere argued, expulsion from the church. In the event that a person in the mission committed a crime for which expulsion would seem too light a penalty, he advised that the offender should be 'handed over to the local chiefs to deal with according to their customs'.[30] In short, the missionaries' power was meant to be 'paternal and not judicial'.[31] However, the challenge of distinguishing between 'paternal' and 'judicial' authority was, as this chapter shows, too great for the missionaries of the precolonial years.

The idea of the top-down strategy was that converting chiefs would help 'root' missionaries into society and convince people it was safe and worthwhile to send children to school.[32] Thus, Christian influence would trickle from the

---

[27] Edward Steere, *Central African Mission, Its Present State and Prospects* (London: Rivingtons, 1873), 133.
[28] Bishop Edward Steere, 'To the Members of the Universities' Mission to Central Africa (Private)', 1882, A1 (3) C, 819, UMArch.
[29] Steere.
[30] Steere.
[31] Steere.
[32] Robert Heanley, *A Memoir of Edward Steere: Third Missionary Bishop in Central Africa* (London: Office of the Universities' Mission to Central Africa, 1898), 291.

top to the bottom of society, converting whole communities. In practice, this meant mission school students were mostly child pawns in mutual exchanges between missionaries and chiefs. In return for students, chiefs expected to be given gifts. Farler initially obliged, but Herbert W. Woodward, who was very junior in the precolonial period, took a sterner stance when he gained influence in the 1890s, arguing that being in the mission should be considered a gift in itself.[33]

The children who were passed from the chiefs to the missionaries were not the chiefs' children, but rather their child dependants.[34] Often, their fathers had died and they and their mothers had been appropriated by chiefs as followers and/or slaves. Other times, they were orphans. Samuel Sehoza and Petro Limo, the founding priests of the UMCA church in Magila, were wards of Semnkai, a chief who will be discussed in detail below.[35] The historian Justin Willis convincingly argued that the fact that as children Limo and Sehoza were so marginal outside of the mission spurred them on to embrace the mission culture fully and find their own social status as they progressed through the mission hierarchy. So, their personhood was shaped by the mission more dramatically than for any other mission dependant or Christian.[36]

The habit of pawning children to have them join mission school was a product of the mission culture for which Farler was largely responsible. Farler enmeshed himself in politics and left behind a generous paper-trail to prove it. Considering much of this chapter relies on Farler's correspondence, it is imperative I outline his position vis-à-vis the UMCA policy and practice of other missionaries. Part of Farler's approach was to support power-brokers who either identified themselves as 'Bondei' or who were Kilindi but claimed they could unite the Bondei. He saw Bonde as a separate and distinct nation, albeit a weak one, oppressed and preyed upon by its neighbours. Farler

---

[33] H. W. Woodward and Mr Roberts, 'Our Bondei School', *Central Africa*, 1891.

[34] Sundkler and Steed suggested that Kibanga sent sixteen of his children to the mission school. It is likely that they were not Kibanga's biological children. Bengt Sundkler and Christopher Steed, *A History of the Church in Africa* (Cambridge: Cambridge University Press, 2000), 545.

[35] Hugh Peter Kayamba encountered the mission in a very similar way but did not become a mission priest and instead worked in the colonial administration. In 1914 he left the employ of the mission in Zanzibar (as a teacher) to become a trader in Magila, reasoning in his memoir that 'I thought I needed some more money to better my prospects.' Martin Kayamba, 'The Story of Martin Kayamba Mdumi, MBE, of the Bondei Tribe', in *Ten Africans*, ed. Margery Perham, 2nd edn. (London: Faber, 1963), 184.

[36] Justin Willis, 'The Nature of a Mission Community: The Universities' Mission to Central Africa in Bonde', *Past & Present*, no. 140 (1 August 1993): 149.

believed that missionaries' influence could be undermined if they allowed themselves to be financially exploited. He wrote many letters about the weaknesses of other missionaries. For example, George Herbert Wilson, a fellow missionary, was said to have paid for things very readily, especially with regards to building projects. But Wilson was also guilty, in Farler's eyes, of ransoming slaves with little hesitation.[37] Farler wrote plainly to Wilson that, 'it will never do for these people to think that we are mere money bags, and that they can squeeze us with impunity whenever they like'.[38] In short, Wilson and Farler were both missionary politicians, but Wilson's approach was more representative of UMCA policy.

While Willis suggests that Farler was representative of an aggressive missionary policy, I suggest that Farler was an outlier who interpreted UMCA policy according to his own interests and beliefs.[39] In other words, Farler went beyond UMCA policy as he thought the mission should endeavour to modify the existing political hegemony, which entangled him in the temporal affairs to which the mission was so averse. The missionaries who formed the 'home committee' in London were concerned about Farler's behaviour and outlook but had very limited power over the missionaries. Edward Steere, who became bishop in 1874, had more potential to influence and discipline Farler, which he eventually did amid the lime-burning crisis.

Even if Farler was controversial, he was also a valued member of the mission with a knack for the work. He claimed he held legend-like status among the Bondei. This was not completely fabricated. Steere observed that Farler had attracted a huge amount of support, noting in a private letter that when Farler returned after a short trip, 'the whole country was very glad to see him'.[40] A fellow missionary vouched for this, remarking in 1878 that the people of Umba treated him like a Sultan, (a fact that will appear ironic by the third part of this chapter).[41] Moreover, Geldart noted that Farler's name was used to invoke truthfulness, for example: 'By the truth of Mr Farler I'm going to Masa (Mass)'. An African adherent put it this way: '"the truth of Mr Farler" means perfect, honest, straightforward truth, because Mr Farler never told us a lie'.[42] Even

---

[37] J. P. Farler to Bishop Edward Steere, Magila, Tanga, 23 November 1881, A1 (6) A, 597, UMArch.
[38] J. P. Farler to George Herbert Wilson, Magila, Tanga, 18 November 1881, A1 (6) A, 702, UMArch.
[39] Willis, 'The Makings of a Tribe: Bondei Identities and Histories', 199–200.
[40] Steere to Robins, October 1879.
[41] Woodward to Farler, Magila, 1878, A1 (4) A, 228, UMArch.
[42] Rev. H. Geldart, 'Umba', *Central Africa*, January 1885.

though respondents' memory of precolonial times was limited, one respondent said that Farler had a nickname, 'a nice face which is good for me'.[43]

Bishop Steere even briefly considered Farler as a suitable successor, though he concluded that, 'Farler would be by far the best [option] if it were not for his want of judgment and his overbearing self-importance.'[44] As Steere's opinion suggests, Farler was oftentimes afflicted with delusions of grandeur. Farler referred to the Bondei as 'my people', and Magila as 'the heart of Bondei' and he was even so bold as to claim that by 1877 there existed the 'Church of Bondei' even though no conversions had taken place, according to the records.[45] He believed the mission was the centre of the country and that other people viewed it that way too.[46] Farler also suffered, like other missionaries, from continual stress, loneliness, vulnerability, overwork and discontent, which tied into excessive drinking habits.[47] In April 1877 Farler suffered his first mental breakdown but he did not take extended leave until things were at an all-time low in 1881.[48]

However, the political significance of Farler was not due to his temperament alone. More importantly, Farler adapted to the political context and Muslim hegemony and seized the opportunities it brought. For instance, he reported in one letter that: '[A] man who has heard that I am going away to *Ulaya*[49] has begged me not to go, and says "we shall have no one to come to *shauri*. All the men will leave, no one will come to class".'[50] Farler also claimed that, 'My room every morning is a kind of *durbar*,[51] where I advise. Help. Teach. And speak a kind word to all who come.'[52] Farler self-fashioned

---

[43] The Bondei phrase is, '*Cheni chedi chanifala.*'
[44] Edward Steere to James C. Yarborough, Zanzibar, August 1882, A1 (3) A, 444, UMArch.
[45] Willis makes the same observations from his reading of Farler's letters. Willis, 'The Makings of a Tribe: Bondei Identities and Histories'; J. P. Farler to Rev. Cecil Deecles, Magila, Tanga, 20 February 1877, A1 (6) A, 413, UMArch.
[46] J. P. Farler, 'A Letter from Archdeacon Farler'.
[47] J. P. Farler to Bishop Edward Steere, 30 September 1876; J. P. Farler to Bishop Edward Steere, Magila, Tanga, 1877, A1 (6) A, 407, UMArch; Bishop Edward Steere to Rev. W. H. Penney, (private, copies made), 19 October 1888, A1 (3) B, 558, UMArch.
[48] J. P. Farler to Rev. W. H. Penney, Magila, Tanga, 2 November 1881, A1 (6) A, 345, UMArch; J. P. Farler to Chauncy Maples, Magila, Tanga, 27 April 1877, A1 (6) A, 411, UMArch.
[49] Europe.
[50] Advice.
[51] A Persian word for a ruler's noble court.
[52] J. P. Farler to Chauncy Maples, 27 April 1877.

himself as a ruler.⁵³ He held feasts, arranged marriages, counselled power-brokers, positioned himself as a broker of coastal influence, took dependants from headmen, and doled out punishments to regulate behaviour.⁵⁴

It is possible that chiefs were only humouring the missionaries in their seemingly humble requests for *shauri* (advice). In the end, very few influential chiefs converted. Farler's legendary status was more ephemeral than he would have anticipated and his local prominence did not lead to much conversion. Farler was seen as a power-broker among power-brokers more than a religious innovator. Thus, Iliffe's claim that proselytising was likely to be more successful in stateless societies does not apply to the Magila case, in which African power-brokers attempted to take advantage of missionaries to further their own ends. UMCA policy was difficult to abide by in practice, especially under the region's political conditions. This was not just because Farler was an outlier, but because missionary ideals were inconsistent and difficult to apply in such a tumultuous political context.

In his authoritative *Modern History of Tanganyika*, John Iliffe attributed the success of Christianity in the region to the history of Bondei political disunity. Bonde was a society in which the old order had collapsed, leaving no adequate substitute, and, thus, providing an opportunity for new religion. Iliffe explained: 'The Bondei had destroyed Kilindi control but relapsed into statelessness. Semboja [a Kilindi chief] was trying to reconquer the area. Slave hunters were active. So too was Islam. Many Bondei therefore saw the missionaries as valuable allies, willing to seek guns for them and exert diplomatic influence on their behalf.'⁵⁵

In short, Iliffe argued that political instability facilitated mission work.⁵⁶ Indeed, missionaries were looked upon as brokers of firearms and agents in local diplomacy. By this logic, Christianity was certain to fare better in areas where there was no existing, religiously constituted power-holder, and it is evident that the missionaries became participants in diplomatic negotiations. However, Iliffe's argument contains some assumptions that demand attention. The first is that, as a result of the ending of Kilindi rule, the Bondei felt an absence that required filling. Iliffe's use of the term 'relapse' distracts from the fact that the various Bondei factions preferred clan-based, decentralised leadership, which is why they revolted against the Kilindi.⁵⁷ The second assump-

---

⁵³ J. P. Farler to Chauncy Maples.
⁵⁴ J. P. Farler to R. M. Heanley, Magila, Tanga, 13 October 1877, A1 (6) A, 394, UMArch; Willis, 'The Nature of a Mission Community', 141.
⁵⁵ Iliffe, *A Modern History of Tanganyika*, 86.
⁵⁶ Iliffe, 87.
⁵⁷ Feierman, *Peasant Intellectuals: Anthropology and History in Tanzania*, 117.

tion was that 'stateless' societies were more willing to take on new religions or seek out missionary allies. Iliffe implied that political alliances with missionaries to secure firearms might accelerate the spread of Christianity. Even if chiefs converted to Christianity as a result of these alliances, what effect would it have had on people who were subject to such minimal political authority? Moreover, conversion driven by such a worldly rationale would not have equalled the missionaries' idea of 'genuine' conversion. What this discussion tells us is that there is a complex relationship between politics and religious conversion. This becomes even more evident in the light of power-brokers' interactions with the mission, which are analysed in the following section.

Missionaries as allies and patrons

In these early years, missionaries were considered exceptionally strange. On the one hand they were isolated as dangerous outsiders, yet on the other, they had connections with the coast. Thus, the missionaries' key project was to expand their 'wealth in people'.[58] Yet they ruffled feathers at every level. Working people, suspicious of these unknown visitors, were far from attracted to the wage labour and education the mission offered. In terms of the mission's success in gaining followers, Justin Willis argued that some of the UMCA's followers may have considered church attendance as 'a way of making a claim upon the church as a patron', much like participation in *fika* (the making of sacrifices to the dead).[59] He has also demonstrated how the combination of the missionaries' insistence on singular social memberships and the political instability of the precolonial period were deterrents. Mission allegiance came at a great cost for commoners. Missionaries condemned Christians who had plural social memberships, yet survival depended upon the ability to make claims upon multiple different communities for indemnity, as Willis has shown.[60]

---

[58] J.M. Vansina, *Paths in the Rainforests: Toward a History of Political Tradition in Equatorial Africa* (Madison, WI: University of Wisconsin Press, 1990); Jane I. Guyer, 'Wealth in People and Self-Realization in Equatorial Africa', *Man*, 28, no. 2 (1 June 1993): 243–65; James Ferguson, 'Declarations of Dependence: Labour, Personhood, and Welfare in Southern Africa', *The Journal of the Royal Anthropological Institute*, 19, no. 2 (1 June 2013): 223–42.

[59] Willis, 'The Nature of a Mission Community', 142–43; The various forms of *fika* are described in detail in: Dale, 'An Account of the Principal Customs and Habits of the Natives Inhabiting the Bondei Country, Compiled Mainly for the Use of European Missionaries in the Country'.

[60] Willis, 'The Nature of a Mission Community', 135.

In one sense, missionaries were treated the same way as other power-brokers of the time: cautiously and opportunistically.[61] The perceived value of having missionaries as patrons or allies constantly changed. Some people valued them as potential brokers of weapons and gunpowder. Others viewed them as rainmakers. Power-brokers who were less concerned about making alliances spoke more candidly. For instance, a slave-trader, who admitted he had captured a woman the UMCA were attempting to protect, stated that, 'the English are also thieves, the only difference being that while I steal on land, they steal on sea'.[62]

What remained constant is that the missionaries were easy to fool, largely due to their often poor language skills. Communication was extremely difficult in these early days. Often, an appointed African Christian would speak for the missionary and, as a result, missionaries frequently suspected they were not privy to the full picture. Consequently, they became extremely frustrated when they found themselves excluded from negotiations that concerned them.[63] Communication was difficult in another way: many misunderstandings and conflicts arose from the exchange of gifts.

Opportunistic and aspiring leaders sought to benefit from missionary alliances to gain access to gunpowder and coastal connections. Coastal trading connections were essential to power-brokers because firearms were essential, as the fall of the Vuga kingdom exemplified. The explorer Keith Johnston lived up to this expectation as he took 20lb of gunpowder to give as gifts on his travels in 1879.[64] On Kibanga's first meeting with Steere in 1875 it was made very clear that the mission would not help him gain access to gunpowder, but Farler was more flexible.[65] This is well illustrated by the relayed words of a man called Chombo, whose uncle was 'a great man in the country'.[66] Chombo acted as a guide for Farler, who summarised Chombo's advice as follows:

---

[61] Much as other authors have noted. E.g.: Willis, 'The Nature of a Mission Community'; Stoner-Eby, 'African Leaders Engage Mission Christianity: Anglicans in Tanzania, 1876–1926', xiv.

[62] H. W. Woodward, 'A Story of a Woman's Wrongs', *Central Africa*, August 1884.

[63] H. W. Woodward.

[64] Keith Johnston, 'Notes of a Trip from Zanzibar to Usambara, in February and March, 1879', *Proceedings of the Royal Geographical Society and Monthly Record of Geography*, 1, no. 9 (1 September 1879): 545. In 1881 Farler criticised the Sultan for seizing Kibanga's gunpowder. Edward Steere to Rev. W. H. Penney, Zanzibar, 8 January 1881, A1 (3) A, 393, UMArch.

[65] Edward Steere to Polly, Marongo, July 1875, A1 (3) A, 226, UMArch.

[66] J. P. Farler to Bishop Edward Steere, Magila, Tanga, 10 October 1876, A1 (6) A, 387, UMArch.

Chombo recommends that our freed men should have some guns so that they may take their part in the defence of the town if the *Wadigo* should attack it, and he says the fact of their having guns would give such confidence that great numbers would ask for permission to settle there and the knowledge that the *Wazungu* were living there with many guns would be the surest prevention against any attack from the *Wadigo*. [67]

It is noteworthy that Chombo's advice reflects his impression that missionaries had access to arms and a desire for political authority, security and followers. Farler endeavoured to follow Chombo's recommendations and utilise his coastal connections. He made two requests (neither of which were granted) to Steere for firearms and powder and to Steere to ask John Kirk to ask Sultan Barghash bin Said to write a letter to Digo leaders to instruct them not to interfere with the mission. [68] Thus, though missionaries rarely fulfilled expectations to provide gunpowder and arms, aspiring big men persisted in seeing an opportunity in them.

Anglican missionaries and British travellers were increasingly perceived as valuable allies as the slave trade continued to thrive and British influence in Zanzibar became clearer.[69] For example, in the early 1880s rumours spread that the Sultan had a fear of white men.[70] This rumour was partly a product of events in 1884, when a missionary named John Key used his connection to Sir John Kirk to free some 'Bondei' people being held captive in a Pangani prison by the *wali* (a representative of the Sultan). The missionary record connects this narrative to another one that conveys intense conflict between the coast and hinterland. In early 1884, Mbaraku, a 'rebel chief' according to the Zanzibar Sultanate, with the support of many neighbouring chieftains, fortified himself in the Magila mountains.[71] The Sultan instructed the *wali* of Pangani to attack Mbaraku, using 'Bondei' forces. The *wali* demanded these forces fight without pay, which the Bondei refused. Consequently, the *wali* labelled the Bondei rebels, along with Mbaraku.[72]

Though the missionaries usefully connect these two narratives, we cannot be sure that the Bondei travellers were captured in the town as revenge for the Bondei refusing to fight for the Sultan without pay. The power of the *wali*

---

[67] J. P. Farler to Bishop Edward Steere, 30 September 1876.
[68] J. P. Farler to Bishop Edward Steere.
[69] Willis, 'The Makings of a Tribe: Bondei Identities and Histories', 198.
[70] John C. Key, 'An Expedition to Ransom a Slave', *Central Africa*, May 1885.
[71] This was probably in order to defend himself but Smythies suggests it was a (further) act of rebellion. Bishop Smythies, 'The Bishop's Visit to Magila', *Central Africa*, June 1884.
[72] J. P. Farler, 'Other Troubles at Magila', *Central Africa*, September 1884.

to capture this group of Bondei travellers was facilitated by Barghash's proclamation of 18 April 1876. This proclamation gave *wali* the power to capture and imprison people who were believed to be bringing slaves to the coast.[73] It is even possible that part of this group of travelling Bondei were slaves, intended to be sold at the coast. It is probable that the group were captured by the *wali* because they were suspected of being slave-traders and were later admonished for representing the Bondei who refused to obey the Sultan's orders to attack Mbaraku without pay. It is not known if the *wali* eventually decided to pay these Bondei forces, or what happened to Mbaraku, who is not mentioned elsewhere.

In any case, it was incidents like this that showed how dangerous it was for Bondei people to venture to the coast, within reach of the *wali*'s authority. However, it was also a time of famine, and food had to be sourced from the coast. For example, in 1884 the mission sent a caravan to Pangani to buy rice and several groups of other Bondei people, who were not connected with the mission, accompanied them. On arrival at the mission house in Tanga, coastal authorities captured them and put them in prison in very poor conditions. The *wali* refused to release them and only after a UMCA missionary came would they compromise and set free the people who were working for the missionaries. The others, some of whom were Christians, remained imprisoned in such terrible conditions that one of them died. Kirk finally wrote to the Sultan demanding their freedom and for the *wali* to be punished. In turn, the Sultan eventually wrote several letters ordering the release of the Bondei and that the *wali* should report to the Sultan in Zanzibar.[74] Following that, the *wali* denied the claims made against him. Instead, he maintained that the few '*kafir*' he had imprisoned were found in the *nyika*, not the mission house in town, which suggests the *wali* was trying to make a case that they were slave dealers hiding in the forest rather than mission agents looking for food. Farler brought five witnesses, and when the *wali* received their evidence, replied that he would not accept the evidence of '*kafir*'.[75]

The *wali* was sent to the fort in irons and the Sultan paid 200 rupees in compensation, 'to replace the money, clothes, and other things that the soldiers had taken from them, also to compensate the family of the man who died in prison'. In the mission magazine that detailed these events, Farler was careful to note that the Sultan acted very honourably, despite his delayed

---

[73] Moses D. E. Nwulia, *Britain and Slavery in East Africa* (Washington, DC: Three Continents Press, 1975), 143.
[74] J. P. Farler, 'Other Troubles at Magila'.
[75] J. P. Farler.

intervention. Farler added that the Bondei were 'greatly impressed with the might and influence of England'.[76]

However, the missionaries' connections with and influence over coastal authority often made African power-brokers and commoners wary. Indeed, many were suspicious of coastal cultures and authority. For instance, one local headman was reported to have looked upon the new lime buildings of Magila mission disapprovingly, muttering, 'This is not Magila, it is Zanzibar'.[77] He may also have been referring to the use of Swahili and the coastal dress styles of mission people. Coastal influence threatened to undermine the cultural hegemony of the mainland and settling disputes through the governor at Pangani or Tanga. Meanwhile, missionaries were prepared to exercise their coastal influence, even when it risked undermining the authority of dignitaries, including local power-brokers and less local *wali*.[78] This all shows that missionaries could get the Sultan to act against his own representatives and that missionaries had to be 'coastal' to be able to act as Christians and Europeans.

As we have seen from the *wali*'s actions in identifying the Bondei as rebels in 1884, Bondei identity had currency and political valence at the time. Willis argued that Bondei identity existed prior to the missionaries' arrival but was elaborated in the 1880s due to a desire to claim support from outsiders (i.e. missionaries). Moreover, members of the Kilindi faction presented themselves as the rightful rulers of Shambaai and used the idea of the Bondei as a way of defining the local constituency to which they laid claim. In this way, as an audience for these elaborations and potential patrons, missionaries played a role in the shaping of Bondei identity.[79] This was a twist on Iliffe's claim that, '[t]he British wrongly believed that Tanganyikans belonged to tribes; Tanganyikans created tribes to function within the colonial framework.'[80] Although Willis asserted that various ethnic identities existed prior to colonial rule, he was in line with Iliffe's observations that Africans emphasised the clarity of 'tribal' identity in order to manipulate outsiders. Farler and the other missionaries had set themselves up as patrons of the Bondei. In turn, the Bondei elaborated their identity. Willis showed that the Bondei were not a unified cultural body, noting that even today the multitude of clans with distinct identities that make up the Bondei is well remembered and valued as part of Bondei identity.[81]

---

[76] J. P. Farler.
[77] 'Our Post Bag', *Central Africa*, December 1887.
[78] J. P. Farler to Rev. W. H. Penney, 30 May 1881.
[79] Willis, 'The Makings of a Tribe: Bondei Identities and Histories', 201.
[80] Iliffe, *A Modern History of Tanganyika*, 218.
[81] Willis, 'The Makings of a Tribe: Bondei Identities and Histories', 202; Vincent William Semkuruto, interview by Zuhura Mohammed, Dar es Salaam, 30

Kibanga, probably the most powerful man in Bonde, was a mixture of Shambaai and Kilindi. However, Farler was never clear if Kibanga was Kilindi or Bondei. The fact that Kibanga attacked some Kilindi in 1884 suggested to Farler that Kibanga was not Kilindi. This indicates that Farler associated Semboja with the Kilindi more than he associated Kibanga with the Kilindi. Farler did not seem to consider Kibanga Bondei either, even if Kibanga had significant authority over Bonde. Thus, it does appear that Farler understood that Kibanga was a non-Bondei ruler over Bonde. Farler wanted Kibanga on his side. Farler believed that if he paid Kibanga enough respect and showed him enough generosity, he would eventually convert. For example, Farler allowed Kibanga to exhaust the mission stores during the 1877 famine. Farler wrote: 'I bought up all the grain I could, sending far and wide; and I think we should have got through fairly well if Kibanga the king of Usambara had not chosen just that time to pay us a visit with numerous wives, slaves and soldiers; he stayed a week, and having to find food for such a mass cleared us completely out.'[82] The fact that Farler did not appear to consider turning Kibanga away, given the prevailing food shortages, is all the more striking, seeing as Kibanga showed such minimal interest in converting. [83]

But what might Farler's generosity towards Kibanga have meant to onlookers? Kibanga's power derived from his rain-making talents, which provided food. Normally, commoners came to him during famines to be fed. Now, missionaries were providing the most powerful man for miles around with sustenance.[84] It must have been clear to most people in and around the mission that Farler did not procure grain through rain magic. He procured grain through his connections to the coast, much as he and other missionaries were able to procure arms from the coast or seek judicial settlements from the coast.

The meaning of the event is ambiguous. Kibanga made himself dependent on mission supplies, but he also considered himself fully entitled. Kibanga's show of entitlement may have been a smokescreen for his dependence. Or it may have been more simple than that. Kibanga had, after all, offered Farler

---

October 2014; Anthony Christopher Mabundo, interview by Zuhura Mohammed, Handeni, 8 October 2014.
[82] Farler to Heanley, 13 October 1877.
[83] It was not for want of trying that the missionaries failed to convert Kibanga. In 1881, Farler requested that the UMCA recruit a missionary for the sole purpose of converting this ruler. J. P. Farler, Magila, Tanga, September 1877, A1 (6) A, 707, UMArch.
[84] This seems a similar situation to the one Kinyashi, the heir to Kimweri's throne, faced. In the last years of the nineteenth century, Kinyashi was begging German Bethel missionaries for food. Feierman, *Peasant Intellectuals: Anthropology and History in Tanzania*, 127.

military protection. Farler probably knew that Kibanga was not Bondei, but Farler also believed that Kibanga had the potential to unite Bondei people. This is all very much suggests that Farler and Kibanga's political visions in some way converged.

Kibanga had little to gain politically from allying with the mission. It was the big men looking to gain from the fall of the Shambaai kingdom by forming anti-Kilindi factions, notably the Bondei, who saw the value in a missionary alliance. With these factions gravitating towards the mission, the Kilindi rulers also saw the value of a missionary alliance. In order to secure alliances with the missionaries, chiefs, aspiring political leaders and petty local headmen presented themselves as 'true' Bondei.[85] They were more likely to do so if they ruled over vulnerable areas.[86] For established powers such as Kibanga, the alliance with the missionaries was less about gunpowder than about controlling the Bondei faction that had allied with the missionaries. This explains why Kibanga, like other members of the Kilindi faction, emphasised his role as protector of the Bondei in his frequent dealings with the mission.[87] This also explains why Semboja, a Kilindi chief, was unconcerned about securing a missionary alliance. Firstly, gunpowder and trade were his strengths prior to the missionaries' arrival.[88] Secondly, he attracted followers through fear and was not very interested in gaining Bondei followers.[89]

Indeed, missionaries struggled to secure high status conversions. There are only five recorded cases of power-brokers converting, or beginning to convert, during this period. These power-brokers were: Mtali, Sekehufya, Austini Sipindu, Michael Kifungiwe and Henry Semnkai. The shortage of prominent converts probably reflects how missionaries did not hesitate to withdraw their patronage and attack the reputation of adherents who had broken the rules, without regard for their social standing, in order to make an example of them. The principle of leading by example underlay the missionaries' approach. In other words, the mission made it almost impossible to be both Christian and politically influential or socially mobile, as shown in a number of conversion stories below.

The case of Sekehufya, an Umba chief and ritual expert, is a good example of a high status convert for whom mission patronage ultimately did not pay off. Sekehufya was, by Farler's account, the wealthiest man in the area and

---

[85] Willis, 'The Makings of a Tribe: Bondei Identities and Histories', 198.
[86] Mr Wallis, 'The Boondei and Digo War: Fighting at Mkuzi'.
[87] Willis, 'The Makings of a Tribe: Bondei Identities and Histories', 201.
[88] Iliffe, *A Modern History of Tanganyika*, 65–66; Feierman, *Peasant Intellectuals: Anthropology and History in Tanzania*, 89.
[89] Feierman, *Peasant Intellectuals: Anthropology and History in Tanzania*, 69.

infamous for his violence towards his slaves. He was made a catechumen, but in 1887 he showed up on the missionary disciplinary radar when he ordered the killing of an albino child, born to one of his slaves. Farler made it known he considered Sekehufya a murderer and attempted to convince the other chiefs to punish Sekehufya but realised they had neither the interest nor power to do so. The chiefs claimed they were too afraid. Farler then threatened to denounce Sekehufya everywhere and, consequently, Sekehufya was reported to have thrown himself 'on his knees' and 'begged for mercy'. Eventually, Sekehufya went to Msalabani Sunday service to 'confess his guilt openly, and beg forgiveness from God and His people'.[90] According to Farler, Sekehufya's public shame meant his slaves were no longer afraid of his violence.[91] The people reportedly announced, 'Now we are not afraid.'

Farler also claimed that this incident reduced Sekehufya to poverty: 'Sekehufya is now going about clothed in rags, meaner in his apparel than the meanest of his slaves.'[92] There is no independent confirmation of these claims and it is likely that Farler exaggerated the effects of his actions on Sekehufya's status or that there were other reasons for his lost status. It is also possible that Farler stipulated Sekehufya should wear simple clothing as punishment, though Farler does imply the Sekehufya had somehow lost his wealth as a consequence of the mission's punishment. Even so, the account of Sekehufya is revealing. If missionary displeasure meant Sekehufya lost his slaves, then it follows that a power-broker might have better control over his slaves if he abided by the missionaries' prohibitions, which sits uneasily with the UMCA's anti-slavery credentials.

Missionaries, whose influence was limited, did not press Christian chiefs to relinquish the slaves they all seemed to have, but they did insist that they abandoned polygamy. Quite often, missionaries would discover that Christian chiefs kept their polygamy secret from them. For example, Michael Kifungiwe, who was also a ritual expert, converted to Christianity but he had never left his wives.[93] Some people, including one of Kifungiwe's wives, who was Christian, came to Kifungiwe's defence and explained to the missionaries that giving up wives meant giving up power. Kifungiwe's town was growing and he had been enjoying more power than usual through Kibanga, his half-brother.[94] Both Kibanga and Kifungiwe were sons of Kimweri, which made them Kilindi and, thus, they were both on shaky ground after the Kiva rebellion of 1868. It was

[90] J. P. Farler, 'The Power of the Gospel'.
[91] J. P. Farler.
[92] J. P. Farler.
[93] 'The Bishop Writes', *Central Africa*, July 1885.
[94] 'The Bishop Writes'.

said that Kifungiwe had been allowed to stay in the region, 'on account of his kindly disposition [...] but he was reduced to a private station'.[95]

Kifungiwe defended his continued polygamy by claiming that he risked offending Kibanga if he abandoned his wives. This prompted Bishop Smythies to visit Kibanga to resolve the issue. In the bishop's meeting with him, Kibanga was said to have, 'acknowledged that if his brother was a Christian he ought to keep the Christian law'. Kibanga also implored the missionaries not to leave Kifungiwe.[96] Kibanga agreed with Smythies that Kifungiwe should give up his wives. Why was Kibanga so accepting of Smythies demands? The missionary record suggests Kibanga supported the missionaries' disciplining of Kifungiwe because Kibanga wanted to protect Kifungiwe and help maintain his missionary alliance.

This might have been accurate but there are other possibilities. For example, Kibanga and Kifungiwe may have been attempting to placate the missionaries together. However, it is more likely that Kibanga stood to benefit from encouraging the missionaries to discipline Kifungiwe. Firstly, encouraged Smythies to discipline Kifungiwe helped Kibanga maintain his amicable relationship with the mission. Secondly, it put a check on Kifungiwe's power. Thirdly, it secured Kibanga's access to Kifungiwe's medicine, which was said to derive partly from the mission.[97] This third point is particularly interesting because it suggests that power-brokers could benefit from alliances with Christian power-brokers, and thus avoid conversion themselves. Indeed, Kibanga, who did not convert to Christianity, appeared to delegate accessing missionary medicine to Kifungiwe, his half-brother. This underlines that secure big men like Kibanga found conversion to Christianity unnecessary and risky. From Kifungiwe's perspective, he was facing a double threat to his alliances. The missionaries would reject him if he did not give up polygamy meanwhile, his half-brother Kibanga might also reject him for losing his missionary alliances. In other words, a missionary alliance was part of a web of political alliances. Kifungiwe is above all an illustration of the dilemmas the less secure big men faced, and the fact that the missionaries were as likely to add to them as they were to help resolve them.

In the end, Kifungiwe had to live in Zanzibar with his Christian wife for two years, 'so as to prevent them returning to his house'.[98] However, an oral history respondent who remembered the name Kifungiwe suggested that the reason for fleeing to Zanzibar had more to do with a fear that he would be

---

[95] Farler, 'The Usambara Country in East Africa'.
[96] 'The Bishop Writes'.
[97] H. W. Woodward, 'Work in the Bonde Country, East Africa', *Central Africa*, 1890.
[98] 'The Bishop Writes'.

bewitched by his kin.[99] Five years after his exile, Kifungiwe returned. The troubles centred upon his status as healer, which had not been forgotten. In 1890 Woodward reported that:

> [Kifungiwe] has been practically ostracised from the clan unless he will make medicine and distribute it amongst them. They will not see him, not even look on his village, lest they should die, and make long circuits to avoid it. Michael now has to choose between Christ and heathen superstitions, only unfortunately it appears he has already made the medicine privately for his own use. The heathen relatives are the more determined because they say David Jangwa[100] died through associating with him.[101]

Michael Kifungiwe's story suggests how essential his alliance with the missionaries must have been to have faced such strife. It also shows how conversion to Christianity could cut off the personal networks that were so essential to power-brokers. Adherents were put in very difficult positions as their attempts to maintain their membership in their other communities were treated as moral crimes.

Semnkai, aged over seventy years old and half-blind,[102] was another power-broker who converted to Christianity. He was from Umba village and was said to be converted in 1881 through the efforts of H. A. B. Wilson, who appeared to have some appeal in Umba, though he was not confirmed until 1884.[103] He took the name Henry in 1882 (soon after Wilson's death).[104] Henry Semnkai was the most prominent Christian chief in the 1880s and the missionaries were initially impressed by his apparently firm stance against 'heathenism'. Geldart hailed him, 'the truest Christian in the country'.[105] However, in 1885 he would be excommunicated for allowing Christians to perform *galo* (male youth initiations), overseeing the making of body markings on young men,

---

[99] John Geldart Mhina, interview by Zuhura Mohammed, Magila, 15 October 2014. Bwana Mhina is a historian, and the author of *Historia ya Magila Msalabani 1848–2012*.

[100] Unidentified person, but he was clearly a Christian, which suggests it might not have been Jangwa's relationship with Kifungiwe alone that put him at risk; perhaps his religious allegiance was an additional challenge that the missionary record did not acknowledge.

[101] H. W. Woodward, 'Work in the Bonde Country, East Africa'.

[102] J. P. Farler to Rev. W. H. Penney, Kiungani, Zanzibar, 26 October 1885, A1 (6) A, 463, UMArch; 'Our Post Bag', February 1886.

[103] Edward Steere to Rev. W. H. Penney, Zanzibar, April 1881, A1 (3) A, 356, UMArch.

[104] J. P. Farler, 'Our Work in the Usambara Country'; Anderson-Morshead, *The History of the Universities' Mission to Central Africa 1859–1896*, 257.

[105] Rev. H. Geldart, 'Umba'.

and practising polygamy.[106] Semnkai's disobedience angered Bishop Smythies so much that he refused to see him when he was on a visit to Umba.[107]

Semnkai was under fairly ineffective missionary surveillance. When it came to his slave-trading activities, missionaries were rarely able to catch him, or other Christianising chiefs. Rather, the slaves of Semnkai saw an opportunity to appeal to the missionaries. There is an incident dating from 1884 that helps illustrate this, in which a woman named Mrashi came to the missionary Herbert Willoughby Woodward to appeal for protection. Mrashi claimed the British consul had proclaimed her legally free, but she had been captured again in Pemba and brought to Umba; her letter of freedom destroyed. Semnkai, the Umba chief, went to the mission about this woman because he was being accused of assisting her to flee there. However, Woodward strongly suspected that Semnkai bribed the supposed thief, named Kombo, to hide from the mission that Semnkai was involved in slave-trading. The events around Semnkai show how suspicious missionaries could be and how difficult it was to be a Christian power-broker, though they no doubt faced challenges no matter their religious allegiance.[108] Despite the fact that Semnkai converted, missionaries complained that Umba was a particularly troubled place to work in, highlighting, again, how converting chiefs did not automatically lead to the conversion of commoners.[109]

Farler described Austini Sipindu, a chief with many followers, as 'the earliest and staunchest of the Christians' at Umba. George Wilson, the aforementioned missionary, played an important role in Sipindu's conversion and, under strange circumstances, the two men died within the same month. However, when he died in 1883 his followers rejected the missionaries. In fact, some of the healers boasted that they had bewitched and killed Wilson and Sipindu. Within a matter of months, Christianity gained a bad reputation around Umba.[110] Umba itself, which was particularly vulnerable to slave-raiding, did not welcome the mission. Farler complained about how difficult it was to maintain the mission at Umba because the area was so heavily influenced by Islam and the coast. Thus, he recommended that the UMCA post 'a

---

[106] Bishop Smythies, 'The Bishop's Visit to Magila'; J. P. Farler to Rev. W. H. Penney, Zanzibar, 24 November 1885, A1 (6) A, 456, UMArch; Farler to Penney, 26 October 1885; Rev. H. Geldart, 'Umba'; H. W. Woodward, 'Usambara Work', *Central Africa*, April 1886; 'Our Post Bag', February 1886.

[107] Bishop Charles Alan Smythies, 'The Mountain Towns of the Bondei Country', *Central Africa*, June 1886.

[108] H. W. Woodward, 'A Story of a Woman's Wrongs'.

[109] J. P. Farler, 'Our Work in the Usambara Country'.

[110] J. P. Farler; 'The Bishop Writes'.

man of great power' there.[111] These power-brokers wishing to maintain their claims on several communities had more to lose than the commoners and displaced peoples who came to the mission, who often only held membership in this one community.[112]

Precisely how African power-brokers weighed up whether to continue their commitment to the mission in the face of being criticised or ostracised is impossible to determine, but there are some conclusions that can be drawn. For the more secure power-brokers, missionaries were more trouble than they were worth. The connection was not necessary for somebody as influential through other means as Kibanga, who managed to keep the missionaries on his side and benefit from them without having to convert. Moreover, for those power-brokers who already had coastal connections and access to firearms, the missionaries' role as a broker between the coast and the hinterland was threatening and interfering, as illustrated in the preceding pages in this chapter. That the relatively minor Bondei big men aligned themselves with the mission was due precisely to their relatively insecure status. In turn, Bondei power-brokers' interest in the mission prompted Kilindi rulers to look to the mission.

Although missionaries were valuable allies, they were not of equal value to all people. Moreover, allying with missionaries tended to compromise other alliances and relationships. Missionaries were brokers of a Muslim authority, namely, the Sultanate, which they were very critical towards, but nevertheless subordinate to and dependent upon. The missionaries' connection with the coast, facilitated by the UMCA's establishment in Zanzibar and relationship with Sir John Kirk (Consul General, 1873–87), was not always advantageous to power-brokers in Magila. Moreover, converting to Christianity posed risks. Understandably, missionaries were not treated as confidants, as Farler appears to have seen it, but as dangerous men.

However, as I have already alluded, missionaries were unpredictable and inconsistent in their allegiance. When power-holders acted against the missionaries' ideals, they were chastised. Meanwhile, when it came to conversion and spreading the word of God, power-holders were awarded with an enormous amount of attention and respect that contrasted with the quite exclusionary attitudes towards upcountry power-brokers held by coastal big men and traders.[113] Farler strived to honour chiefs. For instance, he was anxious to ensure that notables did not have to sit on the floor alongside the commoners.

---

[111] J. P. Farler, 'Our Work in the Usambara Country'.
[112] Willis, 'The Nature of a Mission Community', 149.
[113] Felicitas Becker, *Becoming Muslim in Mainland Tanzania 1890-2000* (Oxford: Oxford University Press, 2008), 83.

At Magila church there was even a 'chief's pew' designed to make them look dignified.[114] Farler was apparently onto something as one chief claimed he would have attended services sooner if it were not for the fact that on the one occasion he tried to do so the church was so full, 'that he had to sit with boys and men of no position, which was contrary to the customs of the country'.[115]

Responding to the expectations of his African interlocutors regarding leadership, Farler insisted that missionaries should be *waungwana* (civilised people, gentlemen). In 1886, Farler wrote, 'It is wonderful how quickly and accurately the native reckons them up, how respectful they are to a gentleman, and how insolent and insulting they can be to a made-man wanting in the tact which education and refinement only can give.'[116] Accordingly, Farler, with his hyper-awareness for status struggles, demanded the mission should recruit men 'of some position' and criticised missionaries he did not deem civilised enough. In particular, Farler believed Africans did not take well to missionaries who were rough in their manner or overly humble.[117] He claimed that one chief had instructed him as follows: 'Tell your chiefs we want a *gentleman*, not an uncultivated man.' Farler was pleasantly surprised by how perceptive they were, adding patronisingly, 'Where they had learnt the word, or how they knew the difference, is more than I can tell.'[118] If we assume the term used to connote 'gentleman' was '*mwungwana*', we can suppose that it was rare to hear the term at this time and place. Moreover, the anecdote suggests that the advantage of associating with the mission was still contested as far as struggling or aspiring big men were concerned. Thus, power-brokers may have interacted with the missionaries to be paid respect, but the reputation of missionaries was measured against the values and styles associated with Muslim coastal hegemony.

The lime-burning troubles, 1880–81

This final section explores the lime-burning troubles with which this chapter began. Even though a significant number of letters exist recounting the events of the conflict, they have never been discussed in published literature.

---

[114] J. P. Farler, 'Our Work in the Usambara Country'.

[115] J. P. Farler to Rev. W. H. Penney, Magila, Tanga, 4 October 1881, A1 (6) A, 364, UMArch.

[116] J. P. Farler to Rev. W. H. Penney, Magila, 20 September 1886, A1 (6) A, 503, UMArch.

[117] J. P. Farler to Rev. W. H. Penney, 24 August 1881; Similar concerns repeated here: J. P. Farler to Rev. W. H. Penney, Magila, 24 May 1887, A1 (6) A, 544, UMArch; Farler to Penney, 4 October 1881.

[118] J. P. Farler, 'Our Work in the Usambara Country'.

These troubles were unusually well documented, probably because the events were dramatic and strange to the missionaries. However, it is as useful as it is problematic as a case study. Although there is a fair amount of detail, most of the letters recounting the incidents were from Farler, either writing to fellow missionaries stationed in neighbouring missions or to the mission office in London. The accounts, therefore, are written mainly from Farler's own perspective. Furthermore, the letters that were written by other missionaries (Steere and Wilson) suggest that Farler had a penchant for hyperbole and readily jumped to conclusions. One of the greatest challenges is navigating the missionaries' categorisation of individuals and groups who played a role in the conflict. The first group was referred to as the 'Umba chiefs', which included Segao (mentioned in the opening of this chapter) and two Christians: Henry Semnkai (the Umba chief) and Austini Sipindu (an *akida* – a soldier), whose conversion stories have already been discussed above. In terms of their role in the lime-burning conflict, Farler did not blame either Semnkai or Sipindu for how it escalated. In particular, Farler noted Semnkai's political fragility, reporting that all the people of the Umba area 'utterly condemned the authority of Semnkai in the matter'.[119]

The second group Farler referred to interchangeably as the '*Wakumba*', 'Umba people' who came from several different villages, including Mkuzi, Mfunte, Vumba, Mdili, Kwa Makumba and Umba itself. Umba was the name of the cluster of villages as well as the biggest village among them. Most of the time it seems that they were referred to generically, along with the people of Mfunte and Vumba, as the 'Umba people'. In this account, 'Umba people' refers to the fractious, disparate and complex group of people working against the mission.[120] The 'Umba people' appear to have encompassed a very heterogeneous group that included the leading headmen, aspiring leaders and commoners. The 'Umba people' were the most obvious group opposing the lime-burning and are crucial to the narrative because they demonstrate the influence of popular action and the role of local people escaping chiefly control.

The third and final category were those Farler identified as 'Magila chiefs'.[121] Farler did not name any of these 'chiefs' that were local to Msalabani. Though they were probably the UMCA's closely allies, these 'Magila chiefs' were

---

[119] J. P. Farler to Bishop Edward Steere, Magila, Tanga, 19 November 1881, A1 (6) A, 354, UMArch.

[120] Dale, 'An Account of the Principal Customs and Habits of the Natives Inhabiting the Bondei Country, Compiled Mainly for the Use of European Missionaries in the Country', 181.

[121] For a list of the actors involved in the lime-burning conflict please consult to Appendix 3.

playing a diplomatic game. On the one hand, they claimed the 'Umba people' were '*wakorofi*' ('troublemakers') who lacked a convincing case against the missionaries' lime-burning. 'Magila chiefs' thus argued that giving in to them would mark the beginning of a slippery slope of submitting to their bold demands. On the other hand, the 'Magila chiefs' warned Farler they would have to withdraw their support of the mission if he refused to pay the Umba people, because the chiefs depended on securing their support as followers and fellow leaders. They claimed they had no choice but to accept the resistance of the '*wakorofi*' because their own authority could be at stake. This suggests, firstly, that their alliance with Farler was not the highest priority. Secondly, it suggests that the missionaries' authority would not have suffered if they were to refuse the demands of the '*wakorofi*' – or, at least, that is what the 'Magila chiefs' would have them believe. Regardless of the motives of the 'Magila chiefs', Farler invested a great deal of trust in them.[122]

Upon their meeting in October 1881, Farler was surprised to find Segao 'very pleasant' considering his previous (apparent) hostility to the mission. Segao claimed people were spreading rumours about him disliking the missionaries and declared, 'Am I not a Bondei, and were not the Bondeis friends of the *Wazungu*?'[123] [...] were not all the Bondeis glad to have the *Wazungu*, and why should he be different from his companions?'[124] Clearly, Segao was trying to keep the missionaries on side without wanting to adopt Christianity. But Segao's declaration also confirms that 'the Bondei' did not act as a corporate group and neither did they straightforwardly ally with the missionaries. Rather, the Bondei consisted of shifting alliances of people who used this label according to context, as Willis has shown.[125] The key differences between the groups discussed was not so much their geographical spread, but rather their social standing. Both commoners and power-brokers worked against Farler but the main difference between them was in the way they organised their attacks. The Magila chiefs maintained cordial relations with the missionaries because their alliance was valued for security, coastal connections, medicinal knowledge and firearms. Commoners had less to lose from organising open resistance.[126] Power-brokers were more vulnerably positioned between the people they hoped to secure as followers and the missionaries they valued as allies.

[122] Farler to Steere, 23 November 1881.
[123] White people, Europeans.
[124] J. P. Farler to Bishop Edward Steere, Magila, Tanga, 16 October 1881, A1 (6) A, 378, UMArch.
[125] Willis, 'The Makings of a Tribe: Bondei Identities and Histories'.
[126] Much like in the case of the erosion control scheme crisis of the 1950s that Feierman explored. Feierman, *Peasant Intellectuals: Anthropology and History in Tanzania*, 23.

Lime-burning was a politically complicated business because it demanded a huge amount of labour and natural resources. The process began with the back-breaking work of stone-quarrying. This was followed by cutting down trees for timber. Once the weather was dry, the wood would be burnt to break down the stone. The lime-burning and tree-cutting was carried out in a *nyika*, half a day's journey from the mission station. *Nyika* land was defined as uninhabited, uncultivated, and, by Farler's reckoning, 'no-man's-land'.[127] The missionaries did not appreciate that so-called unoccupied land might still be important for shifting cultivation, grazing or hunting. The *nyika* could even be a refuge in politically uncertain times such as these.[128]

Though the lime-burning drama reached its height in November 1881, tensions had surfaced four years earlier when Farler began his plans for building. Farler started the lime-burning before consulting anyone living around the *nyika* and he maintained throughout the conflict that even in cultivated country under a chief, it would not be necessary to ask his permission.[129] After a short time, Farler encountered resistance, but successfully secured permission from some of his Bondei allies who were not resident in Umba and whom he referred to as 'Magila chiefs'. The Umba people demanded an exorbitant amount of silver to help burn and carry the stone. Consequently, in 1877 Farler met with a trader he did not get along with to negotiate for *vibarua* (day labourers) to carry lime 'at a reasonable rate'.[130] Farler did not succeed and thus faced having to buy donkeys and hire 'drivers' from Pangani, which would have been more expensive, risky and time-consuming.[131] With all these difficulties combined with a shortage of funds, Farler put the project on hold until 1880.

Thus, it was only in May 1880 that Farler finally began quarrying stone in earnest and he did not begin the lime-burning until the rains stopped. At this time Farler was on good terms with the power-brokers in Umba.[132] After some

---

[127] J. P. Farler to Herbert A. B. Wilson, Magila, Tanga (not for public), 12 November 1881, A1 (6) A, 350, UMArch.

[128] Isaria N. Kimambo, 'Environmental Control and Hunger: In the Mountains and Plains of Nineteenth-Century Northeastern Tanzania', in *Custodians of the Land: Ecology & Culture in the History of Tanzania*, ed. G. Maddox, James L. Giblin, and Isaria N. Kimambo, Eastern African Studies (Athens: James Currey, 1996), 71–95.

[129] Farler to Steere, 23 November 1881.

[130] J. P. Farler to Chauncy Maples, 27 April 1877; Anderson-Morshead, *The History of the Universities' Mission to Central Africa 1859-1896*, 223.

[131] J. P. Farler to Chauncy Maples, 27 April 1877; J. P. Farler to My dear Prof, Magila, Zanzibar, 30 May 1880, A1 (6) A, 335, UMArch.

[132] Farler to Steere, 23 November 1881; J. P. Farler to Bishop Edward Steere, Magila,

weeks spent in Zanzibar, Farler returned to Magila in late September. On his return, a meeting of 'all the chiefs and notables of the country' (about forty people all together) was held to pay their respects to Farler. The proceedings were summarised as follows:

> One made a speech saying how glad they were to see me back, and that they were thankful my health had been restored. I replied and also said how glad I should be if they would accept my message of salvation. We then served coffee, biscuits and some native dainties, and amused them with the musical lot and other things.[133] However, in December 1880 the lime-burning provoked a 'hostile demonstration' in Mkuzi for which there is sparse evidence.[134] Semnkai and Sipindu helped suppress the dispute and supported the mission.[135]

Meanwhile, also in December 1880, a different confrontation took place between Farler and Kibanga, which was only partially related to the resistance to lime-burning. Farler had fallen out with both Barghash and Kibanga, as the latter had refused to support him in a confrontation with the former. According to Kibanga, Farler had retaliated by attempting to tarnish Kibanga's name with Sultan Barghash.[136] What exactly Farler told Barghash is not known, but the consequences were dramatic. On 22 January 1881, 300 of Kibanga's armed men marched to Magila to stop him from building and communicating with the coast. According to Steere, these included 'some of the Bondei themselves, who are no friends of the Magila people', which shows that the Bondei were divided regarding their alliance with the mission.[137] Steere was mortified and condemned Farler's behaviour as 'an act of almost incredible folly'.[138] In spite of his disagreements with Farler a month earlier, Barghash put a stop to Kibanga's attack and instructed that Farler's work should be allowed to continue and that mission goods should be allowed to circulate again.[139] Farler remarked to Steere that by this point there were, 'a hundred chiefs burning to avenge [Kibanga]'.[140] Whether these chiefs were primarily

---

Tanga, 7 October 1881, A1 (6) A, 371, UMArch; Farler to My dear Prof, 30 May 1880.
[133] Farler to Penney, 4 October 1881.
[134] J. P. Farler to Rev. W. H. Penney, 24 August 1881.
[135] Farler to Wilson, 18 November 1881.
[136] Edward Steere to John Wogan Festing, Zanzibar, January 1881, A1 (3) A, 330, UMArch.
[137] Perhaps they were actually Kilindi, not 'Bondei'? Edward Steere to Festing.
[138] Edward Steere to Rev. W. H. Penney, Zanzibar, December 1881, A1 (3) A, 441, UMArch.
[139] Edward Steere to Rev. W. H. Penney, 8 January 1881.
[140] Edward Steere to Rev. W. H. Penney, December 1881.

seeking to avenge Kibanga, whose reputation Farler had attempted to sully, or whether they were also protesting Farler's lime-burning, is very unclear. Farler's lack of diplomatic skill in dealing with coastal rulers may have made him a nuisance to Kibanga by this time, though Kibanga had supported Farler against his half-brother Kifungiwe in the matter of the latter's marriages. In sum, while the reasons behind Kibanga's attack were apparently independent of Farler's lime-burning business, the attack itself must have contributed to the tensions. Kibanga's attack may have also given fuel to further attacks in April and November 1881, when the people of Mfunte attacked Farler's workers.[141]

After the April attacks against Farler's workers, Woodward had to navigate a conflict of interests in May 1881 with Semnkai, the Umba chief who relayed the Umba peoples' dissatisfaction with the lime-burning. It began with a female slave belonging to a Digo trader who a Yao slave-trader captured, after killing her Digo father and uncle. Apparently with Semnkai's support, one of the Bondei Muslim masons at the Mkuzi mission bought the enslaved woman and kept her in his living quarters at the mission compound, which did not go unnoticed. Indeed, strangers were not allowed to sleep in the compound, unless they reported to the missionaries. Woodward gathered that the woman was stolen from Digo slave-traders. He saw this as an opportunity for peace-keeping between the Bondei and the Digo, uniting them against the Yao trader and the people he represented.[142]

Woodward announced at the meeting of Bondei chiefs that he intended to send the woman back to the Digo 'with messages of peace and friendship'. The chiefs agreed with Woodward's plan, but the feeling shifted when, a few days later, some Digo raiders illegally captured five Bondei people, two of them Christians, from Umba.[143] The case did not come to a satisfactory conclusion for Woodward and he never divulged what became of the slave woman. After several meetings with different groups of chiefs, Woodward announced that he would refer the affair to the Governor at Pangani, on the grounds that, first and foremost, the Yao slave-trader and Muslim mason were subjects of the Sultan and neither were Christians. In other words, Woodward tried to decide the fate of this slave in consultation with the Sultan, over the head of Semnkai. Semnkai, who feared for his dignity in the face of coastal interference, tried to stop Woodward.[144]

---

[141] Farler to Wilson, 18 November 1881; Farler to Steere, 19 November 1881; Farler to Steere, 23 November 1881.
[142] J. P. Farler to Rev. W. H. Penney, 30 May 1881.
[143] J. P. Farler to Rev. W. H. Penney.
[144] J. P. Farler to Rev. W. H. Penney.

The last meeting Woodward called on this subject broke up in a frenzy and the captive woman disappeared from sight. Woodward immediately wrote to the Pangani *wali* and on the same day they arranged a night attack on the Msalabani mission station to find the woman, but they were unsuccessful. Woodward sent the Muslim mason as a prisoner to Pangani, blaming him wholly for the debacle. The Yao man was not interfered with and the mason paid him the remaining sum of what the woman was estimated to be worth. The fact that the mason suffered more than other actors in the story shows how missionaries assumed authority not only over their converts, but their employees as well.[145] This case may have contributed to tensions between the mission and the Umba people, especially if the UMCA were already either suspected of being slave-dealers, or considered to be overly interfering.

In May 1881 Farler had an unusual visit to a village called Ndume, to meet a petty chief named Sehiza, who was an 'Umba chief' in this location.[146] However, when Farler arrived at the town, Sehiza was not there: 'The people were very cold, and for a long time we sat out in the middle of the town, no one coming to welcome us. My boys made me some tea, and at length an old woman brought us some native food, *ugali*[147] and *kitoweo*,[148] for we had taken nothing ourselves thinking it would be better to prove ourselves upon this hospitality of the natives.'

When Sehiza finally returned he was very hospitable, and apparently aggrieved that his people had treated Farler so badly. In the morning the atmosphere changed. The people flocked around Farler to hear him speak. He reprimanded them for their 'bad manners', reminding them of how helpful the mission had been over the last six years, particularly during the famine of 1877. Crucially, he added that they should not believe the rumours the 'beach Mohammedans'[149] ('who steal their children, rob and insult them') were telling them. This suggests that, at the time, coastal people (who were probably slave purchasers) and missionaries were competing for the loyalties of these people. According to Steere, this remark made them go on the defensive and,

---

[145] J. P. Farler to Rev. W. H. Penney.

[146] In 1886 he was described as the 'Ndume chief', indicative of his increased power after the death of Segao from a fatal bite from a slave. Bishop Charles Alan Smythies, 'The Mountain Towns of the Bondei Country'; 'Our Post Bag', February 1886; Farler to Penney, 26 October 1885; Chambai remembered Sehiza being an old man, whose death sparked off the Kiva Rebellion. More research is needed to understand his role in the period of rapacity that followed Kiva. George Chambai, interview by Elias Mutani, Mkuzi, 22 April 2016.

[147] Stiff porridge made by boiling maize or sorghum or millet meal flour in water.

[148] Relish. Can also mean spice and seasoning.

[149] This is likely to be a mistranslation of '*Waislamu wa pwani*' (coastal Muslims).

'they tried to put the blame upon other people and admitted that it was bad'. This is when Farler first heard about Segao, a headman who held a strong influence over Sehiza.[150]

In the same month (May) Segao announced that at night an ancestral spirit had visited him, communicating that the people were more vulnerable than ever to being caught by slavers because the lime-burning had rendered their charms and medicine ineffectual. It was said that the mission was burning lime in the *nyika* and 'spoiled'[151] their *mafingo* (charms) and *dawa* (medicine), which explained the Digo raiders' killing spree against the people of Umba.[152] In other words, the people believed missionaries were capable of angering the spirits and consequently compromising the medicinal power that healers held. The 'Umba people' claimed that they required goats to sacrifice to the *mapepo* (spirits) because their charms had stopped working as a result of Farler's activities there.

Despite all this, the missionaries seem to have been on good terms with chiefs, including Semnkai, Segao, Sehiza and Sipindu, who paid visits to Farler in September and October 1881, when he returned from Zanzibar.[153] The dispute peaked in November, partly because gunpowder had suddenly become more easily available. The Zanzibar government had apparently granted the gunpowder to 'the Bondei' in order to defeat Digo raiders. By a great turn of irony, it was this gunpowder that was made use of by the 'Umba people' against Farler's labourers.[154] Stronger chiefs and headmen already had access to gunpowder, but now it had become more widely available. It is striking that they were willing to spare this gunpowder for the cause against Farler when they were said to have really needed it to protect themselves against Digo raiders.

In the same month (November) the two Christians, Semnkai and Sipindu, who had supported Farler during the confrontation in December 1880, demanded on behalf of the Umba commoners that Farler pay 50 MTD and cease to burn lime. As Farler understood it, the commoners claimed to need this sum for buying goats to sacrifice to the ancestors, whom Farler had disturbed, according to Segao's dream. It is unclear whether or not Semnkai and Sipindu had changed sides but Farler was convinced that these chiefs disagreed with the concerns of the commoners. However, because Semnkai and

---

[150] J. P. Farler to Rev. W. H. Penney, 30 May 1881; Farler to Penney, 4 October 1881.
[151] Farler wrote 'bananga'd'; an anglicised version of *kubanga*, 'to destroy'.
[152] The interjections of Swahili words are Farler's. Farler claimed that the Wadigo had been killing their people long before the lime-burning began. J. P. Farler to George Herbert Wilson, Magila, Tanga, 12 November 1881, A1 (6) A, 705, UMArch.
[153] Farler to Penney, 4 October 1881; Farler to Steere, 16 October 1881.
[154] Farler to Steere, 19 November 1881.

Sipindu depended on their followers, they felt there was no other way but to help the commoners make their demand.

It is likely that the commoners made a financial demand, rather than simply demanding the livestock that they claimed to require for sacrifice, because the missionaries' wealth was in cash, not livestock. Farler found the narrative partially convincing because people like Sipindu and Semnkai did not bring up the subject of ancestral spirits with the missionaries if they could help it.[155] However, Farler interpreted the financial demand itself as corruption and exploitation and refused to pay it. He labelled this 'blackmail' and the very antithesis of '*haki*' (justice).[156] As for the claims about the customs surrounding the *nyika*, Farler dismissed them as 'utter rot and *upuzi*' (foolish talk).[157]

Farler's colleague Wilson, who was actually based at Umba, was less certain. In any case, he argued that it was important to promote good feeling among the 'Umba people', 'for they are determined to enforce what they term their right'. Conversely, Farler believed Wilson was 'very ignorant about the people, and green in these things, and his usual plan seems to be to pay all round, make everything smooth with money, promote good feeling with feasts and pay fully every demand'.[158] More than anything, Farler feared that his reputation and position as a power holder was at stake.[159] Farler threatened to call on the Sultan to punish the Umba people.[160] In turn, the people threatened to leave the land, though the 'Magila chiefs' called this '*maumo matupo*' ('empty threats').[161]

Farler was anxious to refute any notion that the missionaries were simply rich men without political or legal support. For the sake of security, but also for the sake of his own vision of himself as a big man, it was important to at least give the illusion that actions against the mission would have serious consequences. Farler believed it was necessary to punish the 'rebels' of Umba villages that Sipindu and Semnkai claimed to represent and 'give them a good frightening' by sending them to prison in Zanzibar.[162] They were, in Farler's

---

[155] I imagine their reasons for requesting MTD instead of goats was two-fold. Firstly, missionaries did not collect goats for trade, only for use. Secondly, money-currency had great value, so they could buy more goats than the actual value of the coins. J. P. Farler, Magila, (copy for publication), 1 December 1881, A1 (6) A, 343, UMArch.
[156] J. P. Farler to Herbert A. B. Wilson, 12 November 1881.
[157] J. P. Farler to George Herbert Wilson, 12 November 1881.
[158] Farler to Steere, 23 November 1881.
[159] Farler to Wilson, 18 November 1881; Farler to Steere, 23 November 1881.
[160] Edward Steere to Rev. W. H. Penney, December 1881.
[161] This is Farler's translation, which is accurate. Farler to Steere, 23 November 1881.
[162] J. P. Farler to George Herbert Wilson, 12 November 1881; Farler to Steere, 19 November 1881.

eyes, unashamed criminals. He wrote to Steere that: 'There never could be a better opportunity of winning the respect of all these people for our power and sense of justice for the whole country is with us on these questions and these thieves are already putting their tails between their legs to bolt or get the whipping they know they deserve.'[163] This, Farler contended, would increase the respect for law and 'common honesty' that was present among the majority of 'well-disposed and respectable Wabondeis'.[164]

Farler believed that the 'truth' of whether he had indeed defiled custom was irrelevant and that his actions would determine the nature of the mission's reputation for miles around: 'They say the whole country is now looking to see whether the Wazungu have any power or not. Whether we are but a few rich men who can be plundered with impunity, or whether we have the authority and force of any law at our back, as the people have always believed that we have.'[165] Thus, Farler pleaded to Steere that force should be used as the mission's 'prestige' was at stake.[166] Indeed, the 'Magila chiefs' suggested to Farler that, while the demand was for money, its subtexts were about power and reputation:

> They say these people are simply thieves that their demand is an act of robbery, and if we yield to it we cannot remain long in the country, for as there is no central authority, every *mkorofi*[167] in the country will be looking out for an excuse to make some other demand, and that even the quiet people in other parts will say 'the country does not belong to these Umba people, if the *Wazungu* have paid them $50[168] he must pay us something too'. They say we should soon find it impossible to meet the demands of black-mail and we should have to go.[169]

Steere was unsympathetic to Farler's requests, and so the Sultan's forces were never requested.[170] Steere warned against appealing to the Sultan and that, equally, 'an Arab governor might give you infinitely greater troubles than these'. Instead, Steere recommended that Farler stop building and negotiate a financial settlement.[171]

According to Farler's letters, by January 1882 harmony was restored. The Umba people accepted Farler's offer of 30 MTD and agreed to grant him, 'the perpetual right to carry lime through their country'. Farler cheerfully reported

---

[163] Farler to Steere, 23 November 1881.
[164] Farler to Steere.
[165] Farler to Steere.
[166] Farler to Steere, 19 November 1881.
[167] Troublemaker.
[168] MTD.
[169] Farler to Steere, 23 November 1881.
[170] Farler, 1 December 1881.
[171] Farler to Steere, 19 November 1881.

that he planned to give them a further present of 20 MTD, 'to show them that it was not money I contended for, but justice'.[172] However, this peace did not last. In 1885 Segao threatened to burn down a mission church. Later that year, in October, he was bitten by a man whom he was trying to capture as a slave and died a few days later from infection. As with the deaths of many prominent men, people talked of how Segao's death was 'a judgment upon him', according to Farler. While this is probably not the whole story, slave dealers like Segao no doubt divided opinion.[173] The different big men's actions and stratagems illustrate what a complex political force-field the mission had to operate in. Bondei identity, in this context, was another stratagem to tap into patronage networks.

Despite his bravado, it appears that Farler's reputation had suffered greatly, just as he had feared. Indeed, there is a total absence of his talk of meeting with dignitaries, which was so typical of his earlier letter-writing, between 1882 and 1886. Admittedly, for much of this time he was either in Zanzibar or in England. In early 1883 Farler, went to England for 'a rest', returning to Magila the next year for a visit with Bishop Smithies. By 1886 Farler seemed to have renewed his characteristic vigour, declaring, 'the mission here is ripe for completely taking possession of the country; everywhere we are honoured guests'.[174] However, this optimism did not last long. Following an extended period of unhappiness, Farler resigned from missionary work in early 1889 and then became Slavery Commissioner in Pemba from 1891 until 1905.[175]

Having unpacked the key historical actors and the timeline, let us now consider the leading grievances against Farler. First of all, it should be noted that the perceived problem was probably a combination of the process of actually preparing the lime and the plans the missionaries had to erect buildings, which was a way of simultaneously claiming territory and creating a new holy site.[176] The grievance against building was important as a spatial demonstra-

---

[172] Anderson-Morshead, *The History of the Universities' Mission to Central Africa 1859–1896*, 223.

[173] 'Our Post Bag', February 1886; Farler to Penney, 26 October 1885.

[174] J. P. Farler to Rev. W. H. Penney, Magila, Zanzibar, 14 October 1886, A1 (6) A, 499, UMArch; Anderson-Morshead, *The History of the Universities' Mission to Central Africa 1859–1896*, 228, 231.

[175] Bishop Charles Alan Smythies, 'Letter to the Clergy of the Mission', Zanzibar (printed), February 1889, A1 (5) A, 4, UMArch.

[176] Unsurprisingly, authors have noted that the politics and symbolism of mission buildings was of great importance: Jean Comaroff and John L. Comaroff, *Of Revelation and Revolution: Christianity, Colonialism, and Consciousness in South Africa*, vol. 1 (Chicago: University of Chicago Press, 1991), 206; Jean Comaroff and John L. Comaroff, *Of Revelation and Revolution: The Dialectics of Modernity on*

tion of their permanent presence. The published works of the UMCA were bound to emphasise the notion that people were challenging the building itself. Indeed, the UMCA official history of 1897 framed the dispute quite specifically. According to this text, Kibanga used armed soldiers to stop the mission from building the church because they mistakenly believed they were building a fort.[177] This was a rather prudent way of depicting the conflict as a simple misunderstanding between missionaries and an individual with great power. It was in the missionaries' interest to depict the conflict as resistance against the building of the church rather than resistance against lime-burning, local beliefs surrounding the *nyika*, and friction with power-brokers.

The lime-burning activities need to be seen in the context of a range of Farler's political and social affronts. It is likely that all kinds of people were challenging *both* the production of the building materials and the building itself. Farler saw the whole debacle as a straightforward test of the mission's strength. In contrast, Steere's theory was that Semnkai had sparked off much of the conflict in response to the fact that Farler did not request permission or offer a gift in return for using the land. It is likely that Farler failed to properly calculate the equivalences of the exchanges of gifts and respect. In fact, Farler did rebuff Semnkai's request for a gift. In a socio-economic context in which big men were enormously tied up in exchange, this was significant. Steere would later regretfully conclude that this debacle could probably have been avoided if Farler had agreed to give Semnkai a gift and consulted more local chiefs.[178]

Both Steere and, more strongly, Farler refused to entertain the notion that that the lime-burning was interfering with the Umba people's medicine. However, this was the only grievance the people actually communicated to the mission. In many ways, it is convincing. The Umba people were probably not concerned about the mission directly making their healing practices ineffectual or their rituals meaningless, it was that they were angering the ancestors, which, in turn, led to other terrible consequences. This was neither the first nor the last time that Africans would claim that *wazungu* were capable of interfering with the spirit world. For instance, in 1886 Farler met Mtoga, a

---

a South African Frontier, vol. 2 (Chicago; London: University of Chicago Press, 1997), 278, 301–6, 485; Julie Livingston, *Debility and the Moral Imagination in Botswana* (Bloomington, IN: Indiana University Press, 2005), 70; Cherry Leonardi, 'Laying the First Course of Stones: Building the London Missionary Society Church in Madagascar, 1862–1895', *The International Journal of African Historical Studies*, 36, no. 3 (2003): 607–33. doi.org/10.2307/3559436.

[177] Farler, 1 December 1881; Anderson-Morshead, *The History of the Universities' Mission to Central Africa 1859–1896*, 222.

[178] Edward Steere to Rev. W. H. Penney, December 1881.

chief, and Farler asked to see a spring he had heard about. They were reluctant because they worried that if a white man drank from the spring it would 'destroy all their charms'.[179] This should come as no surprise as missionaries frequently desecrated rituals. They even encouraged schoolboys to destroy 'spirit trees'.[180] Most memorably, they made a point of climbing the 'spirit mountain', Mlinga, in order to disprove the belief that whoever mounted it would die.[181] Some of their perceived supernatural power derived from their ability to retrieve captive slaves.[182] The missionaries were actors also in the spirit world that the African factions in the region negotiated, but they were not willing to countenance this aspect of their relationship with African groups or leaders.

On the other hand, Farler may well have been right to be suspicious of the claim that the lime-burning was making charms ineffective. First of all, the people did not claim that the decline in effectivity of the medicine had caused drought or disease. They claimed that it made their charms ineffective against attacks by the Digo; a matter that Farler was deeply concerned with. This was the only reason that the Umba people directly put forward to Farler. There were frequent Digo slave raiding attacks, but was this the primary concern? Or was the claim about the lack of security an attempt to appeal to Farler's

---

[179] J. P. Farler, 'Magila News: Extracts from Archdeacon Farler's Diary', *Central Africa*, February 1887.

[180] J. P. Farler to Bishop Edward Steere, 1877; Farler to Penney, 4 October 1881; J. P. Farler to George Herbert Wilson, 12 November 1881; J. P. Farler to Herbert A. B. Wilson, 12 November 1881; J. P. Farler to Rev. W. H. Penney, Kiungani, Zanzibar, 29 August 1884, A1 (6) A, 443, UMArch; J. P. Farler, 'Diary from Archdeacon Farler', *Central Africa*, November 1886; Godfrey Dale, 'Mkuzi', *Central Africa*, 1893; F. E. P., 'Customs and Beliefs of the Washambala', *Central Africa*, May 1915; Samuel Sehoza, 'Some Beliefs and Customs of the Wabondei: II. Spirits of the Dead', *Central Africa*, September 1929; Godfrey Dale, 'The Gender of Spirits', *Central Africa*, September 1930.

[181] H. W. Woodward, 'S. Luke's, Misozwe', *Central Africa*, March 1885; H. Kerslake, 'News of Magila', *Central Africa*, January 1886; H. W. Woodward, 'Usambara Work', *Central Africa*, April 1886; J. P. Farler, 'Magila News: Extracts from Archdeacon Farler's Diary', *Central Africa*, April 1887; Henry Nasibu, 'News from Misozwe by a Native Evangelist', *Central Africa*, July 1887; J. C. Salfey, 'Mlinga, the Spirit-Haunted Mountain', *Central Africa*, 1891; 'Post Bag', *Central Africa*, 1891; George William Mallender, 'Missionary life in Central Africa' (Journal, 1896), A1 (4) B, UMArch; R. K., 'How We Climbed Mlinga (a Holiday Experience)', *Central Africa*, April 1914; C. C. Monro, 'Village Schools in Tanganyika', *Central Africa*, January 1923; A. M., 'Mlinga the Spirit Mountain', *Central Africa*, November 1927; Arthur Roland Lewis, *Twilight over Mlinga* (London: Universities' Mission to Central Africa, 1956).

[182] 'Told by Himself. The Story of a Slave Boy', *African Tidings*, January 1893.

concerns? They must have been aware that Farler was near obsessed with managing the threat of the Digo slave-raiders, which is why he appealed to the Sultan for arms. Moreover, the Umba people used the term '*desturi*' (custom), which Africans commonly utilised to plead with the mission to loosen their prohibitions, because they must have noticed missionaries were sympathetic to what they saw as 'custom'. Indeed, the very idea of tricking people with false stories of magic was actually a trope in local folktales, which suggests it happened in real life, too.[183] Could Segao's dreams have been trickery? To a large extent, this was a case of extraversion, whereby the headmen manipulated the missionaries in order to extract wealth.

Extraversion or not, the story of the magical damage that lime-burning caused clearly indicates true grievances. There are four key grievances I extrapolate. First, there is no doubt that Farler was harming the *nyika*, which was more important than Farler gave it credit. It was essential for agriculturalists to have access to the *nyika* in order to manage it and keep it at bay.[184] Furthermore, people hunted there and the mission was no doubt making that work harder.[185] Second, it is very likely that people were objecting to the imported labour from Zanzibar. The result of Kibanga's attack in January 1881 was that the labourers from Magila refused to continue their work for Farler.[186] Unable to procure local workers, Farler brought the labour over from Zanzibar in two batches. The first group did not stay for long and insisted that they would only do the work if they were given weapons and gunpowder to protect themselves against marauding Digo raiders.[187] Many of these outsourced labourers were ex-slaves from the ex-slave settlement in Mbweni. It is possible that Digo slave raiding attacks were increasing because they saw the mission ex-slave labour force, isolated and unprotected in the *nyika*, as easy targets. Equally, it is possible that these attacks were a springboard for further attacks on Umba settlements.[188]

All of this also indicates that the people were angered by the influx of strangers, namely, the ex-slaves. This is something that comes across in the oral history record. Antoni Mabundo, who was one of the most knowledgeable

---

[183] See 'tale' 14, for instance. H. W. Woodward, 'Bondei Folktales, III (Continued)', *Folklore* 36, no. 4 (31 December 1925): 366–86. doi.org/10.2307/1256210.
[184] Thaddeus Raymond. Sunseri, *Vilimani: Labor Migration and Rural Change in Early Colonial Tanzania* (Portsmouth, NH: Heinemann, 2002), 15.
[185] Kimambo, 'Environmental Control and Hunger: In the Mountains and Plains of Nineteenth-Century Northeastern Tanzania'.
[186] J. P. Farler to Rev. W. H. Penney, 24 August 1881.
[187] J. P. Farler to Rev. W. H. Penney.
[188] Farler to Steere, 19 November 1881; J. P. Farler to Bishop Edward Steere, Magila, Tanga, 9 November 1881, A1 (6) A, 357, UMArch.

respondents about the deeper past, remembered that the people were not welcoming towards the missionaries or the ex-slaves they brought from Zanzibar.[189] Perhaps the Umba people were also angered that Farler excluded them from the wage labour he had the capacity to offer. However, this seems unlikely seeing as people local to the *nyika* refused to be enlisted, probably because they were concerned about being present in case they needed to fend off an attack. All things considered, the fact that Farler outsourced labour probably contributed to tensions, but could not have been the whole story as tensions existed before he started hiring ex-slaves from Zanzibar.

The third grievance I identify revolves around financial gain. Considering that the 50 MTD demand was made over a year after opposition to lime-burning began, it was likely to have been part of longer-term grievances, rather than an end in itself. Yet commercial gain, or rather, resistance against commercial loss, must have been part of the story. Missionaries did not take well to financial exploitation and they were conspicuously exploitable.[190] Just a few months before, the people of Mfunte took advantage of the newly arrived missionary, Wallis, who was building a mud church. People joked that Woodward paid a pice per stick to build a small church at Mfunte that was totally unusable.[191] Indeed, Farler might have had a point with regards to his concerns about missionaries' reputation for being easily exploitable.

The 50 MTD demand was substantial. Farler pointed out that a large piece of land was granted to Wallis at Mkuzi for only 5 MTD.[192] On the other hand, 50 MTD would have amounted to a fraction of Farler's building costs. The lime preparation was a visibly expensive process. Once the lime had been burnt, they were bringing about fifty bags of it a day to Magila, each bag costing 20 pice.[193] Fifty MTD only equalled about half of the expense of wages Farler was spending in a month of building. He reported that for the month of October he spent 53 MTD on wages in addition to 44 MTD on *pagazi* (porters) to carry the lime from the *nyika* all the way to Msalabani.[194] The Umba people may have been protesting against a bizarre way of spending so much money. The logic

---

[189] Anthony Christopher Mabundo, interview.

[190] Here are a few examples of missionaries complaining about being exploited. Woodward to Farler, 1878; J. P. Farler to Herbert A. B. Wilson, 12 November 1881; Herbert A. B. Wilson to Bishop Edward Steere, Umba, 15 July 1881, A1 (6) A, 826, UMArch; Herbert Lister, 'Work at Korogwe', *Central Africa*, March 1892; H. W. Woodward, 'Letter from Magila', *Central Africa*, 1893; J. Zanzibar to Duncan Travers, Mkunazini, 2 March 1904, A1 (13), 200, UMArch.

[191] Wilson to Steere, 15 July 1881.

[192] Farler to Steere, 23 November 1881.

[193] Farler to Steere, 9 November 1881.

[194] Farler to Steere.

may have been that if the missionaries were willing to pay for this, they might as well let the people near the *nyika* see some monetary benefit from it. The production of lime was a clear – if unintentional – demonstration of wealth as bags of lime each worth 20 pice traversed the landscape. The 50 MTD may also have been a way of putting a price on what the Umba people lost out of the destruction of the *nyika*. This makes the 50 MTD demand understandable, while equally showing this was not a clear-cut case of financial exploitation.

Another way of looking at it is that the Umba people were having to face the consequences of the lime-burning, without being able to benefit from the buildings themselves. Indeed, Farler advised Wallis to build his station just outside of Mkuzi to ensure that the Umba people did not become jealous. He foresaw that with this approach, Wallis, 'will be looked upon by all the Umba people as equally theirs, [...] all will feel that they have a right to the church'.[195] Farler was probably not exaggerating these jealousies as Woodward corroborated Farler's claim, reporting that there existed 'deep-seated jealousies' among the Umba people, who, 'compare themselves with Magila people, saying they are not treated as well'.[196]

The fourth explanation I identify is linked to all the other explanations, and is the most fundamental: the missionaries were viewed as a threat because they were living on the land without any investment into it or responsibility for it. Feierman describes the foundational organising principle of political philosophy in the region's African communities at the time as follows: 'dangerous forms of power bring life and fertility rather than death and famine only when the powerful person is given the land as his own'.[197] Perhaps it all comes back to the request made in 1877 for Farler to become 'king of the Bondei'. He had refused it, which must have had diplomatic consequences. Farler's refusal was potentially interpreted as a dangerous rejection of all the responsibilities that came with rule. Lime-burning was one way in which Farler over-strained the generosity of the land and the people.[198] Equally, his refusal may have indicated how anomalous the missionaries were, which probably led both power-brokers and followers to consider missionaries differently, not against the political principles they expected fellow African power-brokers to follow.

All things considered, it is likely that all these explanations played some role in the tensions between the Umba people and the mission. Moreover, by

---

[195] Farler to Penney, 2 November 1881; Farler to Steere, 16 October 1881.
[196] Woodward to Farler, 1878.
[197] Feierman, *Peasant Intellectuals: Anthropology and History in Tanzania*, 48.
[198] The story Feierman details about Kighuunde people giving a ewe to the German missionaries when their king had been killed, in order to ensure the missionaries understood their duty to the people, is analogous. Feierman, 48–49.

exploring the potential causes of the tensions, we get a picture of how uncertain the missionaries' position was, partly because they were considered a threat to survival.

Conclusion

This chapter has set out the context of war, famine and instability that followed the 1868 Kiva rebellion in the Bondei and Usambara regions. In this setting, it was impossible for the UMCA to fulfil their aims operating only as a peaceful, paternal, non-judicial, authority. The missionaries' conversion strategies also demonstrated a lack of understanding. For example, they sought to convert chiefs, hoping that Christianity would be efficiently filtered through the whole of society, but this would not have been possible as the power of the chiefs was very limited. Missionaries' approaches could be further flawed. For instance, they were in favour of bolstering established centralised authority, yet they did not hesitate to chastise chiefs allied to them who strayed from the mission's moral codes, which harmed chiefs' reputations.

Opportunistic big men, chiefs and headmen, were likely to consider the missionaries as valuable allies. This was mainly because they were perceived to facilitate coastal connections and access to gunpowder. Missionaries were also respectful towards chiefs, compared with some coastal dignitaries, who referred to these chiefs as *washenzi* (primitive people) and *wakafiri* (unbelievers). However, these alliances, which usually necessitated Christian conversion, came at a price. Converting to Christianity could very easily undermine a chief's authority if he fell out of favour with the missionaries. Indeed, for many power-brokers, particularly those who already had coastal connections and access to gunpowder, the missionaries were troublesome allies.

At the heart of this chapter was the conflict that arose over the mission's right to burn and transport lime so that the missionaries could build in stone. The conflict demonstrates tensions over resource control and dealings with coastal authorities. The existing power-brokers and the missionaries exploited each other in different ways. Power-brokers claimed Bondei identity and unity to gain the missionaries' respect and trust. As for the missionaries, they tried to use their influence on coastal authorities to ensure obedience, marking missionaries out as volatile allies.[199] Farler believed the source of conflict was the 'rebellious subjects' of local chiefs, as he saw them, who were hoping to financially exploit the mission. However, the 'Magila chiefs' who on the

---

[199] Willis only briefly mentions the political and violent set of reactions and entanglements that lime-burning prompted. Willis, 'The Makings of a Tribe: Bondei Identities and Histories', 200.

surface supported the mission were also working against him. This demonstrates that it was possible to maintain a missionary alliance while simultaneously undermining the missionaries' power. Even so, from the perspective of African power-brokers, missionary alliances, which were usually marked by conversion, were politically risky. For both commoners and elites, conversion to Christianity could undermine a person's social networks, wealth and authority. Missionaries also invoked coastal authorities. Though coastal authority was well-established at this time, the way the missionaries used it was a departure from the norm that could undermine a power holder's authority. Equally, the mission was not a safeguard against slave-raiding as Christians were, at certain points, prime targets for slave capture, partly because they were isolated from kin who may have otherwise been able to protect them. It was also partly because those who had converted lost their kinship protection anyway.

Because this chapter is based mostly on written sources, and too distant to be confirmed or challenged by the oral history record, there are several moments in which we are forced to conjecture. Even though clear conclusions cannot be confidently drawn on all issues, we do get some important impressions of the time. Crucially, as Feierman has shown, commoners were neither helpless nor reactionary and their ideas were constantly developing.[200] In fact, when we consider the lime-burning conflict, the only people who could boldly express their concerns were the commoners, who did not rely on missionary alliances.

Overall, missionaries had limited wealth in people. Those who were in alliance with the mission were generally duplicitous. Even if missionaries met frequently with chiefs, the quality of these relationships appears to have been low.[201] Cordial face-to-face relationships with missionaries were not necessarily indicative of a committed missionary allegiance. Missionaries were not trusted because they were isolated, kinless outsiders. They were perceived as troublesome, interfering and dangerous. Missionaries were not that different, at this time, from some of the stranger-leaders that occurred in local political thought, such as Mbegha, a 'ritually dangerous person' who came to rule the Shambaai kingdom.[202] The major difference between these kinds of rulers, who had the power to heal and harm the land, and missionaries (who may have been perceived to have the same powers) is that missionaries made exorbitant demands on followers to show exclusive allegiance. In other words, missionaries' authority was perceived through the lens of long-standing, local

---

[200] Feierman, *Peasant Intellectuals: Anthropology and History in Tanzania*, 4.
[201] For the qualitative nature of wealth in people, see: Guyer, 'Wealth in People and Self-Realization in Equatorial Africa'.
[202] Feierman, *Peasant Intellectuals: Anthropology and History in Tanzania*, 48.

political terms. They were not yet anywhere near defining these terms and gaining hegemony. Thus, while this chapter addresses missionaries trying to influence elite actors' ritual and way-of-life choices, the next chapter deals with their attempts to influence ordinary people converting to Christianity.

All these challenges considered, the longevity and eventual success of the mission in Magila is better explained by what happened after 1888. Just as Anne Marie Stoner-Eby showed in south-east Tanzania, missionaries were no less dependent on local alliances for their survival once colonial control was consolidated.[203] Nonetheless, this precolonial period provides an insight into how the UMCA shaped its missionizing strategy around their local contexts. Crucially, it also shows how the conditions of the labour in the mission were not considered desirable or worth the risk except for those with few options to survive elsewhere.

---

[203] Stoner-Eby, 'African Leaders Engage Mission Christianity: Anglicans in Tanzania, 1876–1926', xv, 360.

CHAPTER 2

Building the Slave Market Church in Zanzibar, 1864–1900

It was the Christmas Day service of 1879 when the building work of Zanzibar's Slave Market Memorial Church was almost complete.[1] Scaffold poles were adorned with palm branches and the floor was laid with grass mats. Benches and chairs were brought in for the use of the missionaries and other Europeans from the town; everyone else sat on the floor. The congregation, all dressed in their finest attire, was noted as an 'effective and picturesque' symbol of the mission's progress as it included Arabs and ex-slaves, 'Groups so similar, but assembled for how different a purpose!'[2] Six years earlier the site of the church had been 'the last open slave market in the world', now it epitomised the presumed affinity between Christianity and anti-slavery as a 'home of freedom' for 'all colours and races'.[3] The edifice was said to be built by the freed slaves under the mission's care at the Mbweni *shamba* (farm) under the initiative of Edward Steere, a UMCA Bishop (1873–82). The UMCA made much of their choice to employ ex-slaves as labourers, which symbolised their commitment to the anti-slavery cause. The Cathedral still stands today, nearby a building with dark cellars popularly thought to be where slaves were kept. Tour guides routinely inform visitors that the glorious juxtaposition to this dark past is that freed slaves built the Cathedral as part of the missionaries' humanitarian efforts to provide employment and general care to the slaves who had been

---

[1] Edward Steere to Rev. W. H. Penney, Zanzibar, September 1881, A1 (3) A, 384, UMArch.

[2] Robert Heanley, *A Memoir of Edward Steere: Third Missionary Bishop in Central Africa* (London: Office of the Universities' Mission to Central Africa, 1898), 249–51.

[3] Heanley, 120–21; Bishop Edward Steere, 'First Quarterly Statement', 29 August 1875, 5, A1 (3) C, 814, 816, UMArch.

rescued by the British navy; thus, a promising sign of a transition to wage labour in East Africa.[4]

However, in 1883 Steere was posthumously accused (by a member of the same missionary society) of employing slave labour to build this monument to Christianity and anti-slavery. The Cathedral had not, after all, been built solely with free labour. Steere had contracted hire slaves, paying them a wage, only some of which their masters would allow them to keep. Hiring slaves was a common labour practice for Europeans and Indians in Zanzibar, most notably amongst the Imperial British East Africa Company (IBEAC) in the 1890s. This practice offended British audiences, and slave owners saw it as hypocritical.[5] This was quite a different matter from taking in runaway slaves or redeeming slaves, a practice that has been more widely researched.[6] Aside from the controversy of Anglican anti-slavery missionaries employing slaves, this episode demonstrates the immense variety of opinions among abolitionists. These missionaries were from a small – albeit quickly growing – missionary society and had similar backgrounds. Yet their opinions on how to go about ending slavery – or at least, the slave trade – were markedly varied.

This chapter explores the question of divergent abolitionist sensibilities by dealing with the terms on which labour was extracted, how missionaries engaged with the labour market and how they tried to create their own Christian labour force. There is already a historiography on how missionaries all over East, central and southern Africa brokered relations between African workers and colonial economies.[7] This chapter also addresses the origins of

---

[4] Jonathon Glassman, 'Racial Violence, Universal History, and Echoes of Abolition in Twentieth-Century Zanzibar', in *Abolitionism and Imperialism in Britain, Africa, and the Atlantic*, ed. Derek R. Peterson, African Studies from Cambridge (Athens, OH: Ohio University Press, 2010), 176–80.

[5] Moses D. E. Nwulia, *Britain and Slavery in East Africa* (Washington DC, USA: Three Continents Press, 1975), 173–74; Stephen J. Rockel, 'Slavery and Freedom in Nineteenth Century East Africa: The Case of Waungwana Caravan Porters', *African Studies*, 68, no. 1 (1 April 2009): 100; Fred Morton, *Children of Ham: Freed Slaves and Fugitive Slaves on the Kenya Coast, 1873 to 1907*, African Modernization and Development Series, 1990, 138–39; Opolot Okia, 'The Windmill of Slavery', *The Middle Ground Journal*, 45, no. 3 (2011): 1–35.

[6] Landeg White, *Magomero: Portrait of an African Village* (Cambridge: Cambridge University Press, 1987); Robert W. Strayer, *Making of Mission Communities in East Africa: Anglicans and Africans in Colonial Kenya, 1875–1935* (London: Heinemann, 1978); Nwulia, *Britain and Slavery in East Africa*.

[7] John McCracken, *Politics and Christianity in Malawi, 1875–1940: The Impact of the Livingstonia Mission in the Northern Province* (Cambridge: Cambridge University Press, 1977); Johannes Fabian, *Language and Colonial Power: The Appropriation of Swahili in the Former Belgian Congo, 1880–1938* (Cambridge:

this process by focusing on the actual employment of African workers. The first aspect of African labour attended to is the mission's recruitment of hire-slaves, which gives some texture to the understanding of the different terms on which slave labour was extracted. The second issue to address is that of the labour of the potential and actual converts within the mission all of whom had previously been slaves. This includes the labour of students who boarded in the mission and the 'adult' freed slaves on the settlement. However, it is first necessary to contextualise these issues by setting out the UMCA's stance on slavery and abolition.

The UMCA's abolitionism

Bishop Steere was opposed to the freed slave settlements set up by the CMS and the French Mission, arguing in 1873 that it imposed a kind of 'Christian communism' with unnatural and immoral Europeanised values.[8] Andrew Porter and Terrence Ranger have noted that the UMCA was unusual in that it disassociated itself with the project to combine missionary aims with economic development and 'civilisation'.[9] Instead, suspicious about urban life and about migration work, it sought for Africans a life of self-reliance in sedentary rural economies under the paternalistic civilising mission.[10] These ideas were met with criticism. For example, John Hine (who would later become Bishop of Nyasaland, 1896–1908) justified the UMCA as follows:

> But what is a mission? The one great work is to make people Christians, because Christians believe in their religion as much as Mohammadans. To the world at

---

Cambridge University Press, 1986), http://quod.lib.umich.edu/cgi/t/text-idx?c=acls;idno=heb02589; Jean Comaroff and John L. Comaroff, *Of Revelation and Revolution: Christianity, Colonialism, and Consciousness in South Africa*, vol. 1 (Chicago: University of Chicago Press, 1991).

[8] Edward Steere to John Wogan Festing, Zanzibar, 24 February 1873, A1 (3) A, 85, UMArch.

[9] Andrew Porter, *Religion Versus Empire? British Protestant Missionaries and Overseas Expansion, 1700–1914* (Manchester: Manchester University Press, 2004), 225, 227–29, 332–33; Terence O. Ranger, 'Godly Medicine: The Ambiguities of Medical Mission in Southeast Tanzania, 1900–1945', *Social Science & Medicine. Part B: Medical Anthropology*, Special Issue: Causality and Classification in African Medicine and Health, 15, no. 3 (July 1981): 261. doi.org/10.1016/0160-7987(81)90052-1; Charles M. Good, *Steamer Parish: The Rise and Fall of Missionary Medicine on an African Frontier* (Chicago, IL ; London: University of Chicago Press, 2004), 47.

[10] Good, *Steamer Parish: The Rise and Fall of Missionary Medicine on an African Frontier*, 19.

large it is the civilising side of mission work that appeals, as being 'something practical'. In the eyes of those who believe in Christianity, religion is the great thing in life, and they believe that it is infinitely more important that men be religious than that they be carpenters or builders or clerks, or even houseboys and cooks to English residents.[11]

This contempt (or ignorance) of self-congratulatory Victorian industry and urbanisation reflected their class and university backgrounds and nostalgia for a vision of pre-industrial England.[12] Even if they did not necessarily support industrialisation, they did support industriousness. Like many missions, the UMCA at once sought to protect Africa and its traditions from the evils of modernity and civilisation and foster economic change.[13] They advocated the spread of free wage labour, the cornerstone of the capitalist industries that offended them.[14] However, the missionaries valued wage labour specifically because of its association with work ethics that promoted the dignity of labour, better 'habits' and 'improvement'. Missionaries argued that, though the 'Arab' slave owner may not be as cruel as the English slave owner in the Americas, the absence of wages hindered productivity and diligence.[15]

For the missionaries, the biblical significance of labour and servitude was paramount. For example, missionaries preached about the Letter of Paul to the Thessalonians in which it was said, 'if any would not work, neither should he eat. For we hear that there are some among you who walk disorderly, working not at all, but are busybodies.'[16] Moreover, the attitudes to Christian labour being part and parcel of the cure for slavery were connected to the idea that worshipping God was like serving a master. At least some of the African converts seemed to have echoed this notion of being a Christian as a form of servitude towards God. As one freed slave boy ('a Zaramo Boy') described his journey from the slave trade to the mission he narrated that, 'I was going to be

---

[11] J. E Hine, *Days Gone by: Being Some Account of Past Years Chiefly in Central Africa* (London: J. Murray, 1924), 117.

[12] Ranger, 'Godly Medicine', 261; Good, *Steamer Parish: The Rise and Fall of Missionary Medicine on an African Frontier*, 45–46.

[13] David Maxwell, 'Freed Slaves, Missionaries, and Respectability: The Expansion of the Christian Frontier from Angola to Belgian Congo', *Journal of African History*, 54, no. 1 (2013): 80.

[14] Frederick Cooper, *From Slaves to Squatters: Plantation Labor and Agriculture in Zanzibar and Coastal Kenya, 1890–1925* (New Haven, CT: Yale University Press, 1980), 2; Bill Freund, *The Making of Contemporary Africa: The Development of African Society Since 1800* (Basingstoke: Macmillan Press, 1998), 61.

[15] Captain H. A. Fraser, William Tozer, and James Christie, *The East African Slave Trade, and the Measures Proposed for Its Extinction as Viewed by Residents in Zanzibar*, ed. Edward Steere (London: Harrison, 1871), 5–6, 31–64, 34.

[16] *New Testament, 21st Century King James Version*, Thessalonians 3, 3.6-11.

sold away to Pemba, but Jesus carried me away to be His servant, and now I am trying to serve Him.'[17] In addition, UMCA's brand of Christianity was steeped in agricultural metaphors and allusions to church work as a way of serving God, as it was in many Christian missions.[18] For instance, missionaries commonly called themselves 'workers' or 'labourers for the master's harvest'.[19]

Christianity and abolitionism were intimately connected in the Zanzibar mission. One of the missionaries' central self-perceived roles was therefore centred on guiding freed slaves to a new means of livelihood and nurturing a particular idea of freedom. In a pamphlet from 1871, Steere argued that the condition of slavery took away an individual's civil liberties and authority over their bodies and therefore also any incentive for self-improvement or morality.[20] The destruction of slavery in Christendom was the template upon which Bishop Steere conceptualised the solution; slaves had to elevate themselves by converting to Christianity so that they would become such good Christian slaves that they would finally shame their masters into manumitting them regardless of the legal status of slavery.[21] This is a mirror version of the notion in Islamic slave-holding societies that Muslims cannot be enslaved.[22] Steere's reading of St. Paul's perspective provided a point of comparison to the challenges that Moses faced with the slaves he famously freed and also demonstrated that it was up to the slave rather than the master to initiate moral improvement. Moreover, this understanding of slavery suggests that it may have been ideologically acceptable for the UMCA missionaries to employ slaves to build a monument to anti-slavery. In contrast, the transition to free wage labour would, for British government officials, mostly come about through their 'status of freedom', which was materialised by their freedom papers.[23] They were less compromising or trusting with regards to the importance of

---

[17] A. C. Madan, ed., *Kiungani, or, Story and History from Central Africa* (London: G. Bell and Sons, 1887), 62.

[18] 'Sermon by the Rev. Canon King', 30 November 1883, UMArch A1 (V) A, 2, UMArch.

[19] Arthur Nugent West to St. Andrew's College, 1874, A1 (3) A, 5-8, UMArch.

[20] Edward Steere, 'Preface by Edward Steere', in *The East African Slave Trade, and the Measures Proposed for Its Extinction as Viewed by Residents in Zanzibar*, ed. Edward Steere (London: Harrison, 1871), 6.

[21] Edward Steere, *Central African Mission, Its Present State and Prospects* (London: Rivingtons, 1873), 14. This is remarkably similar to Hegel's interpretation of freedom through consciousness discussed in Orlando Patterson, *Slavery and Social Death* (Harvard University Press, 1985), 99.

[22] Paul E. Lovejoy, *Transformations in Slavery: A History of Slavery in Africa* (Cambridge: Cambridge University Press, 2011), 16–18.

[23] Robert Nunez Lyne, *Zanzibar in Contemporary Times: a short history of the southern east in the nineteenth century* (London: Hurst and Blackett, Ltd., 1905), 78.

self-reliance than the missionaries. John Kirk, the British Consul-General for Zanzibar (1870–86), believed the cure for slavery should be just as severe as its malady because 'the freed slave will certainly not work unless compelled'.[24]

All this is to say that the missionaries' stance on the slave trade was far clearer than their approach to slavery. They did not condone slavery – far from it – but neither did they consider legal manumission as a straightforward solution. Rather, freedom would come through Christian conversion. The fact that the UMCA were not straightforwardly against slavery (as opposed to the trade of slaves) helps contextualise the controversy mentioned at the beginning of this chapter regarding the UMCA's hiring of slaves. The controversy was sparked off by an article in *Mission Life* by Robert Needham Cust, an East India Company civil servant and Orientalist, who in 1883 wrote to criticise the Society for the Propagation of the Gospel (SPG) in their Madagascar mission for furnishing their African missionaries' houses with upstairs rooms for their slaves and hiring slaves from local masters.[25] Naturally, Cust's criticisms incited a reaction and so the SPG Reverend Francis Ambrose Gregory, who later became the Bishop of Mauritius (1904–19), but was based with the SPG in Madagascar at the time, wrote a revealing counter-argument to Cust's article, claiming that Cust was out of touch with the compromises missionaries had to make, asking, 'is not Mr Cust guilty of inhumanity in wishing to deprive the slave of any advantages he may get from living with a missionary?'[26] Hence, Gregory was drawing on the quite prevalent assumption that if there must be slaves, they would at least benefit from working for Christians. Steere no doubt would have disagreed with Gregory. In a 1873 pamphlet, Steere fiercely denied the assumption that the fact of having a British person in charge would necessarily improve the African worker and he was extremely mistrustful of any European 'possessed of absolute power' and 'free from the immediate control of home opinion'; even the missionary should try

---

[24] Sir John Kirk, 'Report on an Experiment to Look After Freed Slaves', 22 September 1871, 187, TC E30, UMArch.

[25] Robert Cust, 'Madagascar: Slavery and Christianity', *Mission Life*, May 1883. Cust was reacting to a published extract of one of Gregory's letters, in particular to this comment: 'The students are all married; each has a house, consisting of sitting-room, bed-room, and kitchen, with an upstairs room for his slaves'; Rev. Francis Ambrose Gregory, 'Madagascar', *The Mission Field*, 2 December 1879, 581.

[26] Reverend Francis Ambrose Gregory, 'Slavery in Madagascar', *Mission Life*, July 1883, 305. In Madagascar there was a similar system of hiring slaves and in the mid-nineteenth century it was widely thought that slaves were in a better position than the free wage labourer who was forced into the imperial labour system. Gwyn Campbell, *An Economic History of Imperial Madagascar, 1750–1895: The Rise and Fall of an Island Empire* (Cambridge: Cambridge University Press, 2005), 117–18.

and limit the extent of their authority.[27] Still, the missionaries' central task was to lead the way for drastic changes in society and so it was necessary to claim some sense of authority that extended past clergy members and into the freed slave settlement, industrial training centres and among those employed outside of the mission community. In practice, the missionaries did not simply leave African workers to take on an 'improved' work ethic through Christian teaching alone. Despite the missionaries' criticism of the authoritarian approaches of the Catholic mission in Bagamoyo or the CMS mission in Rabai, not only did the missionaries find themselves extending their authority and discipline past the main nucleus of the clergy but they also had to manage the mission as a whole.[28]

However, Chauncy Maples (UMCA missionary, 1876–95 and Bishop of Likoma, 1895), who was based on the mainland in Masasi at the time, picked up on a different aspect of Cust's article. He noticed that Cust favourably contrasted the SPG mission with Bishop Steere's protest against slavery, which was exemplified by the construction of the Slave Market Church.[29] Maples responded to Cust by declaring that '[t]he memorial church erected by Bishop Steere's skill on the site of the old slave market was built almost entirely by slave labour'.[30] Maples claimed that Steere's reasoning for hiring slaves was that 'all the working-classes, masons, labourers, &c., in Zanzibar, are slaves, and therefore if a church is to be built at all, it must be built by slaves'. Like the SPG in Madagascar, Steere paid slaves but some of their pay was relinquished to their owners.[31] Although he had planned to have the freed slaves build the church, their labour was mainly confined to the Mbweni plantation, where they would harvest coral from the ground to transport to the church for building. Steere therefore sought the labour of skilled hire-slaves, including Hindu masons who were said to be the highest class of manual labourers in Zanzibar despite their slave-status.[32] In one sense, this should not have been surprising. Building the Cathedral required an enormous number of diverse skills that

---

[27] Steere, *Central African Mission, Its Present State and Prospects*, 15.
[28] John Iliffe, *A Modern History of Tanganyika* (Cambridge: Cambridge University Press, 1979), 84–85.
[29] Cust, 'Madagascar: Slavery and Christianity', 193.
[30] Edward Steere, 'To the Members of the Universities' Mission' (1882), A1 (9) B, 121, UMArch; Chauncy Maples, 'Slavery and Christianity (Typed, Unpublished)' (c 1881), A1 (9) B, 160, UMArch.
[31] R. M. Heanley to Rev. W. H. Penney, c. (undated 1883, A1 (8) 154-5, UMArch; Farler to Penney, 17 November 1883, A1 (9), 156, UMArch; William Percival Johnson, *My African Reminiscences, 1875-1895* (London: Universities' Mission to Central Africa, 1926), 33, https://archive.org/details/myafricanreminis00john.
[32] James Christie, *Cholera Epidemics in East Africa, from 1821 till 1872* (London, 1876), 311.

the mission's freed slaves were unable to offer.[33] Maples was probably right – Steere had made the decision to hire slaves in the absence of free labour. There was no recorded attempt at an ideological justification as there seems to be in the case of Gregory's response to Cust.

Despite Maples' stated intention to defend 'our brethren in Madagascar', he was in fact underlining the apparent hypocrisy of the missionary practice of hiring slaves and supporting Cust's view that missionaries should not countenance slavery and that 'we should rather let them remain free heathens than become slave-Christians'.[34] Maples' article was probably also intended to tarnish the memory of Steere's work in Zanzibar and challenge Steere's labour ethics. Maples' coldness towards Steere probably began in the same year (1882). In an attempt to discipline a woman suspected of adultery, Maples had allowed the husband to tie her down and beat her. When Steere caught wind of this he wrote a reprimanding letter: 'When attention is called to it, I have no choice but to forbid altogether all beating of women under your direction or by your order, and to forbid receiving of secret accusations [...] I had very much rather have left all to your discretion, but you have made this necessary.'[35] In the draft article, Maples seemingly praised missionaries who trained their students to be good servants. However, he reserved his highest admiration for his own Masasi mission, where 'very little domestic work' was to be done at all due to their idyllic lack of want for extravagancies such as imposing buildings, like the cathedral to which Steere had devoted much of his life's work.[36]

Horrified by Maples' outspokenness, the UMCA Home Committee managed to censor Maples' response to Cust so in the end the missionaries did not have to justify their use of hired slave labour to their fellow countrymen. Still, they did have to justify it to the Home Committee, who seem to have been previously oblivious to these practices until this debate emerged. Following Maples' accusation, many letters followed, which defended Steere

---

[33] The mission continued to require the building skills of non-Christians outside of the mission community well into the twentieth century, and missionaries often wrote about hiring Muslims as an opportunity to convert them. See for example, Mary W. Bulley, 'Kwa Maizi', *Central Africa*, 1931.

[34] Cust, 'Madagascar: Slavery and Christianity', 231.

[35] Bishop Edward Steere, 'To the Members of the Universities' Mission to Central Africa (Private)', 1882, A1 (3) C, 819, UMArch.

[36] 352 Steere, 146–51; Chauncy Maples, 'Slavery and Christianity (Typed, Unpublished)'. There was also a sense that even Steere himself was embarrassed by the great cost of the Cathedral. In fact, he insisted that it must be called the 'Slave Market Church' rather than 'Christ Church Cathedral,' as it is more widely known, as a way of attempting to minimise any sense of extravagance. Edward Steere to Rev. W. H. Penney, September 1881.

against what was perceived to be an extremely harmful accusation. Most missionaries agreed that the mission had no choice but to hire slaves yet were deeply concerned about the effect this news would have on their financial support from home.[37] For example, John Prediger Farler (who later became Slavery Commissioner in Pemba) insisted that, 'there is a sense in which every Englishman in Zanzibar [...] may have employed slave labour' though this was done either unknowingly or as a result of a complete lack of other options.[38] Even David Livingstone, the head-figure of so many anti-slavery missions, employed slave-porters.[39] There was said to be a constant pool of slave day-labourers available in particular spots in urban Zanzibar waiting for employers, and Europeans did not necessarily – or at least not initially – realise that they were hire-slaves.[40]

Farler argued that the Home Committee were over-reacting; they 'could not understand such a peculiar society, a slave is a slave to them'.[41] According to Captain H. A. Fraser, a British resident who hired slave labour on his sugar plantation, this was 'almost the only labour obtainable in Zanzibar, and is universally employed by *all* foreign residents engaged in commerce; there being some thousands of British subjects besides myself who so employ it'.[42] It was common for all kinds of foreigners to recruit slaves; Europeans, Indians and Americans hired them as domestic servants, soldiers and porters.[43]

---

[37] Farler to Penney, 17 November 1883; Heanley to Penney, November 1883, A1 (9), 154–5, UMArch.

[38] Hodgson to Penney, November 1882, A1 (9), 123–5, UMArch. For some useful insights into Farler's career as Slavery Commissioner see Elisabeth McMahon, *Slavery and Emancipation in Islamic East Africa: From Honor to Respectability*, African Studies (Cambridge: Cambridge University Press, 2013), 28–30, 68, 79, 89, 93.

[39] 'Livingstone's 1871 Field Diary: A Multispectral Critical Edition' (1871), 297c/103, 297c/110, 297c/123, 297c/130, 297b/135, 297b/143, especially 297b/145, http://livingstone.library.ucla.edu/1871diary/; Farler to Penney, 17 November 1883.

[40] Suzanne Miers, *Britain and the Ending of the Slave Trade* (New York, NY: Africana Publishing Corporation, 1975), 150.

[41] Farler to Penney, 17 November 1883.

[42] Steere, 'Preface by Edward Steere', 1, 15. For a summary of the labour arrangements of entrepreneurs in Zanzibar, see Sir Reginald Coupland, *Exploitation of East Africa, 1856–1890: The Slave Trade and the Scramble; with an Introduction by Jack Simmons*, 2nd ed (London: Faber, 1968), 174–9.

[43] Abdul Sheriff, *Slaves, Spices, & Ivory in Zanzibar: Integration of an East African Commercial Empire Into the World Economy, 1770–1873* (London: James Currey, 1987), 149; Christie, *Cholera Epidemics in East Africa, from 1821 till 1872*, 331; Rockel, 'Slavery and Freedom in Nineteenth Century East Africa', 100; Frederick Cooper, *Plantation Slavery on the East Coast of Africa* (New Haven, CT: Yale University Press, 1977), 187–8.

Consequently, both local slave owners and anti-slavery lobbyists criticised them for their hypocrisy. Horace Waller, an anti-slavery activist and former UMCA missionary (1860–63), was one of the most vehement critics of Britons who employed slaves: 'The truth is this: we don't eat the slaves, we work the life out of them instead. We are hand in glove with the slave-dealers themselves. [...] [T]he ferocious Arab half-caste who haunts central Africa is perfectly justified in stating to all who will listen to him that the English are only too glad to use slaves when they can.'[44] Horace Waller's opprobrium aside, the use of slaves as servants or labourers was technically legal for British subjects outside of British dominions, as long as it did not entail, 'a dealing or trading in purchase, sale, barter, or transfer, carrying away, removing, &c., of such a slave'.[45] By 1888 it was illegal for British subjects to hire slaves through the slave master but it was still lawful to do so as long as they arranged a contract directly with the slave and did not go through their slave master or a contractor.[46]

This prevalence of hire slavery demonstrates what Stephen Rockel has long argued, that slavery and wage labour could coexist.[47] As many historians have shown, the slave's condition could vary dramatically on the east coast. The only characteristics the various kinds of slaves had in common, Glassman has argued, was that 'their status as subordinated clients descended from kinless outsiders brought forcibly into coastal society'.[48] In Zanzibar most of the urban slaves were *wazalia*, slaves who were born there and therefore were recognised to be at the height of slave society, having cast away their associations with the *washenzi* of the mainland. As a result, they gained their masters' trust and many became part of a category of hire slaves known as *vibarua*. These *vibarua* were day labourers who were paid wages, a share of which went to their

---

[44] Horace Waller, *Heligoland for Zanzibar, or, One Island Full of Free Men for Two Full of Slaves* (London: Edward Stanford, 26 & 27 Cockspur Street, Charing Cross, S.W., 1893), 7–9.

[45] H. A. Fraser, *A Letter to the Honourable Members of the Select Committee of the House of Commons: Appointed to Enquire into the Question of the Slave Trade on the East Coast of Africa* (London: W. J. Johnson, 1872), 13.

[46] Basil S. Cave, 'The End of Slavery in Zanzibar and British East Africa', *African Affairs*, 9, no. 33 (1909): 24; Nwulia, *Britain and Slavery in East Africa*, 174; Okia, 'The Windmill of Slavery', 9, 11; Rockel, 'Slavery and Freedom in Nineteenth Century East Africa', 87–109, 100.

[47] Stephen Rockel, 'Wage Labor and the Culture of Porterage in Nineteenth Century Tanzania: The Central Caravan Routes', *Comparative Studies of South Asia, Africa and the Middle East*, 15, no. 2 (1 August 1995): 14–24.

[48] Jonathon Glassman, 'The Bondsman's New Clothes: The Contradictory Consciousness of Slave Resistance on the Swahili Coast', *The Journal of African History*, 32, no. 2 (1 January 1991): 298.

masters.⁴⁹ The share varied between different slave owners but in Zanzibar it seems it was commonly a fixed sum of two dollars per month, which would leave about six dollars for some of the best paid slave-workers, two of which would have been spent on their bare necessities.⁵⁰ The work of the *vibarua* was extremely diverse, from manual labour to highly skilled work. Female and child *vibarua* tended to be engaged in more menial labour as cleaners, water carriers and sorters of gum-copal.⁵¹ Hired slaves were, to European observers' surprise, able to accumulate quite considerable capital and therefore tended to aim to buy their own slaves rather than purchase their own freedom as a way of attempting to accrue material and social benefits.⁵² In fact, Livingstone even recounted a case of a free person selling himself into slavery to collect the profit in order to buy slaves of his own.⁵³

The UMCA missionaries were aware of these particular conditions of slaves and had to find their own space as employers within this labour market. On the whole, the mission's approach to recruitment was not that of fanatical abolitionists but rather of employers attempting to understand and interact with particular labour customs. In the end, employing slave labour reflected the missionaries' attitude that outright rejection of local customs was futile. Still, employing slaves risked compromising support from home and the only way of solving this problem was to produce Christian workers from within the mission, which is precisely what they attempted to do in the long-term.

---

⁴⁹ Glassman, 291; Christie, *Cholera Epidemics in East Africa, from 1821 till 1872*, 312; A. E. M. Anderson-Morshead, *The History of the Universities' Mission to Central Africa 1859–1896* (London: Universities Mission to Central Africa, 1897), 83.

⁵⁰ Anderson-Morshead, *The History of the Universities' Mission to Central Africa 1859–1896*, 83; Edward Steere, *Some Account of the Town of Zanzibar* (London: Charles Cull, Houghton Street, Strand, 1869), 11.

⁵¹ Glassman, 'The Bondsman's New Clothes', 291–92; Cooper, *Plantation Slavery on the East Coast of Africa*, 184–89; Laura Fair, *Pastimes and Politics: Culture, Community, and Identity in Post-Abolition Urban Zanzibar, 1890–1945*, Eastern African Studies (Athens, OH; Oxford: Ohio University Press; James Currey, 2001),117.

⁵² Laura Fair, *Pastimes and Politics: Culture, Community, and Identity in Post-Abolition Urban Zanzibar, 1890–1945*, 118; William Cunningham Bissell, *Urban Design, Chaos, and Colonial Power in Zanzibar* (Bloomington: Indiana University Press, 2011), 42–43; Jan-Georg Deutsch, *Emancipation without Abolition in German East Africa, c.1884–1914* (Oxford; Athens, OH: James Currey; Ohio University Press, 2006), 71.

⁵³ David Livingstone and Charles Livingstone, *Narrative of an Expedition to the Zambesi and Its Tributaries; and of the Discovery of the Lakes Shirwa and Nyassa. 1858–1864. With Map and Illustrations.* (London: John Murray, Albemarle Street, 1865), 55.

The farm and the city

The UMCA's presence in Zanzibar was made up of multiple mission stations that each had very different experiences, partly shaped by their proximity to the town. Approximately four and a half miles from the town lay the Mbweni mission station, which consisted of a *shamba* and a girls' school. The Mbweni *shamba* was established in 1874 as an ex-slave settlement.[54] As the missionaries struggled to manage the growing and overcrowded *shamba*, they moved groups to form other ex-slave settlements in Masasi,[55] Pambili (near Magila),[56] Dar es Salaam (also known as the 'Zaramo mission'),[57] and Pemba.[58] The Mbweni *shamba* was also not the only ex-slave settlement in Zanzibar. As the abolition of slavery made headway, increasing numbers of ex-slaves joined the settlements established by the British government and Indian traders. As I suggested, many also sought to move to the town or at least work in the town, but this tendency was less common in the 1870s, as Table 1 suggests.

The often over-crowded Mbweni *shamba* was spread over approximately 130 acres with a fluctuating population of 100–500.[59] Ex-slaves were expected

---

[54] Anderson-Morshead, *The History of the Universities' Mission to Central Africa, 1859–1909*, 95.

[55] Rev. Edward Steere, *The Free Village in Yao Land* (London: Universities' Mission to Central Africa, 1879); Andreana C. Prichard, *Sisters in Spirit: Christianity, Affect, and Community Building in East Africa, 1860–1970* (Michigan State University Press, 2017), 86.

[56] This was extremely short-lived and barely documented, which is why I am unable to use it as a point of comparison. J. P. Farler to Bishop Edward Steere, Magila, Tanga, 10 October 1876, A1 (6) A, 387, UMArch; at the 22nd anniversary meeting of the UMCA in London, Farler pitched the idea to set up a 'Liberia' on an uninhabited stretch of land on the mainland. The objective was to allow the ex-slaves to become independent and no longer be a cost to the mission. Farler's idea was not totally rejected, as the missionaries strongly encouraged ex-slaves to make their own way back to the mainland. 'Twenty-Second Anniversary of the Mission', *Central Africa*, August 1883, 117.

[57] The 'Zaramo' mission was a UMCA ex-slave initiative that the missionaries supported. Edward Steere to Rev. W. H. Penney, Zanzibar, 23 August 1881, A1 (3) A, 338, UMArch; J. P. Farler, 'A Visit to Kichelewe', *Central Africa*, October 1895; G. C. R., 'Small-Pox at Magila', *Central Africa: A Monthly Record of the Universities' Mission to Central Africa*, September 1920, 103–7.

[58] The Pemba ex-slave settlement was established in late 1897. By April 1899 it had eighteen to twenty houses owned by the mission, which were leased out to the ex-slaves. Emily Key, 'Pemba', *Central Africa*, April 1899; 'Our Thirty-Eighth Anniversary', *Central Africa*, July 1899; in 1902 it was estimated that there were 200 inhabitants in the settlement. Emily Key, 'Pemba Notes', *Central Africa*, October 1902; C. C. Frewer, '"extension" Movement in Pemba', *Central Africa*, May 1904.

[59] 'UMCA Zanzibar Diary', 1888 1864, CB1, NT; John Wogan Festing, 'Slavery at

Table 1 Adult ex-slave trajectories, Mbweni, 1874–77

Remained on the Mbweni shamba	171
Sent to the Masasi ex-slave settlement	55
Sent to Magila mission station*	6
Sent to Kiungani**	8
Found a home or employment elsewhere	15
Died	9

In these early years, very few (9%) left the Mbweni shamba to live and/or work outside of the mission, which shows the move to the town may not have been desirable, practical or safe at this time. (Based on figures from 'UMCA Zanzibar Diary', 1864–88, CB1, Nyaraka za Taifa, Zanzibar)

*Another source suggests this figure was actually 14. Perhaps eight of them were children. J. P. Farler to H. W. Woodward, Magila, Tanga, 14 September 1877, A1 (6) A, 403, UMArch.

**Probably as domestic servants rather than as students

to work for the mission in return for daily wages. They were also expected to attend church services, be self-sufficient and self-supporting in return for their use of the land. [60] This level of labour organisation was rarely reached in practice and the mission had little control over the life trajectories of the ex-slaves on this settlement.[61] The level of conversion was apparently quite high; the majority of ex-slaves at the *shamba* were classed as 'adherents', as Table 2 shows.[62] Considering that church attendance was compulsory for those wanting to remain on the *shamba*, the high number of adherents should not come as a surprise. In fact, the aforementioned UMCA missionary Cyril Frewer described the majority of these ex-slaves as 'heathen Africans who have no religion except one of devil and spirit-worship'. [63] This contradicts the missionaries' impression of the Mbweni *shamba* as a site of utter chaos, because these religious practices that involved spirit possession must have necessitated collective action, shared beliefs and cooperation.

Zanzibar', c 1873, C2, 140, UMArch; Edward Steere to John Wogan Festing, Zanzibar, June 1875, A1 (3) A, 198, UMArch.

[60] Sir John Kirk, 'Report on an Experiment to Look After Freed Slaves'; Edward Steere, 'Bishop Steere's Mission at Zanzibar and to Central Africa', 1875, A1 (3) A, 4, UMArch; Rev. W. F. Capel to Edward Steere, Mbweni, Zanzibar, March 1877, A1 (4) A, 69, UMArch.

[61] Edward Steere to Rev. W. H. Penney, Zanzibar, 8 January 1881, A1 (3) A, 393, UMArch; Caroline D. M. Thackeray to Rev. W. H. Penney, Mbweni, Zanzibar, 19 January 1885, A1 (6) A, 754, UMArch.

[62] *Central Africa* (1886, 1891, 1892, 1895, 1900).

[63] C. C. Frewer, 'Mbweni Village Life as It Is', *Central Africa*, May 1908.

Table 2 Adult converts, Mbweni shamba, 1885–99

Year	Hearers		Catechumens		Baptised*		Communications		Total M adherents	Total F adherents	Total
	M	F	M	F	M	F	M	F			
1885	Unknown		90		72		76		Unknown		238
1890	16	10	24	20	70	200	56	161	110	230	340
1892	17	17	16	26	88	220	71	187	121	263	384
1894	7	14	16	16	67	124	35	54	90	154	244
1899	7	20	12	7	62	243	60	183	91	270	351

Most inhabitants were adherents because conversion was compulsory. This table also shows that more women than men stayed on the shamba and converted. Moreover, fewer male converts were residing on the shamba. Conversely, there is a general increase in female converts – with a notable fluctuation in 1894 – living on the shamba. This probably suggests that many female students settled on the shamba once they reached adulthood. The total number of adherents encompasses hearers, catechumens, those who were baptised, and communicants. (Source: Central Africa, 1886, 1891, 1892, 1895, 1900)

* Including communicants

The church local to the mission *shamba* also attracted ex-slaves from non-mission ex-slave settlements in the twentieth century, which shows that there was an attraction to the mission for some, even if they did not rely upon it for sustenance.[64] Though relatively far from the town, the Mbweni *shamba* was not protected from the 'temptations' of urban life, as alcohol and transactional sex could be sought.[65] To put a stop to these practices, missionaries enforced discipline and made use of a purpose-built 'parish prison' when it was considered necessary.[66]

[64] C. C. Frewer, 'Mbweni Village Life as It Is'.
[65] J. P. Farler to Rev. W. H. Penney, Kiungani, Zanzibar, 31 August 1885, A1 (6) A, 572, UMArch.
[66] Farler to Penney; *The Universities' Mission to Central Africa Atlas* (London: Universities' Mission to Central Africa, 1903); school children in both the boys' and girls' schools were also subject to imprisonment or 'solitary confinement' at various points. Frank Weston to H. M., Kiungani, Zanzibar, 16 November, A1 (17) A, 190, UMArch.

North of Kiungani, the Mkunazini mission station was at the edge of the town of Zanzibar and the site of a number of different projects over the period. It contained a boarding house for apprentices, a hospital, the Zanzibar Cathedral and St. Katherine's 'home' for women who were widows, divorcees and ex-sex workers (the missionaries referred to them as 'fallen' women). It also contained a compact residential area containing a small Christian population, which missionaries referred to as a quarter, or, rather whimsically, 'Cathedral Close'. Mkunazini was where many of the mission's Christians were housed because the missionaries understood they needed to be in town to make a living.[67]

Mkunazini was not quite as peaceful and well ordered as the missionary magazines and floorplans suggested.[68] Even so, as a rule, the Christian inhabitants tended to be skilled workers, such as boat builders, 'door-boys', cooks and printers, who were often married to 'Mbweni girls'. Some of the mission-employment was inherited. For example, if the storekeeper for the Cathedral died, his son might well inherit his position.[69] The Mkunazini complex was the closest the missionaries got to establishing the stable Christian community that they had in mind. However, there were not many Christians living there and they could not have survived solely through dependence on the mission, which provided a limited number of jobs and patronage.

Across from Mkunazini lay Ng'ambo. The literal meaning of '*ng'ambo*' is 'the other side', because it was on the other side of the tidal inlet that separated it from the prosperous coral-stone town. While Arabs, Europeans, Goans and Indians populated the main town, it was the '*Waswahili*' who lived in Ng'ambo. One missionary described Ng'ambo as a melting pot in which its inhabitants forgot their mother-tongues, though, he added that, 'their faces light up when one talks about the mainland where many of them were born'.[70] Ex-slaves from the mission who were living in Ng'ambo did not lose their slave status by virtue of their connection with the mission. In fact, the townspeople referred to them as *mateka* (captives).[71]

---

[67] M. F. R., 'William Mabruki', *African Tidings*, October 1902; Margaret Sudi, interview by Irene Mashasi, Zanzibar, 12 September 2014; Tereza Mwakanjuki, interview by Irene Mashasi, Zanzibar, 19 September 2014.

[68] George William Mallender, 'Missionary life in Central Africa' (Journal, 1896), A1 (4) B, UMArch.

[69] By 1881 there were about 100 Christians living in the town. Edward Steere to Rev. W. H. Penney, 'Present Work of UMCA, 1881', 1881, A1 (3) C, 810, UMArch; M. A. Cameron, 'Round about the Cathedral', *African Tidings*, April 1896.

[70] M. R., 'The Other Side', *Central Africa*, January 1916.

[71] C. C. Frewer, 'The Native of Zanzibar and Pemba', *Central Africa*, February 1907.

Though Ng'ambo was not the centre of town, it was, 'just as crowded and just as puzzling', as one missionary put it. Missionaries attempted, but continually failed, to establish a mission station in this area.[72] Ng'ambo was a place in which Christian converts were 'lost' from mission control.[73] From the 1880s onwards Ng'ambo had a gravitational pull for various socially marginal people, including slaves who had left their owners' plantations and the mission ex-slaves.

Missionaries and colonial agents shared an interest in keeping certain categories of Africans out of town, though they followed a different rationale in doing so. While missionaries worried about sin, colonial officials packaged the policies to restrict access into the town as efforts to reduce disease, though their outlook was undoubtedly shaped also by social and racial prejudice. Ng'ambo, with its enormous population but lack of stone buildings, was legally defined against 'town' as a 'native location'. So, while missionaries sought to limit the urban influences on their converts, British colonial agents were simultaneously endeavouring to minimise Africans' access to the town proper, which was visually, and, later, legally, defined by its stone buildings. In the 1920s colonial law prohibited 'huts' being built in the 'town', apparently as part of the effort to reduce the spread of disease. There were 'native huts' erected in Mkunazini and elsewhere, but they were increasingly fewer in number.[74]

Colonial quarantine policies, bolstered by building regulations, made it nearly impossible for Africans to live in the 'town,' as William Bissell and Laura Fair have shown, regardless of whether you were Christian or Muslim. In a way this became less significant over time as Ng'ambo became, by 1930, part of the social life of the town, partly as a result of its greater population. Ng'ambo came to be known in the first decades of the twentieth century as a quickly growing 'working class quarter'. By 1931 it held around 22,000 people,

---

[72] Walter K. Firminger, 'The Ng'ambo Experiment' (4 June 1895), A1 (8), 469, UMArch; V. H. P., 'The Other Side: Ng'ambo', *Central Africa: A Monthly Record of the Universities' Mission to Central Africa*, February 1920; Fair, *Pastimes and Politics: Culture, Community, and Identity in Post-Abolition Urban Zanzibar, 1890–1945*, 2001, 20.

[73] May Allen, 'Women's Work in Zanzibar', *Central Africa*, July 1886.

[74] It was not illegal to build in stone in Ng'ambo but rent laws passed in the late 1920s made it financially prohibitive. Lawrence D. Berg and Jani Vuolteenaho, *Critical Toponymies: The Contested Politics of Place Naming* (Farnham, Surrey: Ashgate Publishing, Ltd., 2009); Henry Vaughan Lanchester, *Zanzibar: A Study in Tropical Town Planning* (Cheltenham: Ed. J. Burrow, 1923); Fair, *Pastimes and Politics: Culture, Community, and Identity in Post-Abolition Urban Zanzibar, 1890–1945*, 2001. Bissell offered a messier depiction than the colonial impression of this stark divide between the town proper and Ng'ambo. Bissell, *Urban Design, Chaos, and Colonial Power in Zanzibar*.

which was a quarter of the whole island's population.[75] In sum, both missionaries and colonial administrators shared the concern that 'contagion' should be limited, yet they defined it differently and had differing opinions about the source of it and how best to manage it.

By the turn of the century, most ex-slaves who stayed at Mbweni *shamba* were elderly, unwell, or disabled. In other words, they stayed at the mission because they had no other options. For most ex-slaves, dependence on the mission was a way to survive, but not to thrive. The only really valuable opportunities the *shamba* offered for a livelihood existed for mission-educated retirees who were able to claim the patronage of the missionaries by virtue of their careers as teachers or priests. The rest remained at the *shamba* in order to survive, but were unable to move on from their slave status or pursue more stable livelihoods on the *shamba*.

The missionaries gave preferential treatment to African students and clergy, continuously stigmatising the Mbweni *shamba* ex-slaves by making them sit at the back of the church, giving them only very menial work and offering few opportunities for education. Missionaries believed the *shamba* ex-slaves were poor 'material' for Christian conversion.[76] Later, in the 1920s, and according to the missionaries, the ex-slaves also came to have a reputation as bad workers and bad citizens among Zanzibar's local employers and patrons.[77] In fact, the Europeans of the town were said to have forbidden their servants from visiting the *shamba* for fear they, too, would be morally contaminated.[78] Thus, people on the mission *shamba* lacked the kind of privileged access to employment opportunities that one might expect them to have enjoyed by virtue of their connection to the missionaries.

The synod of 1884 made two rulings that show that the missionaries' disillusionment with ex-slaves came early on. The first was, 'That all able-bodied freed slaves who are not required for the work of the Mission, should be induced to seek work for themselves independently of the Mission.' The second was, 'That no released slave settlement be founded again on the mainland.'[79] Despite the synod of 1884's resolutions, the *shamba* only came to an end,

---

[75] Fair, *Pastimes and Politics: Culture, Community, and Identity in Post-Abolition Urban Zanzibar, 1890–1945*, 15–16.

[76] 'Our African Postbag', *Central Africa*, January 1884.

[77] Ingrams blamed their poor reputation on the fact that by the 1920s many Zanzibar Christians seem to have been Wanywamwezi (but most were "Waswahili"). William Harold Ingrams, *Zanzibar: Its History and Its People* (London: H. F. & G. Witherby, 1931), 223; C. C. Frewer, 'Mbweni Village Life as It Is'.

[78] Mkunazini, July 1884, TC C1, 1, UMArch; May Allen to Miss Randolph, Zanzibar, 11 August 1884, A1 (4) A, 680, UMArch.

[79] *Acts of the Synods: 1884–1903* (Diocese of Zanzibar: Church of England, n.d.), 13;

for financial reasons, when the mission sold the land (in several stages) in the 1920s, gradually disengaging from approximately 200 elderly and infirm 'stragglers' who remained.[80] This poses the question: why did the missionaries not close it down sooner? The answer has a lot to do with compassion for the people living there and fear that abandoning the Mbweni *shamba* would damage the mission's reputation. In addition, there were two key personalities who kept the dream of ex-slave rehabilitation alive: Cyril Frewer, who I have already mentioned, and Caroline Thackeray, a wealthy missionary and benefactor who is discussed in Chapter 4. Ex-slaves on the *shamba* had to attend church services to remain on mission property, but they did not have to become Christian to find work there. This suggests that becoming Christian did offer these ex-slaves something aside from shelter and work. In summary, the mission had enough influence over these ex-slaves to induce them to become Christian, but at the same time missionaries despaired of their inability to influence the ways they conducted their lives.

Working at the Mbweni farm

Tellingly, these ex-slaves referred to each other as '*wajoli*', meaning 'fellow slaves'.[81] Out of all the potential converts the missionaries encountered in Zanzibar, these ex-slaves were of the least interest to the missionaries. Equally, the mission was usually of little interest to these ex-slaves, who only stayed on the *shamba* as a last resort. This ambition to create a self-sustaining Christian labour force and community out of freed slaves highlights the paradox of the UMCA; namely, that despite their wish to disassociate themselves as a political entity, the only way that they could introduce a new way of life on their terms was to create some semblance of secular authority. In the nineteenth century as the British navy increased its success rate in capturing slaves and 'liberating' them, concerns emerged about their 'disposal' – to use the common contemporary term of British administrators. A significant number of mission enterprises strived to harness these displaced marginalised peoples, particularly children, to help establish mission communities and clergy.

---

see also: Anderson-Morshead, *The History of the Universities' Mission to Central Africa 1859–1896*.

[80] Dale believed the sale of Mbweni should be a gradual process, and that it was. Godfrey Dale to Duncan Travers, Mkunazini, Zanzibar, 4 July 1909, A1 (21), 193, UMArch; A. D. Swainson, 'Work in Zanzibar I', *Central Africa*, September 1920; 'Annual Report, a Review of the Work of the Mission in 1922: II. Diocese of Zanzibar', *Central Africa*, May 1923; 'Central African Mission Diary 1922–1932' (29 December 1924), CB1-9, NT.

[81] C. C. Frewer, 'The Native of Zanzibar and Pemba'.

The missionaries were initially sceptical of the idea of a freed slave settlement, limiting themselves to educating freed slave children only. However, by 1875 the UMCA had begun taking in adult freed slaves and many of the children who had first come to the mission were now adults.[82] They were therefore faced with the dilemma of how to find livelihoods for the members of their growing community. The missionaries quite quickly came to the consensus that this strategy was doomed due to the corrupting effects of slavery.[83] They believed slavery caused these individuals to be incapable of 'pure and honourable thought' and 'utterly immoral, untruthful, and dishonest'.[84] This echoes the prevalent notion amongst both British administrators and missionaries that slavery left a permanent mark on the individual.

The *shamba* was a plot of land of about 12 acres populated by approximately 250 freed slaves at any one time.[85] Though the mission was generally against the idea of taking in adults, supporting and employing and therefore disciplining them, the British government paid a fee towards each freed slave taken in by missionaries and it was an opportunity to establish a Christian labour force and finally relocate them to the mainland mission stations.[86] They were given 'small money payments' that increased over time as the labourers became more skilled until they reached the 'ordinary rate of wages,' hence emulating a system of apprenticeship. Wages would also be revoked in the event that the workers were guilty of drunkenness, immorality, theft or absence at church services.[87] The freed slaves also had to pay a rent of one day's work per week or its equivalent value.[88]

The idea was to impress upon them the value of work for wages but wages were not thought sufficient to maintain discipline. Supervision led by the *msimamizi* or 'overseer' was considered essential to the productivity of the *shamba* workers who sometimes laboured in gangs.[89] In fact, the same term

[82] Foreign Office 84/1357, Letter 47, Dr Kirk, 17 March 1875.
[83] Johnson, *My African Reminiscences, 1875–1895*, 34, 36.
[84] A. C. Madan, The Rectory, Dunsley, September 1884, TC C1, UMArch; W. Forbes Capel to The Lord Bishop of London and the committee of the Universities' Mission to Central Africa, 1884, 10–12, TC C1, UMArch.
[85] Johnson, *My African Reminiscences, 1875–1895*, 36, 51.
[86] Steere, *The Free Village in Yao Land*, 3–5; Henry Rowley, *Twenty Years in Central Africa: Being the Story of the Universities' Mission to Central Africa, from Its Commencement under Bishop Mackenzie to the Present Time* (London: W. Gardner, Darton, 1881), 253; Archdeacon R. G. P. Lamburn, 'Zanzibar to Masasi in 1876: The Founding of Masasi Mission', *Tanganyika Notes and Records*, 1951, 42.
[87] 403 Steere, 'First Quarterly Statement', 4.
[88] H. A. Forde, 'Zanzibar II', *Mission Life*, August 1882, 342; Edward Steere to G. A. Robins, Zanzibar, 27 July 1878, A1 (3) B, 476, UMArch.
[89] Johnson to Waller, 14 August 1894, A1 (9), 33-5, UMArch.

– *msimamizi* – applied to the slave plantations on the east coast of Africa.[90] This was the most senior position a male or female African could have within the mission aside from teaching and clergy posts. Each station had some and they were responsible for keeping discipline on mission farms, settlements and industrial schools.[91] Given the limitations of the freed slaves' condition in the mission plantation, many fled or rebelled.[92] Indeed, it has been noted that many missionaries in Africa accused freed slaves specifically of holding a grudge against their paternal authority and the UMCA missionaries were no different.[93]

One missionary claimed that if the *shamba* was taken over by an Arab the people would have 'rather more freedom, a few less pice, and be a little less discontented than they at present are'.[94] In the end, the *shamba* was deemed unprofitable and the mission was unable to secure skilled jobs in the town. Donors no longer invested into the scheme and the freed slaves were pushed harder than ever to find their own livelihood independent of the mission. By 1884 they refused to accept more adult freed slaves from the consulate.[95]

From the 1890s, aside from the small number of mission teachers, priests and their families, the Mbweni *shamba*'s population consisted of elderly, unwanted, kinless, and maimed ex-slaves who had run out of options.[96]

---

[90] Cooper, *Plantation Slavery on the East Coast of Africa*, 161; James Christie, 'Slavery in Zanzibar as It Is', in *The East African Slave Trade, and the Measures Proposed for Its Extinction as Viewed by Residents in Zanzibar*, ed. Edward Steere (London: Harrison, 1871), 31; Jack Goody, 'Slavery in Time and Space', in *Asian and African Systems of Slavery*, ed. James L. Watson (Berkeley, CA: University of California Press, 1980), 36.

[91] J. P. Farler to Bishop Edward Steere, Magila, Tanga, 9 November 1881, 360, A1 (6) A, 357, UMArch; C. C. Frewer, 'An African Overseer', *Central Africa*, April 1906. Tozer, 'Miss Tozer to Miss Twining, Zanzibar, May 5, 1872,' 250; some *wasimamizi* were women, Eleanor M. Bennett. 'The Industrial Wing at Mbweni', *African Tidings*, December 1892.

[92] UMArch TC C1, Farler to Penney, 12 September 1884.

[93] Maxwell, 'Freed Slaves, Missionaries, and Respectability: The Expansion of the Christian Frontier from Angola to Belgian Congo', 80.

[94] UMArch A1 (4) A, 75, Capel to Steere, 2 March 1877.

[95] UMArch A1 (6) B, 432 Farler to Penney, Algiers 29 April 1883; A1 (4) A, 330, Hodgson to Penney, December 1880; 689 Capel to Randolph, 11 August 1884; A1 (5) A, 15, Pastoral Letter by the Bishop of UMCA acts of the synods held at Lukoma, Newala, Magila and Zanzibar between July 1887 and February 1888, V; Newala, II.; TC C1, Capel to John Jackson [Bishop of London], 1884, 9; Anderson-Morshead, *The History of the Universities' Mission*, 282–3; Lyne, *Zanzibar in Contemporary Times*, 211.

[96] M., 'Sick, and Ye Visited Me', *Central Africa*, November 1915; 'Rogations and Prayers', *Central Africa*, September 1916; C. C. Frewer, 'Mbweni Village Life as It

Mbweni *shamba*'s growing population of elderly individuals had failed to make the move to the town when they were younger, and found themselves with very little option but to remain on the *shamba*. Many failed to secure wage labour in the town due to the competition from indentured labourers and so they returned to Mbweni to settle and start families.[97] In other words, for all ex-slaves, there was a narrow window of opportunity to leave the Mbweni *shamba*. Females from the *shamba* were less likely to move to the town.[98]

Mbweni ex-slaves were inventive in finding new livelihood strategies. Godfrey Dale, a UMCA missionary, once remarked that there existed what today might be referred to as 'livelihood diversification': 'there were more than 30 ways in which pice could be earned, and therefore a living made, by those living on our Christian plantation there'.[99] Moreover, many supplemented their labour on the Mbweni *shamba* with occasional work in the town as gardeners or messengers for Europeans.[100] Indeed, one did not have to live in the town to work in the town.

Living on the Mbweni *shamba* meant being an agricultural labourer because missionaries saw agricultural livelihoods as wholesome. Like many missionaries, Frewer tried to convince these ex-slaves they could make a good living outside of the town and that agriculture was respectable work: '[T]he young African in these parts cordially dislikes taking hold of a hoe. It is to the mind of the rising generation the tool of the slave, the quite ignorant, and the aged and this is just as much the case with the heathen boys who live anywhere near a town, as with our Christian boys from Zanzibar schools who can read and write.'[101]

Frewer was a man of action and in 1905 he set out to harvest coconuts from the 2,180 coconut trees on the *shamba*. The head overseer, a Muslim named Ibrahimu, managed the project and the African priest did the book-keeping.

Is'; Ada Sharpe, 'The Aged and Invalid People of Mbweni', *Central Africa*, March 1898; Ada Sharpe, 'Sick and Poor at Mbweni', *Central Africa*, May 1900; Edward Steere to G. A. Robins, 27 July 1878.

[97] C. C. Frewer, 'Cocoanuts', *Central Africa*, April 1908; C. C. F., 'Mbweni Shamba', *Central Africa*, June 1909.

[98] The proportion of slaves who first came to Mbweni *shamba* as ex-slaves was roughly equal with regards to gender, but more women remained there than men. Arthur Cornwallis Madan to Rev. W. H. Penney, Zanzibar, 12 August 1883, A1 (6) A, 931, UMArch; Godfrey Dale to Duncan Travers, Kiungani, Zanzibar, August 1896, A1 (8), 487, UMArch; to Duncan Travers, 'Letter', Kigongoi, Tanga, German East Africa, 6 January 1909, A1 (21), 133, UMArch.

[99] C. C. Frewer, 'The Native of Zanzibar and Pemba'.

[100] C. C. Frewer, 'Mbweni Village Life as It Is'.

[101] C. C. Frewer, 'Industrial Work in Zanzibar and Pemba', *Central Africa*, April 1905.

The workforce consisted of three men to climb the trees and twenty women to collect the coconuts. It was a substantial agricultural endeavour, making a £200 in profit in 1907, purely from the selling of coconuts. The profits were used to pay wages for thirty to forty ex-slave widows to do odd jobs on the plantation, the wages of African clergy, overseers, and all the repairs and renewals to the many and various houses and buildings on the plantation.[102] However, the more coconut trees there were, the more alcohol people brewed, which shows that the times of relative prosperity were also times of lively 'immorality' as the missionaries termed it.[103]

Frewer preferred Pemban ex-slaves to Mbweni ex-slaves. While he characterised Pembans as contented and independent in spirit, he believed Mbweni people were overly dependent and deferential towards the missionaries. Frewer attributed this problem to contact with the urban cultures of Zanzibar.[104] Frewer's project to make 'yeomen' of the Zanzibar ex-slaves was more successful in Pemba than it was in Zanzibar. In moving the ex-slaves across to Pemba and making new ex-slave followers in Pemba itself, he hoped to see 'the development of the Christian villages or colonies, on land owned by natives themselves'.[105] At Mbweni the ex-slaves did not own any land, but in Pemba there were greater opportunities, which Frewer encouraged, for ex-slaves from the mission to purchase their own land and start their own plantations. Access to land was less restricted in Pemba, which had fewer large landholdings and a greater variety of smaller owners who held a variety of ethnic identities.[106]

There are two key examples of ex-slave 'Christian Yeomen' in Pemba that Frewer cited. The first is Edward Abdallah, who became the owner of a plantation and settlement at Kiloweka, Pemba. By 1907 there were 'much larger and commodious houses' on the plot of land, and Abdallah's own house had two stories and a galvanised roof, which was, Frewer claimed, the envy of 'Arabs'.[107] Fundi Basil provides the second example of a Christian agricultural entrepreneur at his Mbweni *shamba* in Msizima (1.5 miles north of Kizimbani, Pemba). In 1904 this plantation began with three men and by 1907 six property-owning Christians, and about fourteen non-property-owning Christians, lived there. Frewer declared that, 'it has become nothing less than a Christian village'. Eight of these people were from Mbweni, three of whom

---

[102] C. C. Frewer, 'Cocoanuts'.
[103] Durham Kaleza (Selemani), interview by Irene Mashasi, Zanzibar, 10 September 2014.
[104] C. C. Frewer, 'A Flying Visit to Pemba', *Central Africa*, October 1907.
[105] McMahon, *Slavery and Emancipation in Islamic East Africa: From Honor to Respectability*, 8, 63.
[106] McMahon, 8, 63.
[107] C. C. Frewer, 'A Flying Visit to Pemba'.

were only there as temporary migrant labourers to assist with the clove harvest. Frewer attributed the success of these plantations to the 'natural' way they came about, i.e. not through European agency.[108] All things considered, it would be naive to attach too much weight to Frewer's optimistic accounts, which do not square with the lack of evidence that life for a mission ex-slave was any better in Pemba. Indeed, McMahon has showed that ex-slaves faced severe struggles in Pemba.[109]

There were opportunities for developing one's social standing at Pemba and Mbweni. Many ex-slaves living around the Mbweni area were attracted to the religious teaching that took place in the Mbweni *shamba*. Frewer believed ex-slaves were attracted to the *shamba* because 'they wish[ed] to get attached to a community of persons'. This suggests that, even if Mbweni was not an ideal location in terms of economic opportunity, slaves and ex-slaves could have been far worse off as the mission did offer ex-slaves a valuable opportunity for socialisation.[110] It was possible to accumulate followers, adopt children and have one's own children who might come to be educated at Kiungani.[111] In the nineteenth century some ex-slaves acquired slaves of their own (who had also been 'liberated' from the British navy), sometimes selling them in the town or making use of their services in the Mbweni *shamba*.[112]

Throughout the period, Zanzibar's wealth lay in the town in trades and services; not in the country with agriculture and manual labour. This observation from 1876 from a British physician illustrates this point: 'The town negroes look down upon their country cousins with a good deal of contempt, and consider themselves a superior class.'[113] This prejudice persisted well into the twentieth century. Keeping in mind that the dominant societies in coastal Tanzania tended to view manual labour as a sign of slave status, the fact that missionaries placed such emphasis on a work ethic was counterproductive in terms of boosting ex-slaves' social status.[114]

[108] C. C. Frewer.
[109] McMahon, *Slavery and Emancipation in Islamic East Africa: From Honor to Respectability*.
[110] C. C. F., 'Mbweni Shamba'.
[111] Durham Kaleza (Selemani), interview.
[112] C. C. Frewer, 'The Native of Zanzibar and Pemba'.
[113] Christie, *Cholera Epidemics in East Africa, from 1821 till 1872*, 316.
[114] Speke argued that, slavery was 'one great cause of laziness, for the masters become too proud to work, lest they should be thought slaves themselves.' John Hanning Speke, *Journal of the Discovery of the Source of the Nile*, Second Edition (Edinburgh; London: W. Blackwood and sons, 1864), xxiv. Steere similarly noted that, '[t]he very first idea is that if anything is to be done you must buy a slave to do it'. See: Steere, *Some Account of the Town of Zanzibar*, 13. Weston

Shamba people, like other ex-slaves associated with the mission, struggled with their reputation. Part of the problem was that staying on the Mbweni *shamba* did not help one's chances of learning Swahili. Swahili was the long-established language of *waungwana* (gentlemen, free people), with a tradition of poetry and religious instruction that proved very resilient during the rise of Arabic-speaking Omanis in nineteenth century.[115] Speaking Swahili poorly, as many of the ex-slaves on the Mbweni *shamba* did, was a serious obstacle to social mobility.[116] In other words, the mission did not prepare the ex-slaves adequately for cultural assimilation and they struggled for respect in the Muslim town.[117] The ex-slaves from the mission suffered on account of their affiliation with the mission, partly because they were invariably 'fresher' slaves than those living in the town, who claimed more respect by virtue of establishing roots on the island.[118]

Missionaries offered the Mbweni *shamba* ex-slaves little more than a livelihood, or, '*njia ya kuishi*', literally meaning 'way of living'.[119] The dependence the missionaries offered was shallow and of limited value. A large part of the problem was that the missionaries offered ex-slaves day labour, or *kibarua* work.[120] This paid fair wages but was lower-status employment than some

---

argued Christians were better agricultural labourers than Muslims or pagans in Frank Weston, 'Africa: And the Blight of Commercialism', *The Nineteenth Century and After*, 87, June 1920.

[115] Jeremy Prestholdt, *Domesticating the World: African Consumerism and the Genealogies of Globalization* (Berkeley, CA: University of California Press, 2008), 100.

[116] Jonathon Glassman, *Feasts and Riot: Revelry, Rebellion, and Popular Consciousness on the Swahili Coast, 1856–1888*, Social History of Africa (Portsmouth, NH; London; Nairobi; Dar es Salaam: Heinemann; James Currey; EAEP; Mkuki Na Nyota, 1995), 62; Jonathon Glassman, *War of Words, War of Stones: Racial Thought and Violence in Colonial Zanzibar* (Bloomington: Indiana University Press, 2011), 35. Conversely, Woodward identified Swahili as a slave language, on the basis that most ex-slaves in Zanzibar spoke it. Instead, he suggested Arabic was the language of the freeborn. Woodward to Child, Kiungani, Zanzibar, 3 November 1891, A1 (8), 345, UMArch.

[117] C. C. Frewer, 'Industrial Work in Zanzibar and Pemba'.

[118] Glassman, *Feasts and Riot*, 106–9; Bishop Edward Steere, *Collections for a Handbook of the Nyamwezi Language: As Spoken at Unyanyembe* (London: Society for Promoting Christian Knowledge, 1885); R. G. Abrahams, *The Nyamwezi Today: A Tanzanian People in the 1970s* (Cambridge: Cambridge University Press, 1981), 2–3.

[119] John Geldart Mhina, interview by Zuhura Mohammed, Magila, 17 October 2014; Durham Kaleza (Selemani), interview by Irene Mashasi, Zanzibar, 10 September 2014.

[120] Rev. F. R. Hodgson to Rev. W. H. Penney, Mbweni, Zanzibar (private), December 1880, A1 (4) A, 330, UMArch; Rowley, *Twenty Years in Central Africa*, 226.

slave conditions because it lacked an ongoing commitment between labourer and hirer. In contrast, being a slave implied the existence of mutual obligations to employees regarding social entitlements. After emancipation, slave-owner bonds became patronage bonds that were usually stronger than what the mission offered, which largely only involved agricultural work. As a result, the dependence that missionaries offered at the Mbweni *shamba* was broadly rejected in favour of dependence on patrons in the town.

In the nineteenth and very early twentieth century there was much movement of *shamba* ex-slaves between Mbweni, Zanzibar town, Kichwele (on the mainland) and Wete in Pemba.[121] Much of this movement, especially the journeys to the mainland, were owed to the opportunities for commercial porterage. Just as mainland students found it beneficial to visit Zanzibar, there was also a significant amount of interest among ex-slaves to venture to the mainland, joining caravans as porters or working on ships. This reflects how travel was a survival strategy that could also offer opportunities to gain respectability in new places, partly through being anonymous and transient. Importantly, porters operated in crews, as Stephen Rockel has noted, which meant that valuable social connections could be made alongside benefitting from cash wages. Indeed, many coastal-based porters referred to themselves as '*waungwana*', which Rockel explained was being, 'at the cutting edge of African engagement with international capitalism'.[122] Porterage work even attracted some of the mission-educated ex-slaves.

Many who chose to hire themselves out as porters refused to work for non-Europeans because, as one missionary put it, 'A man of ours loses caste if he serves under anyone else'.[123] Another missionary claimed that their porters accepted a wage of four MTD per month instead of the usual five, because the missionaries were known to treat their employees well and offer regular pay.[124] Possibly, this is simply what workers told the missionaries in order to flatter them, and perhaps European employers offered better working conditions and probably also the opportunity to carry extra items to sell on the journey for additional profit. This suggests that working for Europeans was, from an early point, a potential opportunity for making ends meet.

Porterage was desirable work for many able-bodied men, but missionaries feared it destroyed marriages and encouraged immoral behaviour. For

---

[121] C. C. F., 'Mbweni Shamba'.
[122] Stephen J. Rockel, *Carriers of Culture: Labor on the Road in Nineteenth-Century East Africa* (Portsmouth, NH: Heinemann, 2006), xiv; Rockel, 'Slavery and Freedom in Nineteenth Century East Africa', 89.
[123] Edward Steere to G. A. Robins, 27 July 1878.
[124] May Allen to R. M. Heanley, Mkunazini, Zanzibar, July 1877, A1 (4) A, 171, UMArch.

instance, Peter Sudi, an overseer from Mbweni *shamba* was often away for long periods of time, during which Mary, his wife, resorted to sex work. She defended herself when the missionaries found out by claiming it was '*desturi*' (custom), probably because missionaries reacted more kindly to the aim to maintain customs than to attempts to make livelihoods against the regulations of the *shamba*. She was nevertheless expelled from the Mbweni *shamba*.[125] Overall, mission dependents' travel between island and mainland, then, was another object of contention, with missionaries seeing moral dangers, while their charges experienced a tense mixture of danger and opportunity.

Conclusion

While the missionaries believed that only Christianity could heal the wounds of slavery, the mission – and the larger nascent imperialist system – could not be separated from the system of slavery itself. By hiring slaves, the mission was implicit in the business of slavery. Missionaries held varying views on how problematic this was in relation to their cause, but all understood that knowledge of their hiring practices could be detrimental to the reputation of the mission among their supporters in England.

The mission *shamba* did not introduce a new kind of slavery, but neither did it provide many opportunities for ex-slaves to achieve full cultural, social and economic emancipation. The mission was a site for many kinds of livelihood strategies for these individuals, but it was the ex-slaves themselves who creatively made their own trajectories and shaped the opportunities that missionaries offered. The paternal oversight of missionaries was preferable only for those who could not be independent. Ex-slaves who were out of options and wanted to stay at Mbweni for security were forced to show an interest in Christianity and eventually become Christians to avoid eviction. This reinforced missionary views of the corrupting nature of slavery and, consequently, missionaries increasingly tried to wash their hands of the *shamba* ex-slaves because they did not think of them as good converts. However, they were bound by a moral responsibility to continue mission work on the *shamba*. Meanwhile, ex-slaves who were relatively independent did not wish to convert to Christianity and disappeared into the town instead.

---

[125] Farler to Penney, 31 August 1885.

CHAPTER 3

Slave Status and the Mission Boys' School in Zanzibar, 1864–c.1930

In 1901 in Kiungani Boys' School, Zanzibar, at nine o'clock on Christmas Eve, the missionary Frank Weston[1] had a memorable interview with one of his ex-slave students, who he was mentoring. The student had been under Weston's guidance for eighteen months, reputedly progressing and flourishing in his teacher-training, which would, if all went well, lead to priesthood. Weston was, therefore, horrified to hear his student admit that he had 'fallen again' to 'the sin of Sodom'. He immediately coordinated a man-hunt for the other guilty party. Weston narrated the events of the evening as follows:

> There was I until 11.30pm trying to get this second boy to confess, and then both to repent. [...] [T]he repentance of the first boy was beautiful. He told me all I asked without a lie, accepted a flogging which hurt him very much, and prayed with me afterwards for a long time. The tears that he shed when we spoke and prayed were more than he shed over his own whipping, which was severe. That was a compensation.[2]

Weston despaired for his students, lamenting the need to monitor their sexual conduct so closely. The significance of this anecdote to this chapter is not in the fact that same sex intimacy existed between students at mission schools, but in the way Weston explains its existence. He, along with other missionaries, strongly believed that this behaviour was the result of the combined influences of city life and slavery. Weston claimed that: 'It is not a

---

[1] Weston would become the Bishop of the UMCA in 1908.
[2] Frank Weston to H. M., St Mark's College, Zanzibar, 20 January 1901, A1 (17) A, 90, UMArch.

mainland sin, it belongs to this sink of sin – Zanzibar. And my particular boys are nearly all the city type.'³

Corporal punishment was not uncommon on the mission, and Weston was well known for his use of it. For Weston, as the leader of his church, his preferred approach was autocracy. He wrote once in a private letter that 'epoch-making smackings have a wonderful effect! I do not pretend to feel traumatised by using the cane, nor do I find that it hurts me more than the boy'.⁴ He did not reserve physical discipline for ex-slaves and children, adult teachers on the mainland were also targeted, but Weston's disciplining of the ex-slave students reflects a broader history of conflict between missionaries and Africans regarding Kiungani students' ties to the city.⁵

This chapter will explore the issues raised by this episode: what role did the mission play in helping male ex-slave students negotiate their slave status? What kind of dependency did the mission offer to help these students feel secure? What kinds of opportunities did the mission offer for eventual independence? To what extent did the mission further entrench the stigma surrounding slave status? In addition, this chapter discusses the deeply gendered experience of slave status in the UMCA and beyond.

Missionaries were convinced that the presence of even a handful of ex-slaves, combined with the school's proximity to the town, resulted in moral contagion. Weston provided two spatial binary oppositions to explain how the temptation to sin had a certain geography: island and mainland; urban and rural. Slave status was inextricably woven into this moral spatial mapping. Weston, like other UMCA missionaries, diagnosed ex-slaves with a moral problem catalysed by proximity to, and a yearning for, the 'city'. For example, missionaries blamed the influence of the city for the conduct of Rev. Cecil Majaliwa, an ex-slave, and Rev. Samuel Chiponde, who was freeborn, both of whom had been 'living in sin' (with sexual partners they were not married to) for several years, who were purportedly under the impression that the missionaries were turning a blind eye.⁶

---

³ Weston to H. M.
⁴ Frank Weston to H. M., Kiungani, Zanzibar, 12 November 1909, A1 (17) A, 131, UMArch.
⁵ Evidenced, for example, by: Frank Weston to H. M., 4 Hyde Park Mansions, N. W. London, 20 September 1907, A1 (17) A, 187, UMArch; William Ernest Deerr to Duncan Travers, Kiungani, Zanzibar, 9 October 1907, A1 (21) 164, UMArch; Weston to H. M., 20 September 1907.
⁶ H. Maynard Smith, 'Memories of Bishop Weston, (Universal Exercise Book)' (Zanzibar, c 1925), A1 (17) A, 456, UMArch; Malcolm Mackay, Samuel Sehoza, and C. S. P., 'Recollections of Frank Weston' (1925), A1 (17) A, 455, UMArch;

The missionaries saw the mixing of ethnicities in urban environments as part of the problem. For example, another missionary, Cyril C. Frewer, argued that Zanzibar presented Christians with 'numberless sin-traps' because it contained 'the dregs of all nations'.[7] Missionaries considered ex-slaves particularly poorly equipped to deal with the 'temptations' of city life because of the lack of the kind of community self-regulation that kinship and 'tribal' belonging afforded to others.[8] The missionaries' opprobrium often originated from their personal experiences missionizing in urban slums in England. Meanwhile, missionaries associated the mainland's countryside with 'unspoilt', virtuous, and free Africans, regulated by unquestioned forms of authority. For example, Weston reasoned that, 'tribal custom inspires a fine for fornication and for adultery [...] in Zanzibar such customs are not observed much. Tribes are nowhere'.[9] Missionaries treated 'immoral' behaviour very differently in Zanzibar from in Magila. In Magila, 'immoral' activity was considered almost excusable because of the missionaries' unspoken assumption that mainland Africans 'sinned' because they could not be expected to control their 'natural instincts'. Conversely, in Zanzibar, 'immoral' tendencies were treated as a deeply-rooted and personal weakness to sin. For this reason, missionaries preferred mainland students, and so they side-lined and gradually drove out most of the ex-slave students, or 'industrial students' as the euphemism went, from the boys' school.[10] Though the missionaries still hoped that some freed slaves would establish the African ministry, they were increasingly pessimistic about their abilities and sought to provide an 'industrial school' route for the majority of freed slave students in order to prepare them for life as

---

George Herbert Wilson, *The History of the Universities' Mission to Central Africa* (London: Universities' Mission to Central Africa, 1936), 158.

[7] C. C. Frewer, 'Industrial Work in Zanzibar and Pemba', *Central Africa*, April 1905; Other examples of missionaries believing the town to be full of temptation: 'Hazina', *African Tidings*, October 1905.

[8] Pennell, 'A Visit to Kiungani: A Universities' Mission College for Released Slave Boys', n.d., 66, A1 (3) C, 972, UMArch; A. E. M. Anderson-Morshead, *The History of the Universities' Mission to Central Africa, 1859–1909* (London: Universities' Mission to Central Africa, 1909), 350.

[9] Frank Weston to H. M., St Mark's Theological College, Zanzibar, 9 December 1899, A1 (17) A, 53, UMArch; a similar opinion can be found here: H. Maynard Smith, *Frank, Bishop of Zanzibar: Life of Frank Weston, 1871–1924* (London: Society for Promoting Christian Knowledge, 1926), chap. 10.

[10] This resembles the use of the term 'Swahili' as a euphemism for someone with slave status, which came relatively late in the 1920s and 1930s. Laura Fair, *Pastimes and Politics: Culture, Community, and Identity in Post-Abolition Urban Zanzibar, 1890–1945*, Eastern African Studies, Athens, OH; Oxford: Ohio University Press; James Currey 2001, 35–6.

free wageworkers. Missionaries feared that too much emphasis on academic life would render their student's bodies too weak for the manual labour that they would invariably have to face in adulthood, while simultaneously being unqualified teachers.[11]

Missionaries understood that the transition to freedom was more complicated than the distantly positioned anti-slavery activists suggested. For instance, the closest word Johnson could find for 'freedom' in the Yao language literally meant 'of-the-family'. Freedom from slavery could only truly be granted by a family member.[12] It therefore followed that the mission had to establish conditions for freed slaves to start new families and benefit from the paternal and maternal guidance of the missionaries themselves. However, the missionaries, with their characteristic concern for authenticity, worried that true kinship could never be found through an ex-slave settlement. Equally, they were generally reticent to build affectionate relationships with the freed slaves themselves because they were anxious to maintain authority and discipline. Missionaries also believed that the losing of one's family – along with their community and property – served as an explanation for the inevitable failure of their cooperation with freed slaves.

The ex-slave students were referred to as '*wenyeji*' (literally, 'natives') at Kiungani school. '*Wenyeji*' was not in itself a derogatory term and, in fact, on the mainland it had quite positive connotations, in line with first-comer status.[13] However, in this case, '*wenyeji*' was used to distinguish between those who were ex-slaves and those who were born free on the mainland and came to Zanzibar to study, thus, not natives of Zanzibar. The ex-slave students were under extremely close surveillance and received possibly the greatest amount of attention from the Zanzibar-based missionaries. Here, I show that male ex-slaves were not guaranteed elite positions in the mission as teachers or priests; many left the mission, and with it, the historical record.[14]

---

[11] Bishop Charles Alan Smythies, 'Pastoral Letter Addressed to the Clergy and Members of the UMCA', Zanzibar (printed), July 1885, 14, A1 (5) A, 6, UMArch.

[12] William Percival Johnson, *My African Reminiscences, 1875–1895* (London: Universities' Mission to Central Africa, 1926), 35–6.

[13] Felicitas Becker, *Becoming Muslim in Mainland Tanzania 1890–2000* (Oxford: Oxford University Press, 2008), 108; James R. Brennan, 'First-Comers, Chiefs and Republicans: Political Legitimacy and the Shadow of Servitude among the "indigenous" People of Dar Es Salaam, 1890–1968', in 'Post-Slavery Societies in East Africa' conference (Cambridge, 2014).

[14] See Tables 5–6 for the quantitative data and some clues as to what the ex-slave students went on to do. On the surface, the findings presented here seem to diverge from those of Andreana Prichard, who argues that the mission's labour practices actually helped create and maintain pan-ethnic and intergenerational

Slave status in a post-abolition world

In Zanzibar, slave labour was significantly in decline after the anti-slavery decrees of 1897, which abolished slavery, and 1907, which made all slaves legally free so they no longer had to claim their own freedom.[15] Concomitantly, slave status was increasingly difficult to identify through social cues and clothing, though slave status was at odds with any vision of a desirable social identity. In 1907 Cyril Frewer noted that, 'the words "people" (i.e. the people, of so-and-so) and "slaves" are quite interchangeable these days'.[16] Despite the decline in slave labour and the mission's anti-slavery ideologies, slave status was persistent and reinforced in the mission. Thus, the mission simultaneously created a refuge for ex-slaves and perpetuated their slave status. Both missionaries and Africans saw slave status negatively, and the social mechanisms that made them despise slaves were surprisingly similar. Even so, missionaries and Africans expressed their prejudice towards ex-slaves differently and had different ideas about what 'honour' entailed.[17]

Crucially, Elizabeth McMahon has argued that from the late 1890s, in Pemba, respectability, or rather, *heshima*, was a way of overcoming slave

---

relationships and networks. In contrast, this chapter highlights much conflict between ethnicities and between Africans with varying degrees of slave status. The difference in our accounts is down to our differing foci on periodisation (Prichard looks at a much longer period up to 1970). Andreana C. Prichard, *Sisters in Spirit: Christianity, Affect, and Community Building in East Africa, 1860–1970* (East Lansing, MI: Michigan State University Press, 2017).

[15] Frederick Cooper, *Plantation Slavery on the East Coast of Africa* (New Haven, CT: Yale University Press, 1977); Frederick Cooper, *From Slaves to Squatters: Plantation Labor and Agriculture in Zanzibar and Coastal Kenya, 1890–1925* (New Haven, CT: Yale University Press, 1980).Concubinage continued after abolition and there were individuals living on their ex-master's plantations who self-identified as slaves. Ingrams, who was an apologist for slavery in the context of 'Arab civilisation', insisted that some slaves declared their slave status proudly. William Harold Ingrams, *Zanzibar: Its History and Its People* (London: Stacey International, 2007), 36–37, 204–5. Although the German colony of Tanganyika did not abolish slavery until 1920, a process of emancipation had begun in the early twentieth century: Jan-Georg Deutsch, *Emancipation without Abolition in German East Africa, c.1884–1914* (Oxford; Athens, OH: James Currey; Ohio University Press, 2006).

[16] C. C. Frewer, 'The Native of Zanzibar and Pemba', *Central Africa*, February 1907.

[17] Indeed, leading studies have already shown that missionaries and African Christians, especially those of ex-slave stock, did not share the same ideas about respectability and honour. John Iliffe, *Honour in African History* (Cambridge: Cambridge University Press, 2005), 246; David Maxwell, 'Freed Slaves, Missionaries, and Respectability: The Expansion of the Christian Frontier from Angola to Belgian Congo', *Journal of African History*, 54, no. 1 (2013): 79–102.

status. *Heshima*, which came to mean 'respectability' more than it did 'honour', meant being a good, stable member of the community, and had very little to do with what degree of 'Arab' ancestry you could claim, or where precisely you came from on the mainland. *Heshima* was also conferred in a non-hierarchical way. The only way to get a better life was to integrate yourself into the local community. Thus, your place and the honour you received in a community was essential to the way you negotiated slave status.[18] This appears to have been very similar to the Zanzibar case as Laura Fair emphasised how one's duty to the community, epitomised by *ujirani*,[19] was essential to the building of social status and daily survival in the protectorate period in urban Zanzibar town, which was exemplified by Siti Binti Saad's songs on the subject of being a good neighbour.[20]

The missionaries' idea of respectability was not so different as they, too, emphasised the importance of community obedience. However, the missionaries also underlined the importance of being a hard worker, sexually disciplined and humble. Missionaries were concerned that the most successful and 'intelligent' ex-slaves who received a mission education had a predisposition towards 'immorality'. In missionaries' eyes, these ex-slaves had taken the greatest leap in social status, which, missionaries believed, damaged their sense of morality, a sentiment that was underpinned by the missionaries' prejudice.[21] Africans and missionaries also had different ideas about possible ways to shed the stigma of slave status. This was largely because the missionaries' geography of respectability conflicted with the Swahili geography of 'civilization'. As to any slave in Zanzibar, so to mission ex-slaves, the commercial centre of Zanzibar town, and the coastal cultures it was associated with, offered the clearest way out of slave status, while the mainland was the site of '*ushenzi*' ('primitivism'), and associated with slavery.[22] Meanwhile, as I have already established, missionaries believed urban life tainted moral character, and thought more highly of the morals of mainland Africans.

Ex-slaves in the mission, though legally free, were subject to the authority and discipline of missionaries. As ex-slaves were usually short of options, they had to live with these constraints and tried to benefit from relationships of

---

[18] Elisabeth McMahon, '"A Solitary Tree Builds Not": Heshima, Community, and Shifting Identity in Postemancipation Pemba Island', *The International Journal of African Historical Studies*, 39, no. 2 (1 January 2006): 197–219.

[19] Neighbourliness.

[20] Fair, *Pastimes and Politics: Culture, Community, and Identity in Post-Abolition Urban Zanzibar, 1890–1945*, 24–25.

[21] C. C. Frewer, 'The Native of Zanzibar and Pemba'.

[22] Mervyn W. H. Beech, 'Slavery on the East Coast of Africa', *African Affairs*, 15, no. LVIII (1916): 145–49.

dependence as far as they could. There is a rich scholarship on this. Notably, Suzanne Miers and Igor Kopytoff convincingly argued that slaves in Africa saw total autonomy as impractical and instead desired social belonging in their new societies, even if this involved a degree of continuing servility.[23] British observers, including missionaries, made quite the same point that remaining a slave could potentially reap greater rewards due to the security afforded by the patron-client dynamic.[24]

Much like these nineteenth-century British observers, scholars have continued to promote the notion that Africans are predisposed to accept dependence or even to seek out dependence.[25] Put simply, the logic goes that Africans are dependent because they want to be. This viewpoint is one of many that make it possible to shift the blame for poverty onto the impoverished in global developmental discourse.[26] Moreover, it suggests that there is something intrinsically 'African' about accepting dependency as a means to belong. This is why Benedetta Rossi has argued that much of the scholarship has mistaken dependence for something desirable when it is sometimes simply the best option out of many poor ones.[27]

In a similar vein, Jonathon Glassman has argued that people with slave status did not indiscriminately accept forms of belonging or dependency. Rather, they would define, or negotiate, the terms of their belonging. Different types of dependence or 'bonds' could be sought to redefine the relationship between master and slave.[28] This is not to say that dependence was necessarily

---

[23] Suzanne Miers and Igor Kopytoff, eds., *Slavery in Africa: Historical and Anthropological Perspectives* (Madison, WI: University of Wisconsin Press, 1977), 17; This was echoed by many other authors, e.g. Frederick Cooper, 'The Problem of Slavery in African Studies', *The Journal of African History*, 20, no. 1 (1 January 1979): 119; James Ferguson, 'Declarations of Dependence: Labour, Personhood, and Welfare in Southern Africa', *The Journal of the Royal Anthropological Institute*, 19, no. 2 (1 June 2013): 223–42.

[24] Captain Philip Howard Colomb, *Slave-Catching in the Indian Ocean: A Record of Naval Experiences* (London: Longmans Green and Co., 1873), 373.

[25] Sean Stilwell, *Slavery and Slaving in African History* (Cambridge: Cambridge University Press, 2014), 8; Ferguson, 'Declarations of Dependence: Labour, Personhood, and Welfare in Southern Africa'; James Ferguson, *Give a Man a Fish: Reflections on the New Politics of Distribution* (Durham, NC; London: Duke University Press, 2015).

[26] Felicitas Maria Becker, *The Politics of Poverty in Africa: Policy-Making and Development in Tanzania* (Cambridge: Cambridge University Press, 2019).

[27] Benedetta Rossi, 'Dependence, Unfreedom and Slavery in Africa: Towards an Integrated Analysis', *Africa: The Journal of the International African Institute*, 86, no. 3 (2016): 584.

[28] Jonathon Glassman, *Feasts and Riot: Revelry, Rebellion, and Popular Consciousness on the Swahili Coast, 1856–1888*, Social History of Africa (Portsmouth, NH;

the ideal. If slaves did not claim full autonomy, it was not because they wanted or enjoyed being in a state of dependence, or lacked a notion of personal autonomy. As Benedetta Rossi put it, '[i]t is because the institutional and cultural landscape in which they live has in-built barriers to their emancipation.'[29]

While conventional notions of freedom were not achievable for ex-slaves, a degree of personal autonomy, albeit through patronage, was achievable. Missionaries were certainly aware that patronage and dependence were the necessary means to negotiate for a degree of personal autonomy.[30] As Frewer put it in 1907:

> The social position of those who remain slaves [in the households of their masters] of their own choice is now practically the same as that of many of the released slaves. [...] [B]eing under the protection of the Arab houses, they have privileges and opportunities which they use for better or worse much in the same way as those living on plantations under the more immediate protection and supervision of the government or a mission.[31]

Missionaries understood that ex-slaves needed patrons, but they were rarely willing to take up that role. As Jeremy Prestholdt has pointed out, the UMCA missionaries (in addition to British officials, such as John Kirk) perpetuated paternalistic attitudes and dependence in a way that was less advantageous to individuals with slave status than some forms of continued dependency on former slave owners.[32] As he put it, the mission provided very limited scope for ex-slaves' desire to 'define their own place in the social order, to represent their own political and social interests'.[33] The problem was not that missionaries created new relationships of dependency, but rather that they created an undesirable form of dependency by not offering avenues to escape slave status. While Muslim slave owners referred to their slaves as children, brothers, or sisters, missionaries used terms like '*mtumwa*' ('slave'), '*mfanyakazi*' ('worker'), and '*kibarua*' ('day labourer'). Thus, some markers of slave or servile status remained more obvious within the mission environment than outside of it. To get a better sense of how the mission stations related to each other and their surrounding communities, the next section contextualises the mission's geography.

London; Nairobi; Dar es Salaam: Heinemann; James Currey; EAEP; Mkuki Na Nyota, 1995), 113.

[29] Rossi, 'Dependence, Unfreedom and Slavery in Africa'.
[30] C. C. Frewer, 'The Native of Zanzibar and Pemba'.
[31] C. C. Frewer.
[32] Jeremy Prestholdt, *Domesticating the World: African Consumerism and the Genealogies of Globalization* (Berkeley: University of California Press, 2008), 125, 132–33.
[33] Prestholdt, 134–35.

Established in 1866, Kiungani school was the UMCA boys' school with the greatest longevity in Zanzibar. John Iliffe treated it convincingly as an exceptional and unrepresentative example of mission schooling, given its relatively small numbers and high academic calibre.[34] Kiungani school was situated about two miles from the town and, in fact, 'Kiungani' meant 'in the suburbs'. In theory, the school's proximity to the town was a way for students to 'learn how to overcome the struggles and temptations of town life'.[35] However, as the introduction of this chapter shows, the missionaries' challenge was, as they saw it, to manage the moral codes and scope of outside influences. The school was intended, from Bishop Steere's episcopate (1872–83) onwards, to be a filled with 'free' or 'voluntary' children.[36] In Zanzibar, so-called 'voluntary' students were rare as many parents feared for their reputation amongst 'zealous Mohammedans' and they worried that the missionaries would 'bewitch' their children.[37] Thus, the majority of the 'voluntary' students had to come from the mainland. Missionaries preferred these students from the mainland who had something (i.e. familial relations) to sacrifice.[38] In contrast, it was the missionaries' belief that the ex-slaves had nothing to lose and, equally, no better option than to stay in the mission. On this basis, the missionaries believed the overall quality of ex-slaves' academic work was bound to be low.[39]

---

[34] John Iliffe, *Tanganyika Under German Rule 1905–1912* (Cambridge: Cambridge University Press, 2009), 176.

[35] G. W. Broomfield, 'St Paul's High School, Kiungani', *Central Africa*, September 1926.

[36] William George Tozer (UMCA Bishop 1863–1872) initiated the system of adopting and training ex-slaves that was kept in place until Smythies' episcopate (1884–94). Edward Steere to John Wogan Festing, Zanzibar, 7 August 1872, A1 (3) A, 81, UMArch; Edward Steere to John Wogan Festing, Zanzibar, 24 February 1873, A1 (3) A, 85, UMArch; Edward Steere to John Wogan Festing, Zanzibar, 15 December 1872, A1 (3) A, 74, UMArch; Bishop Edward Steere to John Wogan Festing, 5 March 1878, A1 (3) B, 461, UMArch; Edward Steere, *Central African Mission, Its Present State and Prospects* (London: Rivingtons, 1873), 16–17; Bishop Charles Alan Smythies, 'A Letter from the Bishop', *Central Africa*, September 1885; 'The Ordination to the Priesthood of the Rev P. Limo', *Central Africa*, May 1894; W. King and Frank Weston, 'St. Andrew's College, Kiungani', *Central Africa*, December 1899; Frank Weston, 'Our Zanzibar Burden', *Central Africa*, November 1906; Justin Willis revealed how the missionaries' assumption that all mainland children were 'free' was deeply flawed as most, at least initially, entered the mission through pawnship. Justin Willis, 'The Nature of a Mission Community: The Universities' Mission to Central Africa in Bonde', *Past & Present*, no. 140 (1 August 1993): 127–54.

[37] Bishop Steere, August 1881, A1 (3) A, 428, UMArch.

[38] J. D., 'Schoolboys in Zanzibar', *African Tidings*, December 1892.

[39] Edward Steere to G. A. Robins, Zanzibar, 27 July 1878, A1 (3) B, 476, UMArch; Farler to Penney, Zanzibar, 12 September 1884, TC C1, UMArch.

Table 3 Students at Kiungani school, 1864–1901.

Year	Boarders	Scholars baptised*	Total
1864–c.1879	-	-	50
1881	-	-	60–70
1890	96	96	96
1892	103	94	103
1893	73	73	73
1901	-	-	72

The number of students at Kiungani was always kept relatively low. The great majority of students were Christian boarders. In the 1870s and 1880s most of the students were orphaned ex-slaves, which is why they boarded. From the 1890s there were increasing numbers of 'voluntary' students from the mainland, who were also inevitably boarders. In addition to this, there was a culture of boarding in Kiungani that missionaries sought to maintain so that students could be easily policed. (Sources: Central Africa 1891, 1893, 1894; Frank Weston to H.M., St Mark's College, Zanzibar, 20 January 1901, A1 (17) A, 90, UMArch)

* Scholars are not necessarily baptised nor borders. Zanzibar schools were unlike other UMCA schools in that most were both baptised and boarders.

Table 4 Kiungani adults, 1890–99.

Year	Hearers		Catechumens		Baptised (including communicants)		Communicants		Total adherents
	M	F	M	F	M	F	M	F	
1890	20	-	-	-	67	1	67	1	88
1892	9	-	-	-	95	-	88	-	105
1894	-	-	8	-	96	5	85	3	109
1899	-	-	-	-	112	4	108	3	116

Some adults resided at Kiungani, as this table shows. These must have been the African male teachers, priests and domestic servants. It is not explained who the women were, but they may have been teachers' wives. (Source: Central Africa, 1886, 1891, 1892, 1895, 1900)

From 1897, as a result of the growing influence of the town on mission life, many of the ex-slaves in Zanzibar mission stations were sent to the 'dumping ground', as Frewer put it, of the mission stations near Weti, on the exceptionally rural island of Pemba.[40] The ex-slaves selected for this exodus were the ones the missionaries identified as being most troublesome: the adult ex-slaves of the Mbweni *shamba*, the apprentices from Mkunazini, and the industrial students (from both the Mbweni and Kiungani schools).[41] This is not to say that the industrial students at Mbweni were categorically considered 'troublesome', but rather that they were thought of as essential counterparts to the male members of the mission moving to Pemba. In theory, but certainly not in practice, only the academic ex-slave students remained in Zanzibar. The idea was to isolate these students sent to Pemba from their own families and fellow ex-slaves who remained living on the Mbweni *shamba* in Zanzibar.[42] This underlines how the missionaries' primary strategy was to keep the mixing of people to a minimum to manage the influence of urban life.

Wenyeji

It was recorded that the small category of male ex-slaves who received an academic or, more often, 'industrial' education at Kiungani were referred to as '*wenyeji*' or '*watumwa waliyokombolewa*' ('released slaves') as opposed to '*waungwana*' (gentlemen or freemen).[43] Social status was unevenly conferred among the students at Kiungani, largely because missionaries favoured mainland students for high-status life trajectories. Indeed, fewer and fewer ex-slaves engaged in academic studies. Instead, they were taught 'industrial' skills that revolved around trades, including printing.

---

[40] A. F., 'Mbweni Girls in Pemba', *African Tidings*, March 1904; C. C. Frewer, 'Industrial Work in Zanzibar and Pemba'; 'Post-Bag', *Central Africa*, June 1905; D. C. A., 'The Emerald Isle', *Central Africa*, June 1916; *Acts of the Synods: 1884–1903* (Diocese of Zanzibar: Church of England, n.d.), 2.

[41] Emily Key, 'Pemba', *Central Africa*, April 1899; Emily Key, 'From Pemba to Zanzibar', *Central Africa*, September 1898; W. E., 'Hospital Sketches', *Central Africa*, June 1907; Morgan Robinson, 'Cutting Pice and Running Away: Discipline, Education and Choice at the UMCA Boys' Industrial House, Zanzibar, 1901–1905', *Southern African Review of Education with Education with Production*, 19, no. 2 (2013): 9–24.

[42] Robinson, 'Cutting Pice and Running Away'.

[43] Chauncy Maples and Ellen Gilbert Maples Cook, *Journals and Papers of Chauncy Maples: Late Bishop of Likoma, Lake Nyasa, Africa* (Lond. &c., 1899), 216; John Geldart Mhina, interview by Zuhura Mohammed, Magila, 17 October 2014, 01:22.

Kiungani is a prism that offers insight into the difficulty of creating a community from such disparate elements and in the face of multiple layers of prejudice. Missionaries increasingly deepened the division between 'free-born' mainlanders and ex-slaves, frequently complaining that the latter were bad 'material'.[44] For instance, the missionary Herbert Geldart argued that the schoolboys on the mainland were much better mannered than 'Kiungani boys' because 'they have never been demoralised as slaves'.[45] By 'demoralised', he meant that slaves were taken from their homelands, where they had moral duties to their communities, to other places where they did not, a view that was pervasive among missionaries, as I suggested in the introduction to this chapter.

It was near impossible to convince local Zanzibaris to bring their children to Kiungani. Moreover, unlike the girls' school, the children of ex-slaves were much less likely over time to send their male children to Kiungani because it had more stringent admissions policies designed to exclude children with slave status. Moreover, missionaries worried that the school risked attracting students from too many different backgrounds, which they thought might increase tensions. Nevertheless, before Kiungani became a school primarily aiming to educate mainland students, it was a great mix of students, including apprentices, 'the young men about town sort', 'boys fresh from slave dhows', boys from Mbweni *shamba*, and finally, boys and young men from mainland schools, which is the subject of the next section.[46]

Kiungani and the mainland

Missionaries expected very little from ex-slave Kiungani graduates when the initial optimism (during Tozer's time as bishop, 1863–73) about rehabilitating ex-slaves had subsided. By the twentieth century, it was considered 'remarkable' for an ex-slave to become a Kiungani teacher.[47] Yet all the African clergy were ex-slaves until 1893, when Petro Limo, of mainland origin, became a priest. Thus, the ordination of Petro Limo was exceptionally significant because he was 'the first free boy who has gone from a mainland station to Kiungani and from there has come back to teach his own people'.[48] Missionaries were not alone in their preference for mainland priests and teachers. Godfrey Dale received a letter from one of his Kiungani mainland students (who was

---

[44] 'Our African Postbag', *Central Africa*, January 1884.
[45] Mr. Geldart, 'Boys at Umba', *African Tidings*, October 1885.
[46] Godfrey Dale to Duncan Travers, Mkuzi, 1894, A1 (8), 445-6, UMArch.
[47] 'Henry Kaleza', *Central Africa*, December 1906.
[48] 'The Thirty-Second Anniversary', *Central Africa*, 1893.

presumably not an ex-slave) in which he emphasised the importance of Limo's assonance: 'I feel sure that it will be the greatest possible benefit to us all to have one of our tribe amongst us to tell us of the things of God. I feel sure that the cause of God will be successful in the country now that we have one of our race to teach us.'[49]

In fact, missionaries worried about sending their best students to Zanzibar and consequently risk exposing them to moral contagion, not only from the town, but also from ex-slave fellow students. Dale insisted that, 'it is my deliberate conviction that boys sent to Kiungani more often than not come back morally deteriorated' and 'utterly degenerated'.[50] Mainlanders shared these concerns. Even though Rev. John Swedi, an ex-slave, sent two of his sons to Kiungani, he maintained that it was still a place of immoral influences in 1894.[51] Even so, according to a mainland student who had gone to Kiungani, the school had gone downhill around this time. Dale relayed the boys' words: 'Boys mock at religion altogether and the whole place is insolent [...] all round the place hover women of doubtful character and drink is got at by the boys at the *shamba*.'[52] Indeed, the Mbweni *shamba* was a place where Kiungani boys could escape the strict surveillance of the school. Moreover, it was a safer place to visit than the town, which did not always welcome Christians and had its own system of surveillance as communities were strongly self-regulating. In fact, missionaries claimed that it was not uncommon for the mission's educated pupils to be taunted for being 'infidels' ('*kafiri*') by townspeople.[53]

In 1894, Newala students (from mission stations in southern Tanzania) similarly claimed that, 'When we left home, we loved our Lord Jesus Christ but now we are always being tempted to do wrong.'[54] Another mainland student at Kiungani was overheard saying to his peers, 'why do the *wazungu* waste their time in Zanzibar trying to convert the people there, why do we not all pack up our things and go back to the mainland, and teach our brethren who are so miserably losing themselves?'[55] These unnamed students had apparently associated themselves closely with the missionaries, and even Dale suspected that they were exaggerating how bad things had become in Kiungani, though he reasoned that missionaries had given similar reports. Curiously, the fact that Dale suspected the students were exaggerating implies that they

---

[49] This was probably a translation. 'The Thirty-Second Anniversary'.
[50] Dale to Travers, 1894.
[51] Dale to Travers.
[52] Dale to Travers.
[53] 'Native Lads Preparing for Ordination', *African Tidings*, 1888.
[54] Dale to Travers, 1894.
[55] 'Child Life in the Mission', *Central Africa*, March 1883.

were conscious of the missionaries' concerns and saw an advantage in buying into them. Nevertheless, the fact that these impressions about Kiungani going downhill were second-hand, translated, and paraphrased, suggests we should be wary of taking them at face value. On the other hand, the impressions themselves are significant.

The oral history record shows from a different angle why Kiungani was a difficult place for mainland students. For example, Ernest Chambo recalled the stories that it was *mapepo* (spirits) that made life difficult for a Kiungani student in Zanzibar. For example, it was said that the students would go to bed in the night and in the morning one could find himself at the beach without knowing who had carried him there. Tales were also told of an enormous hand coming through the window in the middle of the night. The hand would disappear when the students made a noise. It was said that the demons even reached Tanga, at Chumbageni, in the form of cats and if you saw a cat on the road and threw a stone at it, the cat would ask you questions. It was believed that the *mapepo* were working against Christianity and sought to disturb the mission students.[56] This speaks to the ways in which witchcraft is closely connected to the fear of strangers and the moral and physical dangers in an unfamiliar place.[57] Examining these stories, it is impossible to separate prejudice instilled by the mission from mainlanders' mistrust against the islands, or even to know whether that existed regardless of the mission.

Mainlanders nevertheless valued coastal and urban connections, and Zanzibar was clearly influential. But they had to be the right kind of coastal and urban connections. The mainland students were probably best placed to benefit from a brief sojourn in Zanzibar and return to their homes with tales, gifts and mannerisms they had picked up in Zanzibar. Indeed, the mainland boys took an interest in learning some of the 'town ways' in Zanzibar. This included Zanzibari ways of parsing social status, new greetings, clothing and food preferences.[58] Indeed, missionaries complained that mainland students who had been educated in Kiungani returned with bigger egos and were 'stuck up'.[59] Weston believed that these educated youths were guilty of

---

[56] Ernest Chambo, interview by Zuhura Mohammed, Muheza, 19 October 2014. Bishop Charles Alan Smythies, 'Pastoral Letter Addressed to the Clergy and Members of the UMCA', July 1885.

[57] Jean and John Comaroff, *Modernity and Its Malcontents: Ritual and Power in Postcolonial Africa* (Chicago, IL: University of Chicago Press, 1993), 5.

[58] Henry Nasibu, 'News from Misozwe by a Native Evangelist', *Central Africa*, July 1887.

[59] Dale to Travers, 1894; J. P. Farler to Duncan Travers, Mkunazini, Zanzibar, 23 October 1896, A1 (6) A, 638, UMArch; 'The Anniversary', *Central Africa*, June 1913.

'swagger'. The cure was 'epoch-making smackings'.[60] Put less dramatically, in 1915 Woodward complained that the Magila boys who had been educated in Kiungani 'assumed a worldly superiority, objected to manual work or to dish up their own food etc.' on their return to Magila.[61] Respondents relayed the same message. Their peers and even elders would marvel at them, while others found their arrogance exasperating.[62]

To some extent, the ex-slave students shared the missionaries' and mainlanders' moral concern about the town's immoral influence. The accounts Arthur Madan collected from the ex-slave students at Kiungani demonstrate that they, too, believed that Zanzibar lacked the communalism of their mainland origins. For instance, a Zaramo 'boy' observed that people in Zanzibar were much less ready to help their neighbours if they found them to be in difficulty.[63] A Nyasa 'boy' said he was eager to return to his homeland because the people there 'are not hard-hearted, like the people of Zanzibar, who resemble Pharaoh'.[64] Likewise, a 'Makua Boy', noted that in his own mainland village, 'there is a great tree, and by it a place for holding meetings. Each family goes out and takes its meals together.'[65] In contrast, he added that in Zanzibar people ate separately at their individual homes. This is factually untrue, which suggests the 'Makua Boy' was feeding off the information the missionaries gave him about Zanzibari eating habits rather than first-hand information about living in Zanzibar. This highlights how sheltered ex-slave students were from everyday life in Zanzibar and perhaps even relied upon missionaries to provide this knowledge. Clearly, mission educated Christian ex-slaves felt it was difficult to fit into the town, but it is also possible that they were critical of Islam and the Muslim modernity that prevailed. Equally, ex-slaves had a complicated relationship with the mainland and rarely permanently settled or 'returned' there. With all the prejudice missions had against Zanzibar's cultures in mind, it is no wonder that they had trouble developing meaningful relationships with ex-slave male students. To illustrate this, one of the printing apprentices wrote to his patron in England that, 'We are trying to obey Mr

---

[60] Weston to H. M., 12 November 1909.
[61] Herbert Willoughby Woodward to Duncan Travers, Masasi, 9 September 1914, A1 (21), 223, UMArch.
[62] For instance, George Chambai said that if you lived in a village where someone thinks he is very smart, you let him think so while you know he is not the proverb goes, 'mpumbavu au mjinga ni ya kwako'. George Chambai, interview by Zuhura Mohammed, Mkuzi, 18 October 2014.
[63] A. C. Madan, ed., *Kiungani, or, Story and History from Central Africa* (London: G. Bell and Sons, 1887), 63.
[64] 'Child Life in the Mission'.
[65] Madan, *Kiungani, or, Story and History from Central Africa*, 55.

Mallender as [well as] we can to obey him [with] God['s] help and he himself is trying very hard to show us he cares.'⁶⁶

The ex-slave pupils struggled to come to terms with their lack of kin and belonging, in contrast to the students who had come from the mainland. In 1895 Dale observed that, '[t]hese lads here seem to realise bitterly how isolated they are in the world how the family tie exists for all but them, how all the other boys have a home and country and position of their own but they nothing of the kind.'⁶⁷ Indeed, missionaries observed that Kiungani at this time was very 'cliquey' as groups separated according to ethnic group and ex-slave or free status.⁶⁸ Students with ex-slave kin were rarely in the top class, which meant that they were usually under the leadership of mainland boys who had become prefects and were known for abusing their power. Prefects were responsible for disciplining their peers, and were even allowed to use the cane at their own discretion, although they were expected to keep a record in a book of the punishments they dispensed. Missionaries also facilitated the creation of cliques, even building separate areas for Nyasa and Bondei students at Kiungani.⁶⁹ All this threatened the peace at Kiungani as fights broke out between students of different ethnic identities.⁷⁰

However, to some extent the hostility between Kiungani students dissipated as slave status faded somewhat over time, and mainlanders' personal networks became vastly broader. The broader impact of this fading of slave status is explored in the work of Elizabeth McMahon and Laura Fair, who also both note its continuing importance.⁷¹ The UMCA's official perspective was more positive because they could not admit that they held such limited sway in

---

⁶⁶ This letter from Owen Makanyassa, a printer, was written in English on 27 January 1891 to Mallender's mother and sister. George William Mallender, 'Missionary life in Central Africa' (Journal, 1896), A1 (4) B, UMArch. In 1879 Makanyassa was the head of the printing office. For more on Makanyassa, see: Steere, *Central African Mission, Its Present State and Prospects*, 17; Robert Heanley, *A Memoir of Edward Steere: Third Missionary Bishop in Central Africa* (London: Office of the Universities' Mission to Central Africa, 1898), 248.

⁶⁷ Godfrey Dale to Duncan Travers, Kiungani, Zanzibar, 15 November 1895, A1 (8), 241-2, UMArch.

⁶⁸ Godfrey Dale to Duncan Travers, Kiungani, Zanzibar, August 1895, A1 (8), 481, UMArch.

⁶⁹ *The Universities' Mission to Central Africa Atlas* (London: Universities' Mission to Central Africa, 1903).

⁷⁰ Dale to Travers, August 1895.

⁷¹ Elisabeth McMahon, *Slavery and Emancipation in Islamic East Africa: From Honor to Respectability*, African Studies (Cambridge: Cambridge University Press, 2013); Fair, *Pastimes and Politics: Culture, Community, and Identity in Post-Abolition Urban Zanzibar, 1890–1945*.

improving the social struggles of slaves and ex-slaves. The 1921 UMCA annual report charted this significant historical shift: 'Formerly the different tribes there [at Kiungani] did not agree at all well, and there are stories of fights with knives. Those days are now past, and while many things may have contributed to the change, we may believe the main cause of the change is the Faith.'[72]

The suggestion of this neat resolve to tensions is doubtless over-simplified. Even if students no longer resorted to violence, the stigma of slave status in the school remained and was vividly remembered. For example, John Mhina, part of a large and established family of mainland Christians, many of whom were priests and teachers for the mission, contended that the ex-slaves and their descendants were not considered to be truly 'free'. Father Geldart Mhina, John's father, had told him that at Kiungani, mainland students enjoyed greater respect than those born in Zanzibar.[73] Alice Ott has similarly found that UMCA missionaries and Bondei people in Usambara viewed freed slaves negatively.[74]

The moral stigma surrounding Zanzibar Christians and their supposed lack of 'roots' remains today. For example, a respondent in Magila (who wished to keep some of his comments anonymous) criticised the retired Bishop John Ramadhani, a descendant of ex-slaves, for being out of touch with his mainland roots and over-dependent on Europeans.[75] In a similar vein, Canon Samuel Sepeku said that the Magila Central School was a space in which all children were treated equally, even those who were descendants of slaves from Kiungani.[76] Even Sepeku's comment, though intended to be positive evidence of inclusivity, echoed the Christians' prejudice towards ex-slaves.

The standing of Kiungani-educated ex-slave men among ex-slaves was a different story. In particular, they were able to take up prominent positions in the Mbweni *shamba* or other 'experimental' mission stations on the island. For instance, Kiungani-educated Sheldon Mabruki (c. 1858–1909) was said to have, 'won the respect of all the people on the Mbweni *shamba*' by 1908.[77] He was one of the 'primitive Christians' of Bishop Tozer's first baptism. He married an 'Mbweni girl' called Gladys and did independent missionary work

---

[72] 'Annual Report: A Review of the Work of the Mission in 1921', *Central Africa*, June 1922, 134.

[73] John Geldart Mhina, interview, 15 October 2014.

[74] Alice T. Ott, 'The "Faithful Deacon" and the "Good Layman": The First Converts of the UMCA and Their Responses to Mission Christianity', *Studies in World Christianity*, 24, no. 2 (6 July 2018): 140. doi.org/10.3366/swc.2018.0217.

[75] Anonymous, Magila, October 2014.

[76] Canon Samuel Sepeku, interview by Zuhura Mohammed, Dar es Salaam, 29 October 2014.

[77] Bp. J. E. H., 'In Memoriam: Sheldon Mabruki', *Central Africa*, May 1909.

in Ng'ambo and Mtoni, encumbered but not impeded by elephantiasis.[78] Similarly, John Swedi returned to the Mbweni *shamba* around the late 1890s. As a deacon he ran the Mbweni ex-slave village.[79] Perhaps the most obvious example, however, was Cecil Majaliwa, who bought land and hired workers from the Mbweni *shamba*.[80] These men were notable examples of how Kiungani students could and did achieve social mobility despite the struggles for respect in the school.

The city was a space in which one could overcome slave status, but this was not an easy process. Finding new patrons in the town and becoming incorporated into kinship groups, while a preferable scenario for many, was likely to have involved a great deal of conflict.[81] Moreover, those who chose to adhere to Christianity after moving into the town ran the risk of losing employment. Though Muslims employed Christians, they did not employ workers who were recent converts, perhaps partly because until the early twentieth century recent converts were likely to be recently captured by the British Navy, and this recent association with the mainland and slave status made them undesirable cohorts.[82] Missionaries tried to broker this process of finding local patrons with their ex-slave apprenticing scheme. Through it, the mission sponsored some selected ex-slave young men – who would cease their academic education – to become apprentices in the town, on the condition that they slept at the mission at Mbweni and lived under its rules and regulations.[83] The missionaries eventually deemed this scheme a failure, because the apprentice-masters apparently had no interest in training them and saw them as cheap labour borrowed from the mission.

Even though missionaries believed the town was the source of materialistic evils, they nevertheless felt it was the best place to gain professional training. Another possible reason why the apprenticeship scheme failed is that it was not clearly superior to other existing opportunities to move on from slavery. For one, the apprentices were supposed to save part of their small wages to be able to complete their apprenticeship, in a manner that reinforced the idea of

---

[78] Bp. J. E. H.; D. Y. Mills, 'Sheldon Mabruki', *African Tidings*, June 1909.

[79] Anderson-Morshead, *The History of the Universities' Mission to Central Africa, 1859–1909*, 361, 378; C. C. Frewer, 'Mbweni Village Life as It Is', *Central Africa*, May 1908; Weston to H. M., 9 December 1899.

[80] Weston understood it that he stole money from the mission in order to do this. J. Zanzibar to Duncan Travers, Mkunazini, 2 March 1904, A1 (13), 200, UMArch.

[81] Justin Willis and Suzanne Miers, 'Becoming a Child of the House: Incorporation, Authority and Resistance in Giryama Society', *The Journal of African History*, 38, no. 3 (1997): 479–95.

[82] A. Foxley, 'Faraji's Cure', *Central Africa*, June 1905.

[83] Bishop Charles Alan Smythies, 'Our Schools', *Central Africa*, June 1885.

their slave-like status. Frewer explained that: 'The lad gets only a small wage at first. This is gradually increased during his engagement of 3-4 years. At the end of that time he is "redeemed" by himself or his parent or guardian on payment of a premium of 30 rupees (£2), which he is supposed to have saved from his earnings.'[84] Frewer accepted that the apprentice-master would expect the apprentice to act as his servant in order to learn all facets of the trade, but he checked up on them to ensure the young men were not being exploited. Once, to Frewer's horror, he found one of the apprentices looking after his master's children.[85] The apprenticeships were of limited educational use and did not always prepare ex-slaves to compete with the artisans of the town.[86] In effect, the scheme became another way in which the missionaries unwittingly highlighted and reinforced ex-slaves' lack of status even as they tried to help them move on.

In a way, apprenticeships were not necessary because students at Kiungani were quite independent and capable of earning a living in the town, even without a special skill. In 1873 Bishop Steere, who had an unusual tendency among missionaries to highlight ex-slave agency, asserted that: '[I]t must be remembered that the boys are better able to teach us agriculture than we to teach them, they could any of them get a living at that at once, don't imagine that any of them are as helpless as English boys of eighteen or so without a trade.'[87] Yet rather than simply becoming country folk, ex-slave students bought into Zanzibari urban identity and asserted that they were civilised in the same way as ex-slaves who were not connected to the mission.[88] Moreover, whether or not ex-slaves were talented agriculturalists, they avoided agricultural livelihoods. One way in which they distanced themselves from the mission and agriculture was to dress extravagantly once they left the school, in which the dress code was intentionally simple. Missionaries were amused to observe the civility of the students. For instance, in 1893 a missionary noted that one 'dignified young man' wore, in addition to his cassock, 'a most wonderful knitted cap of marvellous colours'.[89]

Indeed, the term for Kiungani ex-slave students, 'wenyeji', had a bitter irony because they did not enjoy the benefits one might expect to reap from

---

[84] C. C. Frewer, 'African Boys', *African Tidings*, May 1909.
[85] C. C. Frewer.
[86] May Allen to Miss Randolph, Zanzibar, 11 August 1884, A1 (4) A, 680, UMArch.
[87] Edward Steere to Festing, 24 February 1873.
[88] Fair, *Pastimes and Politics: Culture, Community, and Identity in Post-Abolition Urban Zanzibar, 1890–1945*, 2001.
[89] G. H. Du Boulay to Vicar and friends, Kiungani, Zanzibar, 3 December 1893, A1 (6) B, 1682, UMArch.

being a 'native'. They were isolated from the town, a problem that concerned both missionaries and ex-slaves, and which Weston expressed in 1916:

> Zanzibar Christians are a very small, isolated body. They are shut off from the town population by the Cross, from fellow Christians – European and Goanese – by colour, and from us by social customs and education, or the want of it. They depended on masters and early missionaries; and they do not easily acquire the independence that our present methods and growth require of them. Many of them accepted Baptism because they lived with us and owed us their daily bread.[90]

Unsurprisingly, missionaries worried that these isolated Christians would be 'lost' to the town. Shutting their converts off from the opportunities the town offered was problematic because they believed that 'genuine' conversion was impossible for individuals who simply had no other choice but to be mission dependants.

According to Percy L. Jones-Bateman's 1890 census (see Tables 5 and 6), 140 out of 272 (51 per cent) students who had by then passed through Kiungani had left the school and continued to live as Christians. Only thirty-one (11 per cent) gave up Christianity. Other evidence suggests Jones-Bateman's survey may have been overly optimistic. Indeed, in 1899 Sir Arthur Henry Hardinge (Colonial Head for the British East Africa Protectorate) claimed that after leaving the mission school, the only ex-slaves who remained Christians were those who had positions in government service and administration, which would have been an extremely low number.[91]

The most striking figure in the census is the first one regarding the death rate. The threat of disease, violence and malnutrition meant that 29 per cent of Kiungani students died soon after moving to the town.[92] Even if some of these individuals had been admitted to the school at the age of fifteen on the school's establishment in 1864, they would have been forty-one at the time this survey was conducted. Hence, they were not dying of old age. This is a striking indication of the struggle ex-slaves faced.

Jones-Bateman's survey was based on second-hand information collected from what African Christians still living at mission stations could glean from individuals who no longer lived with them, usually having moved to Ng'ambo.

---

[90] H. Maynard Smith, *Frank, Bishop of Zanzibar: Life of Frank Weston, 1871–1924*, chapter x, part II.
[91] 'Our Thirty-Eighth Anniversary', *Central Africa*, July 1899.
[92] It is likely that many of these deaths took place in the cholera epidemic of 1871–72. James Christie, *Cholera Epidemics in East Africa, from 1821 till 1872* (London, 1876).

Table 5 Kiungani student life trajectories.

How employed at the present time	Varieties of religious profession				
	Professing Christians	Without any profession of Christianity but refusing Islam	Apostates to Islam	Unclassified	Totals, as regards employments
In Holy Orders	2				**2**
Readers and other Missionary Teachers	32				**32**
Master Craftsmen	31	3		1	**34**
Interpreters	1				**2**
Overseers	3	1			**4**
Soldiers	2	2			**4**
Servants or Porters	18	11	3		**32**
Traders or Salesmen	2	1			**3**
Temporarily unemployed	2	3	2		**7**
Labourers or Cultivators	15	10			**25**
Apprentices	30				**30**
In slavery	2				**2**
Dead					**79**
Unaccounted for				16	**16**
Totals (as regards religious profession)	**140**	**31**	**5**	**17**	**272**

This excluded the small number of mainland male students who had come to Kiungani by 1890. (Source: 'What Becomes of Your Mission Boys When They Leave You?', Central Africa, 1890)

Table 6 Percentages of life trajectories of male ex-slave Kiungani students, 1890, based on Table 5.

	%
Dead	29
Master craftsmen	12.5
Readers and teachers	11.76
Servants or porters	11.76
Apprentices	11
Traders or salesmen	11
Labourers or cultivators	9.19
Unaccounted for	6.6
Unemployed	2.57
Overseers	1.47
Soldiers	1.47
Clergy	0.73
Interpreters	0.7
In slavery	0.7

It is telling that the African Christians who gathered the data for Jones-Bateman could track the lives of so many who had left the mission. Often, the mission's Christians attempted to maintain ties with those who had left the mission, though the desire to maintain contact probably went both ways between those who stayed at the mission, and those who left. Even the 'backsliders', who moved to Ng'ambo and cut off their ties to the missionaries, tellingly, retained some place in African Christians' social networks. Thus, while striving to conform to the standards of coastal culture and rejecting the missionaries, they were likely to form and maintain personal networks with other mission ex-slaves. Indeed, ex-slaves from the mission tended to try and settle together in the town and maintain networks with Zanzibar Christians, even if they themselves had converted to Islam.[93] Christians were isolated from settled Muslims but they were at least able to draw upon contacts made at the mission beyond the time when they lived there.[94]

---

[93] C. C. Frewer, 'The Native of Zanzibar and Pemba'.

[94] Percy L. Jones-Bateman, 'What Becomes of Your Mission Boys When They Leave You?', *Central Africa*, 1890; 'Our Thirty-Eighth Anniversary'.

To remain a Christian in town was difficult as Christian practices could make people undesirably conspicuous, particularly on Sundays when Christians were not supposed to drink, dance or work.[95] Missionaries endeavoured to have their Christian presence felt in the town by orchestrating processions and public reading groups to imitate the practice of reading the Koran in public.[96] This never really caught on, probably due to the reluctance of ex-slaves to reveal their association with the mission. Thus, on the one hand, outward demonstration of their faith signalled their slave status. On the other, Muslims criticised Christianity for being a 'prayerless religion', on account of prayers being conducted relatively privately and quietly, and less frequently.[97] Whether or not Christians chose to accept or believe anti-Christian slurs, they found themselves in a precarious social situation. Muslims refused to eat with them, and women refused to marry them.[98]

Missionaries interpreted this as religious persecution and political vulnerability. For instance, Dale argued that, prior to Zanzibar becoming a British protectorate, the Sultan threatened the mission by saying that any Christian converts would lose the Sultan's protection.[99] This line of thinking was convenient for the UMCA because it placed blame on the prejudice of Muslims. However, while Zanzibar was a British protectorate, Christians were at least legally protected from persecution and Christian affiliation was much less socially harmful than the fact that ex-slave and Christian identity were impossible to separate. Even so, ex-slaves from the mission underwent great struggle in their attempts to integrate into town life that may have exceeded the struggles ex-slaves faced on the mission *shamba*. Mission ex-slaves were first and foremost like other ex-slaves: they were people who had to struggle to move on. This was a generation of ex-slaves that were between the moment of emancipation and the relatively assertive plebeian urban community that Laura Fair has described.[100]

---

[95] Failing to partake in drinking would have suggested a lack of generosity on mainland Tanzania. This is represented in the Swahili word for 'to pay tribute' – 'kushikana' – which literally means 'to hold each other'. Derek R. Peterson, *Ethnic Patriotism and the East African Revival: A History of Dissent, C.1935–1972* (Cambridge: Cambridge University Press, 2012), 122; J. P. Farler to Rev. Cecil Deecles, Magila, Tanga, (20 February 1877), A1 (6) A, 413, UMArch.

[96] Edward Steere to Festing, 24 February 1873; Mr. Lister, 'Industrial Work at Mkunazini', *Central Africa*, January 1894; J. P. Farler to Duncan Travers, Mkunazini, Zanzibar, 4 July 1895, A1 (6) A, 614, UMArch; 'Home Jottings', *Central Africa*, March 1899.

[97] J. W. T., 'Mohammedan and Christian', *Central Africa*, September 1900.

[98] 'Our Thirty-Eighth Anniversary'.

[99] Godfrey Dale, 'Muhammadanism in Zanzibar', *Central Africa*, May 1905.

[100] Fair, *Pastimes and Politics: Culture, Community, and Identity in Post-Abolition Urban Zanzibar, 1890–1945*.

Conclusion

As William Bissell and Laura Fair have shown, town and urban life were undoubtedly potential arenas in which slave status could be modified.[101] There was a multitude of trajectories and possibilities open to ex-slaves. Most of these were unpredictable, often undesirable, but ex-slaves made their own choices, with their own values and worldviews in mind. Kiungani boys took a number of paths, none of which were exclusively to self-differentiate or conform. Some distanced themselves from the townspeople and attached themselves to the missionaries, who they believed to be their benevolent patrons. Another route was to move to the town and conform to Muslim, non-Christian norms. Thirdly, missionaries were not necessarily helpful to ex-slaves in search of a better life.[102] Very often, they simply modified the already existing social stratification previously based on slave status.

The influence of the missionaries on religious practice and cultural self-expression was therefore ephemeral for the majority of male educated ex-slaves. By contrast, the mission sites had diverse uses for the pursuit of livelihoods and for diverse forms of socialisation. For the most-part, ex-slaves used mission spaces, but did not cultivate mission identities to be used outside them. This is reflected in the way Zanzibar Christians could diffuse and disappear into urban life. Through its terminology and its insistence on keeping its dependants separate from the town, the mission simultaneously undermined and perpetuated slave status: insisted that its dependants were 'freed' while keeping them marginal. Considering the pull of the Muslim-dominated town, it is remarkable that there remain any Anglicans in Zanzibar.

Crucially, it was often the mission network, rather than the missionaries, that provided valuable tools for emancipating both Christian and non-Christian ex-slaves. The fact that they retained ties to fellow mission ex-slaves, regardless of their religious affiliation and sometimes even in preference to sustaining their allegiance to missionaries, is very striking. This point illustrates how the mission was a site in which valuable personal networks could be fostered, even if many avoided the missionaries themselves.

---

[101] William Cunningham Bissell, *Urban Design, Chaos, and Colonial Power in Zanzibar* (Bloomington: Indiana University Press, 2011); Fair, *Pastimes and Politics: Culture, Community, and Identity in Post-Abolition Urban Zanzibar, 1890–1945*.

[102] Paul V. Kollman, *The Evangelization of Slaves and Catholic Origins in Eastern Africa* (Maryknoll, NY: Orbis Books, 2005); Maxwell, 'Freed Slaves, Missionaries, and Respectability: The Expansion of the Christian Frontier from Angola to Belgian Congo'; McMahon, *Slavery and Emancipation in Islamic East Africa: From Honor to Respectability*.

The educated ex-slave Christians faced different advantages and challenges from those of the ex-mission, non-Christian dependants who disappeared into town. While they benefitted from their early investment in Western schooling, they also faced the stigma attached to them by missionaries and mainland African Christians. They were marked out as more susceptible to sin, because of their estrangement from their 'roots'. Yet they also had to modify their behaviour in the setting of the Muslim town, which was an important site in their lives.

Amid the multiple forms of dependency and varying attitudes to *heshima*, slave status and its implications in post-abolition Zanzibar, the missionaries' first impulse was to categorise and morally judge ex-slaves. Consequently, the missionaries struggled, usually in vain, to direct particular categories of ex-slaves into the particular livelihood trajectories that missionaries deemed fit for them. Ex-slaves, in turn, did what they could to survive or prosper, without deferring much to the missionaries' preferences. In conclusion, the mission certainly offered opportunities for social mobility, but it did so very selectively, and the options provided were not nearly as advantageous as one might expect from a missionary society that was so deeply engaged in the anti-slavery movement.

CHAPTER 4

Raising 'Mbweni Girls' in Zanzibar, 1864–c.1926

In his hypercritical review of the Mbweni *shamba* in 1884, a missionary named Forbes Capel complained that, 'Compared with their fellow country women the girls are being brought up as <u>ladies</u>' (his emphasis).[1] Thoroughly disillusioned with the UMCA's enterprise, Capel protested that 'the girls were suffering from want of more active employment'.[2] Similarly, in 1884 May Allen despaired that, '[t]he state of the insubordination of the girls here is something dreadful'.[3] Farler also complained that the Mbweni girls were 'so pampered' and consequently impertinent, disobedient, as well as being indifferent to Christianity.[4] Similarly, Smythies believed they were far too educated for their own good, arguing that, 'as yet the country is not prepared for the higher education of women, all they need is a good elementary education'. He believed Mbweni girls were, 'apt to be conceited and not to give their husbands that obedience which is the custom here to exact from them'.[5] Finally, Hine was also extremely negative about the Mbweni girls' school, complaining that, 'no sane person would send mission girls from upcountry to be brought

---

[1] Rev. W. F. Capel to Edward Steere, Mbweni, Zanzibar, January 1877, A1 (4) A, 60, UMArch.

[2] W. Forbes Capel to The Lord Bishop of London and the committee of the Universities' Mission to Central Africa, 1884, TC C1, UMArch. For an excellent account of Capel's findings, see Andreana C. Prichard, *Sisters in Spirit: Christianity, Affect, and Community Building in East Africa, 1860–1970* (Michigan State University Press, 2017), chap. 3.

[3] May Allen to Rev. W. H. Penney, Mbweni, Zanzibar (private), May 1884, A1 (4) A, 283, UMArch.

[4] J. P. Farler to Rev. W. H. Penney, Kiungani, Zanzibar, 28 July 1885, A1 (6) A, 478, UMArch.

[5] Bishop Charles Alan Smythies, 'A Letter from the Bishop', *Central Africa*, September 1885.

up at Mbweni'.⁶ This epistolary debate represents a constant tension in the missionaries' reports regarding the balance between 'work' and 'education', which reflects the gender conflict among the missionaries and the different African perspectives with which the missionaries sympathised.

This chapter concentrates on the trajectories of the educated female ex-slaves, referred to as 'Mbweni girls' or, in Swahili, *'geli za Mbweni'*.⁷ The female students were just as closely monitored as the Kiungani students, but unlike at Kiungani, the ex-slave character of the Mbweni school was celebrated and valued. This was unusual in the wider context of slave status in Zanzibar as slave antecedents were socially shamed. Indeed, Mbweni girls were unique among women associated with the mission for their high level of education, but this did not necessarily ease their troubles when finding marriage suitors or work. Moreover, as Andreana Prichard has argued, adherents at Mbweni took 'opportunities to [...] embed themselves more forcibly and securely into the mission community'.⁸

Female education in Mbweni began in 1865 but the Mbweni Girls' School (also known as St Mary's) was only established in 1871. It was a relatively small school, never exceeding more than 110 boarders, and usually with an additional ten to fifty day-girls.⁹ Initially, it housed and educated female children and adolescent ex-slaves, and, increasingly, the children of these ex-slaves. Almost all the pupils were ex-slaves, usually sourced from British navy ships from the captured slaving dhows. Only a handful of local parents not already associated with the mission were willing to send their children to this school, partly because people feared the missionaries would steal or harm their children.¹⁰ Pupils were only loosely categorised by age. The oldest students were in their late teens (i.e. 'old enough to be married').¹¹ In the event that a woman completed her studies at the school and lacked a spouse, they would often remain on the Mbweni mission land, offering their domestic and agricultural

---

⁶ J. Zanzibar to Duncan Travers, Mkunazini, Zanzibar, 17 January 1905, A1 (13), 257, UMArch.

⁷ Respondents usually used the English version of the phrase, so I follow that convention.

⁸ Prichard, *Sisters in Spirit*, 84.

⁹ *Central Africa*, August 1889, 128; 'UMCA Zanzibar Diary', 1888 1864, CB1, NT; Caroline D. M. Thackeray to Rev. W. H. Penney, Mbweni, Zanzibar, 11 May 1885, A1 (6) A, 762, UMArch.

¹⁰ Edward Steere, Zanzibar, 22 August 1881, A1 (3) A, 422, UMArch.

¹¹ 'Child Life in the Mission', *Central Africa*, March 1883; Caroline D. M. Thackeray to Rev. W. H. Penney, Mbweni, Zanzibar, 19 January 1885, A1 (6) A, 754, UMArch; missionaries considered sixteen a suitable and normal age. M. A. B., 'A Home of Work', *African Tidings*, December 1893.

services to the mission. They would have maintained contact with the school and probably still spent much time there, but they were not students.

The school was adjacent to the Mbweni *shamba*, but it was almost entirely separate from it. The relationship between Mbweni school and Mbweni *shamba* was complex. Ex-slave girls who had recently been recaptured by the British would usually be sent to adoptive mothers on the Mbweni *shamba*, to be inducted into mission life before they joined the mission school. Thus, they must have fostered some kin-like networks in the Mbweni *shamba*. However, Mbweni girls were known to treat the ex-slaves on the Mbweni *shamba* as inferiors, referring to them as 'slaves'.[12] Much as David Maxwell has found in his study of freed slaves in the Congo, these female ex-slaves took on notions of Christian respectability and used them to their own ends, which was often a source of disapproval amongst the missionaries. For example, former slaves would attempt to separate themselves from those they believed to be uncivilised and un-modern in order to attain dignity.[13]

Female missionaries oversaw the female ex-slave students and domestic servants in the 1860s. Helen Tozer, Bishop Tozer's sister, was one of the missionaries who established the school. Her approach was later criticised for its worldly emphasis on 'manners'. Indeed, her students were, 'distinguished by their peculiarly sweet accent and pretty manners'.[14] In fact, in the first mission building in which they housed ex-slave girls – only twenty-three in number by this point – they had a 'governess' and taught English.[15] On the whole, female students had closer ties with missionaries than did the male Kiungani students.[16] This had a lot to do with Caroline Thackeray, who arrived in 1877 and remained at Mbweni until her death almost fifty years later (1877–1926). For most of the period, 'Mbweni girls' benefitted from the benevolent rule of

---

[12] It was said that these educated ex-slaves aimed to procure slaves of their own once they married. Rev. W. F. Capel to Edward Steere, Mbweni, Zanzibar, (January 1877), A1 (4) A, 60, UMArch.

[13] David Maxwell, 'Freed Slaves, Missionaries, and Respectability: The Expansion of the Christian Frontier from Angola to Belgian Congo', *Journal of African History*, 54, no. 1 (2013): 80–81.

[14] M. A. Cameron, 'Round about the Cathedral', *African Tidings*, April 1896; Lincoln, 'A Primitive Christian', *Central Africa*, December 1906; Foxley noted that it was important in Helen Tozer's time to prove that African women could reach 'a high degree of Christian virtue and good manners'. Alice Foxley, 'The Higher Education of Women', *Central Africa*, June 1909.

[15] Nugent West to Seale, English Mission, Zanzibar, July 1873, A1 (4) A, 1a, UMArch.

[16] Edward Steere to Rev. W. H. Penney, 'Present Work of UMCA, 1881', 1881, A1 (3) C, 810, UMArch; Margaret Sudi, interview by Irene Mashasi, Zanzibar, 12 September 2014; Tereza Mwakanjuki, interview by Irene Mashasi, Zanzibar, 19 September 2014.

Thackeray, who was a woman with substantial private financial means and became the UMCA's longest-serving missionary.[17] William Johnson, a missionary who arrived in the same year as Thackeray, applauded her efforts because she took, 'a loving and enthusiastic delight in our work with the girls', and because she provided 'a wholesome link with the world of reality, with method, discipline, and English life'.[18]

Yet other male missionaries despaired at Thackeray's 'extravagance' and the way she promoted European-style activities, such as tea parties and picnics, in addition to 'extravagant' clothes that followed European fashions. Nevertheless, even colleagues critical of her work valued Thackeray's devotion.[19] Thackeray, who self-identified as 'mother' and 'grandmother', frequently referred to her Mbweni network as 'my large family'.[20] While some male missionaries complained that the girls were 'haughty', Thackeray doted on the girls unapologetically.[21] She held tense relationships with both male and female missionary colleagues, yet maintained devoted and affectionate relationships with African converts. Thackeray's efforts contributed to the school's longevity as an institution, though its dependence on her also explains why Mbweni School closed when Thackeray retired in 1914. From 1917 most female students were taught in St Monica's, situated in the Mkunazini quarter of Zanzibar Town, and the hubs of UMCA women's education moved to the Mkuzi and Hegongo mission stations on the mainland.[22]

---

[17] Thackeray donated liberally to the mission and even declined offers for the mission to pay for visits back home, to Steere's delight, as he was anxious to save costs. Edward Steere to Rev. W. H. Penney, Zanzibar, September 1881, A1 (3) A, 384, UMArch. She also purchased much of the expensive land around the Slave Market Church. William Bishop to Viner, Mkunazini, Zanzibar, 26 March, A1 (6) B, 1620, UMArch.

[18] William Percival Johnson, *My African Reminiscences, 1875–1895* (London: Universities' Mission to Central Africa, 1926), 36.

[19] We get a sense of the materialism she encouraged from her letters describing the great pleasure her students got from opening presents from her friend in England, Mrs Leeke, who was a very generous patron. Caroline D. M. Thackeray to Mrs Leeke, Mbweni, Zanzibar, 26 September 1887, A1 (6) A, 775, UMArch; Caroline D. M. Thackeray to Mrs Leeke, Mbweni, Zanzibar, 29 September 1897, A1 (6) A, 812, UMArch.

[20] Caroline D. M. Thackeray to Rev. W. H. Penney, Mbweni, Zanzibar, 27 July 1884, A1 (6) A, 747, UMArch; Caroline D. M. Thackeray to Duncan Travers, Queen's Hotel, Keswick, 19 August 1910, A1 (21), 80, UMArch.

[21] Laura Phillips, 'The Girls' Home at Mbweni', *African Tidings*, February 1897.

[22] Rev. J. F. Christopher Fixsen to Mother, Kizara, 15 March 1914, A1 (22), 671, UMArch.

Mbweni girls were in some ways better off than any other kind of female ex-slave because at the mission they lost much of their sexual vulnerability. This was all largely thanks to the environment that Caroline Thackeray helped create as she fostered a positive outlook towards Mbweni girls among mainland Christians and missionaries. [23] For example, Weston's assessment of Thackeray in 1899, when they first met each other, reveals male missionary's stereotyped views of conflict among female colleagues but ultimately, also, respect for her commitment and influence over the UMCA bishops (Steere, Smythies and Richardson):

> [Thackeray] 'managed' with Steere, dodged Smythies, and ruled Richardson. [...] She is a force to be reckoned with. Her 'girls' are her craze. She has a large staff of able [missionary] women who all rebel at her ineffectiveness. She rules them with an iron rod. They are clever, she more so, they are experienced *à l'Anglaise*, she *à l'Afrique*. They are cowards, she is a mistress of words. Therefore, she is supreme.[24]

Though Thackeray believed that the Mbweni *shamba* was a mistake (albeit one that the mission could not abandon), Mbweni school was, for her, another matter. In her eyes, it was the jewel of the mission.[25] Thackeray and her students were mutually devoted to each other and she acted very much like a 'big woman', or, 'Lady Bishop', as Frank Weston nicknamed her.[26] The memory of Thackeray remains very strong until this day. In fact, it is said that the Christians living at Mbweni after the death of Thackeray in 1926 could no longer bear to hear the audible ghostly coughs of her *pepo* and, consequently, relocated to the town. According to some respondents, without Thackeray, the Mbweni community fell apart.[27]

---

[23] Thackeray reported that she got on quite well with Capel (the ex-slaves' greatest critic), though she admitted, 'he does at time provoke me horribly by things he says about the children and people and I don't agree at all with his very despairing tone about them'. Caroline D. M. Thackeray to Penney, 19 January 1885.
[24] Frank Weston to H. M., St Mark's Theological College, Zanzibar, 9 December 1899, A1 (17) A, 53, UMArch.
[25] Weston to H. M.
[26] Weston to H. M.; William Harold Ingrams, *Zanzibar: Its History and Its People* (London: Stacey International, 2007), 82.
[27] Margaret Sudi, interview; Bibi Shishi, interview by Irene Mashasi, Zanzibar, 17 September 2014.

Industrial students and domestic labour

Following Capel's condemning report on the Mbweni Girls' School, the UMCA set out to separate 'industrial' students, who focused on manual labour, from academic students. This was done with the help of the new Industrial Wing in 1887. Thackeray reported the separation was for the best, even if she would have liked to keep all the students together. Although Thackeray saw 'industrial girls' as somewhat troublesome, she was quite optimistic about them, too:

> I am sure it is better for those who would never make 'scholars', that they should be put to work. A girl nearly grown up wants some way of working off her superfluous energy, and if she is too poor a scholar for her lessons to be an interest to her, one must give her some other if she is to do well. It does not at all follow either, that a girl who is slow at books is stupid at other matters.[28]

Even so, the industrial students received very little tuition and acted as the domestic servants for the Mbweni school.[29] While Kiungani boys' school was divided between those with slave status and those who had come from the mainland, the division at Mbweni was different because the students were exclusively ex-slaves or children of ex-slaves. Moreover, at Kiungani there was a similar divide with one significant difference: academic students were overwhelmingly non-ex-slaves from the mainland while industrial students were all ex-slaves. From 1884 the school was split between 'academic' and 'industrial' students. Industrial students tended to be older but were largely still children. They provided the domestic labour to make the running of Mbweni possible. From the beginning of the twentieth century, schoolchildren rarely worked as domestic servants and the mission transitioned to employing wage-earning adults, usually men. The exception to this rule was the case of Mbweni girls' school, where students were more likely to have domestic skills as part of their curriculum than male students in the twentieth century. This reflected two key characteristics of female mission education. First, the missionaries intended to help rear good Christian wives who could look after their households. Second, for much of the period, female mission schools consisted of ex-slaves and orphans who were more likely to depend on the opportunity to provide domestic service to the mission than freeborn women with kin. Female students were more likely to have been kinless and, thus able to devote their energies to the mission household rather than their own households.

There existed a fluid distinction between education and domestic service in UMCA boys' schools too (see Chapters 3 and 5), with two important

---

[28] 'Our African Postbag', *Central Africa*, October 1884.
[29] 'Our African Postbag'.

differences. First, while missionaries dramatically reduced the domestic service responsibilities of male students to a minimum by the turn of the century, the role of schoolgirls as domestic servants persisted. Meanwhile, industrial students continued to carry out the household labour until the school shut down in 1914 when Thackeray retired. Second, girls' domestic service never became a paid profession with routinised expectations of payment.[30]

Usually, these female students were not personal servants. Rather, they worked in groups with certain students being periodically appointed as overseers.[31] This excerpt of a letter from 1911 (to the mission magazine editors) helps to explain how duties were shared at Mbweni:

> Certain girls had definite duties to perform. There were no trained servants in the house beyond the cook, everything else being done by the children. Rooms had to be swept, lamps collected and cleaned, the table laid for our breakfast, and so on. The room-girls would be busy in the Bibi's rooms, probably with a number of companions to hinder, or perhaps help, in carrying out the necessary duties.[32]

Thackeray herself used the term 'house-girl' for the ex-slave girls living in the mission, as opposed to the 'day-girls' who had a family to stay with, usually the children of ex-slaves. They even donned different uniforms to signify this distinction.[33] However, the communal character of 'industrial' work, which in fact meant predominantly shared domestic tasks, probably offset some of the social stigma attached to it. In fact, given that the Mbweni girls' school was relatively isolated, it is possible that the social stigma attached to agricultural or 'industrial' labour was inconspicuous to most of the students at the school, perhaps because their work tended to be of a more domestic, rather than agricultural, nature.

The so-called 'house-girls', who received intermittent wages, boarding and food at Mbweni, were expected to attend scripture lessons, but considered too old to join the school. Some of them were married. Others used the term 'industrial girl' to describe this Mbweni girl category. They did all the catering

---

[30] There was actually quite a demand for domestic servants in the Mbweni mission but very few women – or men – wanted to live so far from the town, especially in the period following the First World War. A. D. Swainson, 'Work in Zanzibar I', *Central Africa*, September 1920. Female missionaries in the Mbweni mission started training ex-slave female maids as early as 1865: Edward Steere to Polly, Zanzibar, August 1865, A1 (3) A, 39, UMArch.

[31] M. E. W., 'Among the School Children in Zanzibar', *African Tidings*, 1888.

[32] 'A Typical Day at Mbweni', *African Tidings*, June 1911.

[33] Caroline D. M. Thackeray to Mrs Leeke, Mbweni, Zanzibar, 3 October 1889, A1 (6) A, 779, UMArch.

and housekeeping for the school.[34] One of their chief chores was to make *vitumbua*, a kind of fried rice cake that the students had for breakfast most days. This involved pounding the grain, which was a labour-intensive and gendered process as this passage shows:'Two girls generally pound together; when one "*mche*"[35] is out the other goes in; this pounding goes on every day, and is woman's work entirely; men never pound. [...] as many as 220 "*vitumbua*" are made in the course of a morning, as the industrials cook for the school side as well as for themselves.'[36]

The missionaries' belief in the educational potential of *vitumbua*-making is striking, as the next passage demonstrates: 'Two girls are supposed to pound the rice together, but they often like to do it all by themselves one day, and then have nothing to do the next day, sometimes one girl is lazy and leaves her companion to do it alone. Occasionally, when the evening comes, we find they have put the rice away and not ground it at all, then they have no supper, and have to do their work instead.'[37] Missionaries admitted that the *vitumbua* could not be made more cheaply at the mission than they could be bought in the town. In fact, missionaries valued *vitumbua* preparation as a character-building exercise that taught traditional gender roles.[38]

Personal domestic service in Mbweni could lead to careers in teaching, just as in boys' schools. For example, Thackeray had a 'bed-room girl' who she hoped would one day become a teacher.[39] What all these girls and young women in Magila on the mainland and Mbweni in Zanzibar had in common is that they were kinless due either to famine or slavery. To some extent, missionaries in both locations were making use of the labour they had at hand, namely, socially marginal girls and women who had lost their kin. But the Magila mission stations were much less likely to give intermittent payments to schoolgirls in return for domestic labour. This was largely because it was considered less controversial for mission dependants to receive wages in

---

[34] Laura Phillips, 'The Girls' Home at Mbweni'; 'In School at Mbweni (Continued)', *African Tidings*, August 1911.

[35] Pestle.

[36] Eleanor M. Bennett, 'The Industrial Wing at Mbweni', *African Tidings*, December 1892.

[37] M. E. W., 'Among the School Children in Zanzibar'.

[38] Eleanor M. Bennett, 'The Industrial Wing at Mbweni'; M. A. B., 'A Home of Work'; A. E. M. Anderson-Morshead, *The History of the Universities' Mission to Central Africa 1859–1896* (London: Universities Mission to Central Africa, 1897), 281; R. Webb, *A Visit to Africa, 1896* (London: Universities' Mission to Central Africa, 1897), 9; Laura Phillips, 'The Girls' Home at Mbweni'.

[39] Caroline D. M. Thackeray, 'Letter from Miss Thackeray about the Girls' School at Mbweni', *African Tidings*, 1887. This is similar to what Nancy Rose Hunt found in the Congo: Nancy Rose Hunt, *Colonial Lexicon of Birth Ritual, Medicalization, and Mobility in the Congo* (Durham, NC: Duke University Press, 1999), 117–18.

Zanzibar, where a monetised labour market was more firmly established than on the mainland. Mbweni girls did not have to pay for food or boarding, which explains why these intermittent payments appear to have been spent largely on imported clothes and fabrics.[40] Comparing Mbweni with mission stations on the mainland that took in kinless girls, the privileged status of Mbweni becomes even clearer.

Industrial girls' lower status was reflected in their clothing, which was more worn and simpler than that of the academic students who all wore white, sometimes with a *kaniki* (dark blue calico) cloth for further coverage, in addition to many types of beads and necklaces.[41] However, the attire of industrial students was superior to, and certainly covered more flesh than the clothing of the women working on the Mbweni *shamba*, which was similar to that of female manual labourers on the island.[42]

Matchmaking Mbweni girls

According to Thackeray, a good Mbweni girl had to be obedient, neat, educationally ambitious and hard-working.[43] A Christian wife, so the syllabus taught at Mbweni, had several duties to society and to her husband. Hilda Siyenu, a young teacher at Mbweni, wrote out for one of her assignments the chief duties of a Christian wife of a teacher or priest:

1. To know well herself the things of God, that she may help her husband to know those things. To care for the sick in her villages.
2. To show a good example in keeping her house in order.
3. To be like a mother and gentle to all.
4. To care for children who are orphans.
5. To care for widows.
6. To get people to come to church.
7. To wash the church-linen, to light the lamps, to keep the church in order, to do needlework for the church.

---

[40] Caroline D. M. Thackeray to Mrs Leeke, Mbweni, Zanzibar, 25 November 1890, A1 (6) A, 783, UMArch; Caroline D. M. Thackeray to Mrs Leeke, 29 September 1897.
[41] C. D. M. Thackeray, 'Work amongst the Mbweni Girls', *Central Africa*, June 1897.
[42] 'In School at Mbweni (Continued)'; K., 'Mbweni Incidents', *African Tidings*, January 1893; Ethel Younghusband, *Glimpses of East Africa and Zanzibar* (London: J. Long, 1910), 226.
[43] Caroline D. M. Thackeray, 'Letter from Miss Thackeray about the Girls' School at Mbweni'.

8   To cook for her husband (this she was reminded of – possibly she thought no. 2 included this).

9   To teach those who are not yet baptized.

10 Not to regard their bodily state so as to despise them, nor their clothes.

11 It would be a good thing to collect on a fixed day the grown-up women to teach them to sew.[44]

The kind of woman Siyenu was describing could easily have been an English woman interested in church, charity and community affairs. This was one way in which missionary observers claimed that Thackeray 'spoilt' her female students, who were, it was claimed, too likely to be circumspect about the kind of manual labour they engaged in.[45]

The highest-achieving 'Mbweni girls' were introduced to African clergymen.[46] Because of the lack of success in converting mainland women, missionaries had to supply Christian brides for African clergymen. In other words, at Mbweni 'The girls [...] are absolutely necessary as providing wives for the boys.'[47] Despite what Thackeray's critics said, mission-educated male ex-slaves sought Mbweni girls as wives. Thus, Steere wrote in 1874: 'I have been greatly amused at the utter contempt of the elder boys for any girls not brought up by us; they treat the idea of looking for a wife anywhere else as utterly preposterous.'[48] Equally, there was a demand for educated wives, on the mainland as well as in Zanzibar.[49] The wives of the elite Christian teachers and clergymen were ideally expected to act much like middle-class women

---

[44] Thackeray probably translated this into English. It is unlikely it was originally written in English. C. D. M. Thackeray, 'Work amongst the Mbweni Girls'.

[45] Caroline D. M. Thackeray to Randolph, Mbweni, Zanzibar, June 1881, A1 (4) A, 425, UMArch; Bishop Charles Alan Smythies, 'A Letter from the Bishop'.

[46] J. P. Farler to Bishop Edward Steere, Magila, Tanga, 9 November 1881, A1 (6) A, 357, UMArch; Justin Willis, 'The Nature of a Mission Community: The Universities' Mission to Central Africa in Bonde', *Past & Present*, no. 140 (1 August 1993), 141. Willis notes that the practice of patrons finding wives for their dependents was common in the Tanga region among Africans.

[47] Nugent West to Seale, July 1873; W. Forbes Capel to The Lord Bishop of London and the committee of the Universities' Mission to Central Africa, 1884; A. C. Madan, The Rectory, Dunsley, 14 August 1884, TC C1, 5, UMArch.

[48] Bishop Edward Steere, 'First Quarterly Statement', 29 August 1875, A1 (3) C, 814, 816, UMArch; Thackeray offers a similar observation here: Caroline D. M. Thackeray, 'Letter from Miss Thackeray about the Girls' School at Mbweni'.

[49] Caroline D. M. Thackeray to Mrs Leeke, 26 September 1887; C. D. M. Thackeray, 'Work amongst the Mbweni Girls'; C. D. M. Thackeray, 'The African Woman of the Future', *Central Africa*, June 1910; Anne Marie Stoner-Eby, 'African Leaders Engage Mission Christianity: Anglicans in Tanzania, 1876–1926' (PhD, Pennsylvania, University of Pennsylvania, 2003).

in Europe. Thus, missionaries tried to generate interest in needlework and other domestic occupations that they deemed respectable. Missionaries made themselves responsible for making matches between Mbweni girls and male Christian professionals, such as soldiers, masons, printers, cooks or teachers.[50] However, few educated African young men from the mainland could consider marrying someone from Zanzibar. One of the few examples of mainland Christians who married Mbweni girls that I came across among the ancestors of my respondents was a priest called Michael Mhina, who was nicknamed Michael bin Sefu due to what his relations indicated was an unhealthy interest in Muslim culture.[51]

Mbweni girls were certainly desirable, and as wives they were sometimes better educated than their husbands.[52] Sometimes these women made careers for themselves, regardless of their husbands' career trajectories. For instance, Kate Mabruki had a long career as a teacher even though her husband, Francis, was forbidden from preaching in 1879 and he was never restored (the reason is not recorded).[53] Mainland African Christians, too, tended to value educated women as potential brides from very early in the mission's history.[54] Though African missionaries in Magila were more likely to marry Christian women local to them, marrying someone taught at Mbweni had its advantages. Most importantly, they were educated and likely to share teaching responsibilities. The downside was that they were unlikely to take to agricultural work and they had ex-slave status. [55]

A key feature of Mbweni girl weddings was that brides would spend much of the day weeping.[56] This echoed a ritualised event in East Africa.[57] The UMCA

---

[50] 'Miss Berkeley's Girls at Mbweni', *African Tidings*, 1886; Eleanor M. Bennett, 'The Industrial Wing at Mbweni'.

[51] John Geldart Mhina, interview by Zuhura Mohammed, Magila, 15 October 2014.

[52] Bishop Charles Alan Smythies, 'A Letter from the Bishop'.

[53] Anderson-Morshead, *The History of the Universities' Mission to Central Africa 1859–1896*, 110.

[54] Anne Marie Stoner-Eby, 'Not Merely Cooks: The Missionary Wives of the African Leadership of the Universities' Mission to Central Africa, 1880–1940' (London: Institute of Commonwealth Studies, University of London, 1999); Andreana Prichard, 'African Christian Women and the Emergence of Nationalist Subjectivities in Tanzania, 1860–1960s' (PhD, Evanston, Illinois, Northwestern University, 2011).

[55] 'Our Women Christians', *African Tidings*, March 1908.

[56] 'Editor's Notes', *African Tidings*, July 1902; M. G., 'A School Wedding', *African Tidings*, November 1911; M. G., 'A School Wedding', *African Tidings*, October 1911.

[57] Birgitta Larsson, 'Haya Women's Response to Revival', in *The East African Revival: History and Legacies*, ed. Kevin Ward and Emma Wild-Wood (Farham:

printer in Zanzibar, George William Mallender, noted this with some surprise in 1896: 'after the feast all the guests amused themselves as best they could. the brides staying in the house, very often spending the happy day crying! for what reason no one exactly knew except it be the custom.'[58] Whether the brides' tears were customary or not, it's likely this behaviour says something about the particular situation of women in Zanzibar who, most likely, were slaves. When married to either Christians or non-Christians, Mbweni brides were likely to have been more subordinate to their husbands than other brides because they lacked families who could intervene if the relationship went sour.[59] Their tears may have indicated their fear. For the married woman, the mission did not act as defender and patron in quite the same way a family would have done. The most the mission could do was to provide a place for a woman escaping a marriage that had gone wrong, at either Mkunazini or Mbweni. In other words, Mbweni brides faced a life of powerlessness especially if they were marrying someone from the mainland, which was not only associated with '*shenzi*' but, perhaps more importantly, represented the unknown. It is possible these emotions were heightened by missionaries' representations of marriage. The female missionaries in charge of Mbweni, who were single, may have had reservations about married life that they inflected in their teachings. In the late nineteenth century women and children were very vulnerable to kidnapping and (re)enslavement.[60] Indeed, without 'protectors', women and children were especially vulnerable.[61] This danger of isolation, in turn, suggests that belonging was particularly essential.

Yet, even if Mbweni girls lacked the security kinship afforded, Thackeray was true to her self-identified role as matriarch as she was known to provide a safety net for her pupils who wished to leave their husbands, even those who had engaged in mainland marriages. For example, after Kate Mabruki's

---

Ashgate Publishing Limited, 2016), 122; Angéla Molnos, *Cultural Source Materials for Population Planning in East Africa: Innovations and Communication* (East African Publishing House, 1972), 203; S. H. Fazan, *Colonial Kenya Observed: British Rule, Mau Mau and the Wind of Change*, ed. John Lonsdale. (London: I. B. Tauris, 2015), 269.

[58] George William Mallender, 'Missionary life in Central Africa' (Journal, 1896), 34, A1 (4) B, UMArch.

[59] George William Mallender, 92–93; Anderson-Morshead, *The History of the Universities' Mission to Central Africa 1859–1896*, 281.

[60] Elisabeth McMahon, 'Trafficking and Reenslavement: The Social Vulnerability of Women and Children in Nineteenth-Century East Africa', in *Trafficking in Slavery's Wake: Law and the Experience of Women and Children in Africa*, ed. Benjamin N. Lawrance and Richard L. Roberts (Athens, OH: Ohio University Press, 2012), 32.

[61] McMahon, 34.

marriage fell apart, she returned to Mbweni as a teacher and oversaw sewing classes.[62] Thackeray even made a point of visiting her former students in their mainland homes and insisted they keep in epistolary contact. However, even if Thackeray had wanted to, it would have been impossible for her to protect all the Mbweni girls from unhappy marriages. Support for future brides or young women who had just reached puberty could also come from African Christian women, who often stood in for absent (Christian) mothers by appointment of the church. These women would ensure the young woman remained chaste in her engagement period and also ensured she was properly educated for married life.[63] It is likely that these pre-marriage mentors continued to offer their support after a bride's wedding.

Mbweni girls' networks

Mbweni girls stood out, but the slave status that they carried with them, by virtue of their connection to the mission, was less likely to undermine marriage prospects than it was for men. In addition to being well educated, Mbweni girls gained a reputation for being well fed and well dressed.[64] Mbweni women's fashion was diverse and they had privileged access to European fashions and a voracious appetite for fabric from a donor in Hereford.[65] Some favoured Arab-style dress. For instance, Kate Mabruki wore 'Arab dress, tight trousers to the ankles and a tunic of figured cotton material', which shocked Christians in Msalabani on the mainland because they had never seen clothes like it before.[66] In an article comparing the Zanzibar mission in 1909 to that of 1921, Dora Mills noticed there was a change in fashion. While women previously had 'their heads dressed up mountain high' they now 'modestly draw their *sheeties* over them like a veil'. Mills was pleased about this and took it for evidence of 'far greater reverence and intelligence'.[67] Whether this change in fashion meant the

---

[62] 'Mama Kate: An African Saint', *African Tidings*, July 1908.
[63] 'Central African Mission Mbweni and Mkunazini Diary 1919–1946' (17 March 1919), ZNA CB1-8; 'Central African Mission Mbweni and Mkunazini Diary 1919–1946' (4 May 1919), ZNA CB1-8; Neema Heri, a woman 'who does not want to be married' was recorded as needing special assistance: 'Central African Mission Mbweni and Mkunazini Diary 1919–1946' (21 August 2918), ZNA CB1-8.
[64] M. G., 'A School Wedding', November 1911.
[65] 'Something of a Scramble', *Central Africa*, April 1906.
[66] 'Mama Kate: An African Saint'; Kate's dress sounds very similar to the description of Arab women's dress in this source: Younghusband, *Glimpses of East Africa and Zanzibar*, 35.
[67] D. Y. Mills, 'Africa Revisited III', *Central Africa*, October 1921.

Mbweni girls were fitting into the town is unclear, but it does indicate that they were exposed to and interacted with the world outside the mission.

The male missionaries who criticised Thackeray and the Mbweni girls pointed out that the ex-slave wives from Mbweni struggled to get along with people from the mainland. Eight months into her and her husband's new position as priest at Kwa Kibai, near Magila, Blandina Limo was evidently struggling to accustom herself to the people. She was, reportedly, snobbish about another African priest's wife, who was her assistant teacher and 'no scholar; she cannot help me to do anything'. Blandina had received a very high standard of education under Caroline Thackeray, which probably explained why she felt 'quite alone' on the mainland. She added that, 'I do miss my Mbweni friends and companions'.[68]

Some Mbweni girls pursued 'Swahili marriages with Mohammedans', as one missionary phrased it. This suggests that, for Mbweni girls, African Christian men were not necessarily the best or only option as future husbands. Missionaries did not support this, but they accepted it, given that Zanzibar had a majority Muslim population.[69] However, there is no evidence to suggest that non-Christians especially sought out Mbweni girls. Mbweni girls lacked an essential education: that of *unyago* (female initiation). Mbweni girls were referred to as *wasungo*, women who had not been initiated, and were thus inexperienced in the matters of sex.[70] This meant they were not usually seen as ideal wives from the perspective of non-Christians. However, not all suitors valued *unyago*. Many Muslims rejected initiations because *unyago* was believed to undermine Islamic values of chasteness.[71] It is also possible that Mbweni girls were more valued for their education in the 1920s, when mission education became more popular in Zanzibar, as one of the Muslim Zanzibari respondents suggested.[72] At any rate, the occurrence of such marriages does show that the Mbweni girls were connected to the Muslim society around them.

Christian networks were valuable to Mbweni girls. They formed cohorts of their own accord, but the missionaries attempted to manage them through

[68] Blandina Limo, 'A Letter from Blandina Limo', *Central Africa*, April 1895; Louisa Mumbi is another example. See: Caroline D. M. Thackeray to Mrs Leeke, 25 November 1890. All of these letters appear to have been translated by Thackeray into English.
[69] Janet Phillips, 'St Monica's Sewing Class', *Central Africa*, May 1901.
[70] Esther Musa, interview by Irene Mashasi, Zanzibar, 11 October 2014.
[71] Corrie R. Decker, 'Biology, Islam and The Science of Sex Education in Colonial Zanzibar', *Past & Present*, 222, no. 1 (13 December 2013): 215–47. doi.org/10.1093/pastj/gtt016.
[72] Nasoro Ali, interview by Irene Mashasi, Zanzibar, 12 September 2014.

establishing the Guild of All Saints. The guild had many rules, including attendance at Sunday service, being selective about their choice of friends, monitoring the spread of rumour and trying to draw others into the mission. The idea was also to unite the Mbweni girls with other African Christian women on the mainland, who would all come together for a meeting twice a year. In practice, very few mainland female Christians were involved.[73]

There were other ways that ex-Mbweni students maintained their cohorts. One of the major functions of St Katherine's Home for Women in Mkunazini was to provide a meeting point for 'old Mbweni girls' who had married and moved to live on plantations, often with Muslims. These women would use this space to reconnect with their old friends, and the town, 'showing off their children with the greatest pride'. The women enjoyed the 'home' so much that one woman came announcing, to the alarm of the missionaries, she was there for a 'holiday' and would stay one month.[74] Thus, Mbweni girls maintained mission networks and the mission stations were spaces in which they united and reunited, even if their everyday lives had moved on into Muslim communities.

Gender and domestic service

Although Mbweni girls tended to be well educated, they did not (unlike their male counterparts at Kiungani or elsewhere) tend to have the option to make a career out of their domestic service skills. Girls and women, across all UMCA mission stations, contributed significantly to the domestic labour that the mission demanded, but they were rarely paid a regular wage and the conditions of their labour could not be described as 'professional'. There were some exceptions to the rule that Europeans did not employ women as wage-earning domestic servants. To cite one notable example, in 1905 in Kota Kota on the mainland it was decided that missionaries should make a transition to female house servants in order to offer destitute women an opportunity to earn a wage. These women were usually elderly because young women were under their parents' or husband's control and, thus, prohibited from this line of work.[75] Predictably, there were more opportunities in the more commercial setting of Zanzibar than on the mainland for women to become wage-earning

---

[73] R. B., 'Guild of All Saints, Mbweni', *African Tidings*, June 1896; 'Mbweni', *Central Africa*, 1898. Andreana Prichard has written about some other UMCA-based groups for female adherents established in the mid twentieth century, namely the Community of the Sacred Passion and Chama cha Mariamu Mtakatifu (Community of St. Mary), see Prichard, *Sisters in Spirit*, 202.

[74] A. D. S., 'Work in Zanzibar II', *Central Africa*, November 1920.

[75] K. M., 'My "Boy"', *African Tidings*, November 1905.

domestic servants. By the 1900s there were opportunities in Zanzibar town for women to earn a wage as water-carriers to Europeans or *ayah* (nannies or maids) for English settlers. The mission station in town also employed women in various jobs, including hospital work and sewing.[76] This was partly because there was a greater demand among wealthy potential employers looking for specialised skills, but also because there was such a large population of women, especially ex-slave women who were more likely to be kinless and in need of an independent living.

The women and girls at Mbweni did needlework, weaving, laundry (*dhobi*) and cultivating.[77] These women who had learnt these kinds of skills were not so much encouraged to earn a wage but rather to become mothers and settle into a life of 'domestic comfort and respectability'.[78] Though in Zanzibar and nearby mainland areas needlework was strictly man's work, at the mission it was women's work.[79] This reflected the missionary urge to draw in at least some aspects of English feminine ideals of domestication.[80] There is no evidence to suggest that Mbweni girls translated their needlework skills into livelihoods. Rather, it was work they could do for themselves, their families and the Christian community at large.

At the hospital in Mkunazini, Zanzibar, the women of St Katherine's mission station – who were a mixture of mission-educated Christians and destitute 'saved' women[81] from the town – were the primary domestic workers. In addition to helping around the hospital, these women also performed delicate laundry work for the European residents of the town from the base of the mission station.[82] Even so, the opportunities for women were extremely limited in town, as one female missionary noted in 1901: 'There is no domestic service

---

[76] M. A. A., 'S. Katherine's Zanzibar', *African Tidings*, February 1904; The situation had not changed very much by 1920. Swainson reported that, 'Many of the [Christian] women are engaged as servants in the Mission, while others are ayahs to Eurnopeans in town or in the Government hospitals [...] but the majority have no regular work to do.' A. D. S., 'Work in Zanzibar II'.

[77] Anderson-Morshead, *The History of the Universities' Mission to Central Africa 1859–1896*, 281.

[78] Ingrams, *Zanzibar*, 222.

[79] Ingrams, 222.

[80] As discussed in: Deborah Gaitskell, 'At Home with Hegemony? Coercion and Consent in the Education of African Girls for Domesticity in South Africa before 1910', in *Contesting Colonial Hegemony: State and Society in Africa and India*, ed. Shula Marks and Dagmar Engels (London: British Academic Press; New York: Distributed by St. Martin's Press, 1994).

[81] Probably a euphemism for women coming out of sexual slavery.

[82] Rev. William C. Piercy, 'Round Zanzibar', *Central Africa*, February 1904; 'Our Women Christians'.

for women, except for a few *ayahs*.[83] Men and boys do all the housework; even laundry work is almost all in the hands of men.'[84] Indeed, the mission trained men and women in *dhobi*, though it was more often men who secured employment in *dhobi* inside and outside of the mission. *Dhobi* was an Indian skilled trade, carried out by men, that spread throughout Africa.[85]

Alongside the gendered divisions of wage labour, it is worth reflecting on the division of culinary labour and food preparation. For instance, both in Zanzibar and on the mainland, pounding grain was considered strictly women's work. The UMCA official history, published in 1897, describes how cooking came naturally to ex-slave girls at the school yet the missionaries did not attempt to impose on these girls any, 'civilized method of cooking', as they put it. The author added, '[the girls] do not learn European cookery, as that is done by men'.[86] European cookery was a special skill that gave a worker valuable knowledge and employment oppotunities. The imparting of this knowledge to men only had wider implications as it compromised women's ability to obtain employment and made women dependent on men for access to cash.

Conclusion

At first glance, the Mbweni girls were kept isolated and protected from their wider social context. Yet Mbweni girls' life trajectories reflect more typical patterns of women with ex-slave status, with their limited livelihoods and precarious claims to belonging. Unlike their male counterparts, female ex-slaves in the mission were less likely to pursue social mobility in the public eye. As Felicitas Becker has suggested, women grappling with slave status more often fought their battles in domestic arenas, which were 'intrinsically political units'. [87] In the case of the female UMCA mission ex-slaves, they used their leverage as members of Caroline Thackeray's tight-knit community, largely by strengthening their networks among themselves. Association with the mission appears to have been more profitable for Mbweni girls than for any other category of ex-slave. Nonetheless, they entered their husbands'

---

[83] Nannies.

[84] Janet Phillips, 'St Monica's Sewing Class'.

[85] Lincoln, 'A Primitive Christian'. For its history in Natal, see: Keletso E. Atkins, 'Origins of the Amawasha: The Zulu Washermen's Guild in Natal, 1850–1910', *The Journal of African History*, 27, no. 1 (1 January 1986), 41–57.

[86] Anderson-Morshead, *The History of the Universities' Mission to Central Africa 1859–1896*.

[87] Felicitas Becker, 'Transformations of Inequality in a Former Slave Plantation Settlement: Mingoyo, Tanzania', in *Islam and Memories of Slavery* (New College, University of Toronto, 2009), 2.

family networks (if any) in a subordinate position and risked losing the protection of the mission when leaving school.

One major reason why missionaries tended to offer Mbweni students more support than male Kiungani students was that they were concerned the girls were more vulnerable when finding work in the town.[88] Bishop Smythies insisted in 1885 that, 'The girls cannot go out in this country to earn their own living'. The subtext was that they would fall into disreputable work in the town, such as sex work. In addition, Smythies was concerned that if a mission educated girl was forced to find work in town, she would inevitably find a Muslim marriage suitor.[89] The problem of finding 'suitable' livelihoods for Christian women outside the mission persisted into the twentieth century. In the 'coast towns' of Dar es Salaam and Zanzibar, 'a recognised sect of Arabs' were in charge of distributing the work of drawing water for townspeople among women, and would favour Muslim women. Fetching firewood was also out of the question because of the lack of appropriated land from which to gather it. Female missionaries worked together to arrange a solution: to develop 'home industries' such as plaiting mats. The problem was that the only buyers for their crafts work were Europeans in Zanzibar. Instead, these female missionaries hoped to export the women's handiwork to England, where UMCA supporters would purchase them.[90] Needless to say, the pay was too infrequent to constitute a full livelihood.

The Mbweni girls provide a rare glimpse into the lives of ex-slave women, a group even harder to trace in sources than men in the same position. They were clearly exceptional, even within the mission, and more so beyond it. The level of education they were offered and the material goods they had access to, without depending on a husband or other male guardian, made them privileged oddities compared to other females grappling with their slave status on the island. Yet despite the advantages they enjoyed, they lived precariously and were in some ways unprotected from post-abolition struggles. Limited livelihood options and labour market participation meant limited income generating possibilities.

---

[88] Kate Mabruki was an unusual but notable example of a female Zanzibar Christian gaining sustained working opportunities in the town for Europeans. She would mend the clothes returned from the washermen. Lincoln, 'A Primitive Christian'.

[89] Bishop Charles Alan Smythies, 'A Letter from the Bishop'. Similar concerns about the lack of respectable employment for young women, outside the context of the mission, can be viewed here: The Industrials, 'An Appeal for Frocks', *Central Africa*, June 1899; Janet Phillips, 'St Monica's Sewing Class'.

[90] G. B. L., 'Solving a Problem', *Central Africa*, January 1928; For more on Christian women selling mats see D. Y. Mills, 'Africa Revisited III'; A. D. S., 'Work in Zanzibar II'; M. G., 'A School Wedding', October 1911.

Marriage was important yet involved great risks to these kinless individuals, prompting teary farewells to mission folk on the brides' wedding days.

Still, the mission provided some security and, perhaps more importantly, a place to gravitate to even when they had moved away from it. The centre in Mkunazini where they congregated is now defunct, and the descendants of Thackeray's exalted Mbweni girls melted into the population of the town. Inasmuch as this means that slave status has faded, the school has met its original purpose, albeit in a manner very different from what Thackeray set out to achieve. In this sense, the 'Mbweni girls' again demonstrate the unpredictability and variability of ex-slave trajectories.

CHAPTER 5

Domestic Service in Magila and Zanzibar, 1864–c.1930

In the nineteenth century, schoolchildren provided all or most of the labour the UMCA mission household demanded. Missionaries, in keeping with the habits of other Europeans, referred to these students-cum-domestic servants as 'boys'. These 'boys' divided their time between domestic service, study and play, as explained by this ex-slave student's letter from Zanzibar to his patrons in England: 'My work it is to cook food for the children. [...] I study in the evening and Acland Sahera is my teacher, we learn to read English. In the morning my work is to cook, and later my companions take turns with me that I may walk or go to football.'[1] The distinction between students and domestic servants was equally blurred in Magila on the north-eastern mainland of Tanzania. For example, at Umba, the missionary Herbert Geldart oversaw thirteen boarding school boys from neighbouring areas. He wrote that: '[they] do all my housework – sweep, cook, lay table, wash up, &c.; they receive no pice, and often work very hard indeed; yet they are pleased to do it, and a grumble is about the last thing you would hear.'[2]

This close connection between children's education and domestic service declined in the twentieth century. From the early twentieth century, school

---

[1] This is a missionary translation. As with most UMCA translations of schoolchildren's letters, the missionaries applied an infantilised style of English. 'Letter from the Cirencester Boy', *African Tidings*, 1886.

[2] Mr Geldart, 'Boys at Umba', *African Tidings*, October 1885. It is difficult to say how old these children would have been, but the fact that they were students suggests that they were adolescents or younger. This is partly because missionaries targeted this younger age group due to their belief that they would be more open to converting to Christianity, but also because so many children were displaced in the late nineteenth century, and mission schools often provided them with a refuge.

boys' and – to a lesser extent – school girls' household labour was confined to their own familial homes. By this time, there was an emerging – albeit ambiguous – distinction between 'boys' who were schoolboys and 'boys' who were adult, professional wage-earners.[3] In contrast, during my fieldwork it was made patently clear in the interviews that child labour was totally unacceptable, and the attitudes towards child labour are neatly illustrated by Figure 1.

The missionaries' use of children as servants in the late nineteenth century correlated with the high numbers of children who were left kinless and unprotected due to war, slavery, or famine at this time. In other words, humanitarian crises made children widely available as workers. Missionaries, who were anyway in the business of finding children to proselytise, took advantage of this and merged domestic work and religious education. The increasing clarity of the distinction between work and education also owed something to the emergence of domestic service becoming a professional labour category in the early twentieth century.

Few studies have explored domestic service in the mission context. Nancy Rose Hunt's study of the British Baptist Mission in the Congo is a notable exception as she points out the close link between domestic chores and medical expertise.[4] Barbara Cooper has also noted how domestic service and education went hand in hand in the missions of the Muslim Sahel.[5] This body of scholarship shows that the history of domestic service can provide a lens into the many varied trajectories of socialisation into and out of the mission. Working off the basis of this literature, this chapter shows that the missionaries' domestic service training inadvertently led mission-trained domestic 'boys' to leave the mission behind in favour of new employment possibilities. This is significant because it demonstrates how, especially for socially marginal youths, schooling was not just about getting an education; it was a way to make a living and survive in a context of limited, often undesirable, options.

The first section of this chapter explains the demand for domestic service in the mission and the kind of training missionaries offered. The next part brings in other key employers: the colonial administrators and European travellers who would often hire mission-trained domestic servants. The final section compares domestic servants of varied trajectories through their clothing choices and general appearance. First, though, it is imperative to set out what it meant to be a 'boy' domestic servant in the broader history of Africa.

---

[3] H. A. M. Cox, 'My Boy, and What He Does', *African Tidings*, March 1908.
[4] Nancy Rose Hunt, *Colonial Lexicon of Birth Ritual, Medicalization, and Mobility in the Congo* (Durham, NC: Duke University Press, 1999).
[5] Barbara MacGowan Cooper, *Evangelical Christians in the Muslim Sahel* (Bloomington, IN: Indiana University Press, 2006).

Figure 1 Signpost near Korogwe, 18 August 2014. This sign encapsulates William Kamna's sentiment regarding child labour, 'Epuka ajira za utotoni', which translates as 'child labour must be avoided'. It was accompanied by other signs nailed onto trees surrounding Korogwe cathedral that declared the importance of children's human rights, such as: 'pigavita ndoa za utotoni' ('wage war on child marriage'); 'toa taarifaza unyanyasaji kwa watoto' ('report child abuse'); 'ilikupata haki yako timiza wajibu wako' ('in order to get your rights fulfil your duties') [translations by the author]. (Photograph Michelle Liebst).

'Boys' over time and space

Scholars have not failed to point out that the domestic service industry in colonial Africa was male-dominated, so much so that as a labour category it was often referred to as 'boy-work'.[6] 'Boy-work' has a broader history in Africa,

---

[6] Robyn Allyce Pariser, 'The Servant Problem: African Servants and the Making of European Domesticity in Colonial Tanganyika', in *Towards a Global History of Domestic and Caregiving Workers* (Leiden; Boston: Brill, 2015), 286. In some areas of Africa, especially South Africa, the fear of rape determined the gender of domestic servants. Shireen Ally, 'Slavery, Servility, Service: The Cape of Good Hope, the Natal Colony and Witwatersrand, 1652–1914', in *Towards a Global History of Domestic and Caregiving Workers*, ed. Dirk Hoerder, Elise van Nederveen Meerkerk and Silke Neunsinger (Leiden; Boston: Brill, 2015), 260–3.

beginning with European explorers in the nineteenth century. Notably, Henry Morton Stanley's personal servant, Kalulu, was one of the first and most famous 'boys' in East Africa. In his short life, Kalulu travelled to Europe, had a book dedicated to him, attended David Livingstone's funeral, and even had a model of himself in Madame Tussaud's.[7] Even beyond the nineteenth century, men took pride in being 'boys', which is striking considering how notions of domesticity were so closely entangled with notions of femininity in Europe. Equally, in Africa chores such as preparing food or carrying water was usually considered a women's or slave work.[8] Much like the experience of slavery, professional domestic service imposed a kind of disorder on gender roles.[9] John Iliffe explained that domestic service in Africa remained male-dominated for a long time because male servants defended the profession for its reasonable pay and status, and colonial officials preferred that African women concentrate on family life. In addition, white women did not want their husbands anywhere near black women, and, finally, African men, likewise, did not want their wives and daughters near white men.[10]

The transnational spread of the English term 'boys' is worth noting. Intriguingly, Christine Deslaurier has shown how the term 'boy' was even used in French-speaking Burundi.[11] The term has also been used to describe African male workers more generally, as Carolyn Brown showed with regards to Nigerian miners in the early twentieth century.[12] In the specific

---

[7] T. Jack Thompson, *Light on Darkness? Missionary Photography of Africa in the Nineteenth and Early Twentieth Centuries* (Grand Rapids, MI: Wm. B. Eerdmans Publishing, 2012), 111–17, 120–33; Chantal Zabus, *Out in Africa: Same-Sex Desire in Sub-Saharan Literatures & Cultures* (Oxford: James Currey, 2013), 62–73.

[8] Karen Tranberg Hansen, *Distant Companions: Servants and Employers in Zambia, 1900–1985* (Ithaca, NY: Cornell University Press, 1989); Janet M. Bujra, *Serving Class: Masculinity and the Feminisation of Domestic Service in Tanzania* (Edinburgh: Edinburgh University Press for the International African Institute, 2000), 1–15; John Iliffe, *Honour in African History* (Cambridge: Cambridge University Press, 2005), 287; Pariser, 'The Servant Problem: African Servants and the Making of European Domesticity in Colonial Tanganyika'.

[9] Lisa A. Lindsay and Stephan F. Miescher, eds., 'A "Man" in the Village Is a "Boy" in the Workplace: Colonial Racism, Worker Militance and Igbo Notions of Masculinity in the Nigerian Coal Industry, 1930–1945', in *Men and Masculinities in Modern Africa* (Portsmouth, NH: Heinemann Educ Books, 2003).

[10] Iliffe, *Honour in African History*, 287.

[11] Christine Deslaurier, '"Boys" in Bujumbura (Burundi), or How to Domesticate Politics', in *Domestic Workers in Africa (19th–21th Centuries). Historical and Socio-Anthropological Perspectives* (European Conference for African Studies, Paris, 2015).

[12] Carolyn A. Brown, 'A History of the Development of Workers' Consciousness

case of Tanzania, the term 'boy' and other related terms such as 'houseboy', 'cook-boy', 'dispensary boy', and 'donkey-boy' came into use as early as the 1870s and the term was later widely employed to describe African civil servants or messengers.[13] Occasionally, as Nancy Rose Hunt noted, girls and women could be 'boys', which reflects just how deeply ingrained the term 'boy' was in colonial vocabulary.[14] In the twentieth century, and perhaps earlier, 'boy' was Swahilized as *'boi'* while *'uboi'* refers to the labour itself and the identity associated with it.[15] Thus, *'uboi'* refers to what we might call 'boyness' or 'boyship'. The term *'uboi'* will be used in this chapter to refer to the profession of domestic service in the early twentieth century in Tanzania, unless the discussion is of a source that specifically uses the term 'boy'.

In essence, *uboi* is another word for domestic service but it also represents much more complex ideas about social status or 'race'. 'Boy' has been employed as a derogatory and infantilising term, particularly as 'boys' were often adults. In fact, there is one case of a mission 'dispensary boy', in a Pemba UMCA mission station, who had grandchildren.[16] Still, *uboi* was generally an occupation for younger generations. Yet respondents insisted *boi* work was desirable, respectable and scarce, even for non-youths. It was even said (albeit, by missionaries) that African mission teachers were at times jealous of *boi* and their relative intimacy with the missionary employers' daily lives.[17] *Boi* were part of a small and relatively well-to-do category of colonial servants that tended to have uniquely intimate exposure to European cultures.[18] Training into domestic service was a form of education, which is partly why *uboi* came to be seen as privileged.[19] Most importantly, despite the strictures associated with it, *uboi*

---

of the Coal Miners at Enugu Government Colliery, Nigeria, 1914–1950' (PhD, Columbia University, 1985).

[13] Carol Eastman, 'Service, "Slavery" (Utumwa) and Swahili Social Reality', *AAP*, no. 37 (1994): 87–107.

[14] As Nancy Rose Hunt shows, there were female "boys" in the Yakusu mission in the Congo. Hunt, *Colonial Lexicon of Birth Ritual, Medicalization, and Mobility in the Congo*.

[15] For the first reference to the term *'boi'* I could find in UMCA literature, see: C. C. Frewer, 'The Native of Zanzibar and Pemba', *Central Africa*, February 1907.

[16] E. M. V., 'A Faithful Servant', *Central Africa*, May 1927.

[17] 'The Lord Bishop's Zanzibar Carrier-Corps' (Transcript, 1917), 12–13, A1 (21/22), UMArch.

[18] In the twentieth century some domestic servants working for Indians or Arabs could also be described as *'boi'*. Kelly Askew, *Performing the Nation: Swahili Music and Cultural Politics in Tanzania*, PAP/COM edition (Chicago: University of Chicago Press, 2002), 58; Pariser, 'The Servant Problem: African Servants and the Making of European Domesticity in Colonial Tanganyika'.

[19] For the 'labour aristocracy' debate in the African context see: Richard Sandbrook

was also a way people could shape their own personhood. This is not to say that the social status of *uboi* was unambiguously high, but domestic service for Europeans was a way people could claim status, even if precariously.

The desirability of *uboi* became more ambiguous over time, especially when the domestic service industry grew exponentially in the 1940s in Tanzania.[20] As domestic service grew as an employment sector, the status associated with it declined. Indeed, Matthew Lockwood explained that from the 1950s onwards, the cost of living in Tanzania was increasingly less favourable to a domestic worker who was categorised as 'unskilled'.[21] Today, *uboi* is connected with the hospitality and tourist industries more often than with domestic service. In some common tropes, barmen and waiters proudly refer themselves as *boi*. The term can be used lightly as a joke, or as an expression of their servile status. A '*boi*' might jest, 'I can't buy you a drink because I am just a *boi*', or 'I will buy you a drink even though am just a boy'. Another use of the term is to criticise workers for being too close to their *wazungu* (European, white) bosses. These critics might say, '*Yule ni boi wa mzungu*', meaning, 'he is a puppet', (lit., 'he's the white person's boy'). Or, if a person in a position of authority gives a pupil or employee an assignment that is not compulsory, they might boldly refuse by saying, '*mimi sio boi wako*', meaning 'I am not your *boi*'.[22] In sum, the term is still alive in the language and is used playfully and dynamically to say something about social status, economic means, and relationships of power with *wazungu*.

Having painted some broad brushstrokes to suggest what *uboi* meant, let us now consider the linguistic links between *uboi*, *utumwa* (slavery) and *utumishi* (service). Jonathon Glassman argued that the condition of slaves ('*watumwa*') varied widely – but tended to be quite debased, especially for women.[23] For instance, Randall Pouwels has shown how there was much simi-

---

and Robin Cohen, *The Development of an African Working Class: Studies in Class Formation and Action* (Toronto: University of Toronto Press, 1975).

[20] It was in the 1940s that domestic labour came to make up a particularly significant proportion of the wage earning population. The Labor Office estimated that 6,000 men and 1,000 children worked as domestic servants, representing 47 per cent (7,000 of 14,770) of the city's wage-labourers. Pariser, 'The Servant Problem: African Servants and the Making of European Domesticity in Colonial Tanganyika'.

[21] Matthew Lockwood, *Fertility and Household Labour in Tanzania: Demography, Economy, and Society in Rufiji District, c.1870–1986: Demography, Economy, and Society in Rufiji District, c.1870–1986* (Oxford: Clarendon Press, 1998).

[22] Email correspondence with Elias Mutani.

[23] Jonathon Glassman, 'The Bondsman's New Clothes: The Contradictory Consciousness of Slave Resistance on the Swahili Coast', *The Journal of African History*, 32, no. 2 (1 January 1991): 277–312.

larity between *watumwa* and 'uprooted mainland settlers' who were likely to be labelled as *washenzi* (uncivilised or primitive people).[24] The same was true of *boi* who were migrants and consequently faced alienation. UMCA *boi* were not exempt from this experience. This letter from 1885 written by Aaron Amwitamno, a 'cook-boy', who travelled from the Zanzibar mission to work at the Magila mission station, illustrates this point: 'I came on the mainland to cook; if there had been no cook's work I should not have come. [...] I am greatly troubled now because I have no father here.'[25] The word 'father' may refer to a father through kinship but is more likely to have referred to a missionary patron, possibly a priest. As his words suggest, this ex-slave 'boy' was socially disadvantaged as a kinless stranger lacking a patron, recently re-confronted with his slave status.

Carol Eastman's sociolinguistic work made the point that the term '*utumwa*' became, from the late nineteenth century onwards, abstract and a binary opposite to '*uungwana*' (civilisation) and later, *ustaarabu* (Arabness). In the early twentieth century, the term '*utumishi*' largely replaced '*utumwa*', which reflected the changes occurring in the cultural definition of household membership and structure. As such, according to modern dictionary definitions, '*mtumishi*' (a person who serves) refers to a servant who carries out his or her employers' wishes, as opposed to '*mtumwa*' (a slave), who works for nothing and receives inhumane treatment.[26] As the meaning of *mtumwa* became more extreme, it also came to be distanced from male *watumishi*, and female wives or concubines who were integrated into a family.[27] Thus, the notion that *utumwa* is or was part of Swahili society is greatly contested in the twentieth century. In other words, Eastman argued that '*utumwa*' came to be understood as an extreme condition once slavery had become a thing of the past.

Initially, then, *uboi* (along with terms like *kibarua*, *mshenzi*, *mtumishi*, and *mjoli*) connoted servile status and a lack of Swahili, coastal or civilised identity.[28] Yet as slavery declined in the early twentieth century, those who identified as Swahili were often slaves or ex-slaves.[29] *Uboi* was simultaneously

---

[24] Randall L. Pouwels, *Horn and Crescent: Cultural Change and Traditional Islam on the East African Coast, 800–1900* (Cambridge: Cambridge University Press, 2002), 76.

[25] 'Letters from Native Boys', *African Tidings*, October 1885. This was a translation, I have not been able to find the original Swahili letter.

[26] Eastman, 'Service, "Slavery" (Utumwa) and Swahili Social Reality'.

[27] Eastman.

[28] Eastman.

[29] Ethel Younghusband, *Glimpses of East Africa and Zanzibar* (London: J. Long, 1910), 30.

a way of self-fashioning oneself as *mwungwana* (a gentleman). Eastman made the point that, often, when a household grew too large, some male members would be sent to find wage labour in Asian households or on the docks.[30] These Swahili non-freeborn males 'gained a reputation as excellent cooks and valets (houseboys) – with distinctive dress'.[31] She noted that,

> Ironically, the costume of the coveted Swahili cook or valet in colonial homes emulated the clothing long associated with the *mwungwana* par excellence of nineteenth century Lamu or *Siyu* (*kilemba* 'turban' and long flowing robe with a decorated sword or [side-blown] horn *siwa* to bring out on fancy occasions). This outfit contrasts with that of the *mtumwa mjinga*,[32] capless, shoeless, without even an umbrella.[33]

Thus, servant status:

> [...] eventually became associated with this particular form of dress, some education, and a certain amount of prestige. People from various coastal ethnic groups would aspire to have their sons become domestic servants and seek to apprentice them to Swahili households where they would learn the skill and style necessary for them to be sought after to work in colonial homes.[34]

For Eastman, this condition of 'boyness' was a development of *utumwa* and also a product of colonialist and neo-colonialist ways of life that valued Swahili domesticity.[35] However, Eastman's observations did not generally apply to *uboi* in the mission context, as this chapter will make clear.

Uboi status was fluid and ambivalent, always depending on the observers' own relationship to the history of domestic and unfree labour, and the exact nature of the work, employer and social environment. Employers varied from missionaries, Indians to German and British settlers and officials. Colonial officials tended to be employers who offered the highest wages, partly because they usually operated from coastal or urban areas in which wages were expected to be higher. On the one hand, *uboi* was fairly well-paid work that came with status. On the other, women were usually the ones in charge of domestic servants and it was humiliating to follow women's orders. In an interview with

---

[30] Eastman writes about the Kenyan, coastal context but the same case can be made for Tanzania. Eastman, 'Service, "Slavery" (Utumwa) and Swahili Social Reality'.
[31] Eastman; Iliffe makes the same point. Iliffe, *Honour in African History*, 287.
[32] Lit. 'foolish slave'.
[33] Eastman, 'Service, "Slavery" (Utumwa) and Swahili Social Reality'.
[34] Eastman. Again, Eastman is referring to the Kenyan case. There is no evidence to suggest that there existed indigenous employers of domestic servants in the Tanga region or in Zanzibar during this period.
[35] Eastman, 'Service, "Slavery" (Utumwa) and Swahili Social Reality'.

Gerrard Michael Francis Kiongoa Yambi, who proudly spoke of his father who was a 'cook-boy' for the UMCA mission in the 1920s, he insisted that *uboi* was a profession of great *heshima*, requiring an education. His words noticeably startled my research assistant, Zuhura Mohammed, a Muslim woman from a younger generation.[36] Among many Tanzanians, *uboi* denotes a conspicuously servile, colonised condition. For example, when positing that they are from freeborn ancestry, the Manyema, who originate from the Congo Basin and Kigoma, have been known to say '*Manyema hatutoki boi*'.[37] If we take *boi* to be a synonym of *utumwa*, this statement roughly translates as, 'the Manyema were no slaves'. The use of the term '*boi*' rather than '*utumwa*' underlines its connection to slave status.[38]

On journeys around the Magila area, the missionaries and African teachers of the party would do some of the cooking, but this was restricted to warming up tinned food or boiling potatoes. The cooked food, usually consisting of *ugali* (maize-meal porridge) and *mchicha* (cooked amaranth leaf), would be sent for from a woman's kitchen in a nearby village.[39] This suggests an advantage of employing a young boy as a domestic servant as there came a certain age at which young men refused to cook certain dishes such as *ugali* because it was considered unmanly labour.[40] The same can be seen in Zanzibar. For example, during a beriberi outbreak in 1902 the students in the Kiungani boys' school were so ill that they were unable to cook for themselves. Even in these dire straits, the paid adult cook flatly refused to prepare *ugali*. This caused the mission great expense because they had to source local women to come and cook the *ugali*, which the schoolboys normally prepared.[41] Thus, we see that there were limits to the feminisation of men's work as domestic servants, with great symbolic value ascribed to the mundane nature of everyday cooking, which evidently was an inescapable marker of femininity. Considering how awkward the gendered division of household labour could be, it is not surprising that missionaries experimented with hiring married couples to be domestic workers together in order to cover all bases. However, these experiments failed early on without explanation and were never repeated as far as my reading

---

[36] Gerrard Michael Francis Kiongoa Yambi, interview by Zuhura Mohammed, Tanga, 25 October 2014.
[37] Katharina Zöller, '"Manyema Hatutoki Boi": Manyema Group Identification and the Issue of Slavery in Urban Tanganyika' (Post-Slavery Societies in twentieth century East Africa, University of Cambridge, 2014).
[38] Zöller.
[39] J. E. Griffin, 'A Journey to Kologwe', *African Tidings*, November 1893.
[40] Gerrard Michael Francis Kiongoa Yambi, interview.
[41] Frank Weston, 'Kiungani', *Central Africa*, August 1902; H. B., 'Native Views of Slavery and Food Arrangements', *Central Africa*, October 1900.

of the sources suggest.[42] Many couples resisted this due to the missionaries' policy of paying only the male counterpart for their labour, assuming that his wife's labour should come as part of the package, as was the case with priests and their wives. Other explanations are plausible: that men did not wish for their wives to work for wages; or that men felt uncomfortable or emasculated working with their wives as equally qualified colleagues.

There was an important distinction between 'boys' who could cook and those who could not. Unlike the general 'boys' of the mission, the position of cooks in the mission was much more professional. Cooking was typically left to more specialised employees. Missionaries did not entrust female Africans with the task of preparing European-style food, a responsibility entrusted only to paid, professional, cooks.[43] Because it was difficult to procure Goan cooks in Magila, who were valued for their extensive cooking abilities and familiarity with European cuisines, missionaries from a very early point set out to train African male cooks for the mission.[44]

For example, at Korogwe in the 1890s there was a highly-trained (unnamed) African cook who was, as Webb put it, as good as if not better than a 'well paid English' cook. This cook was also 'a man of some learning', owning several books he kept in his kitchen library including devotional Swahili texts and a copy of Mrs Beeton's Cookery-book in English.[45] Similarly, in the 1909 issue of *African Tidings*, a cook named Yohana Chamalanda at Msalabani was commended for his cooking and for the fact that he was writing a cookery book.[46] Indeed, cooks in the mission seem to have had a particularly strong interest in literacy throughout the period. Whether this interest in literacy was part of a conscious effort to make their roles masculine and distinct from female work is difficult to gauge in the light of the available evidence. Drawing upon the oral history, it is indicative of how securing a job as a cook demanded a high level of education because they were desirable and scarce jobs.[47]

Historians have long-since noted the significant historical change that occurred with regards to domestic labour in colonial Africa. For instance, Bill

---

[42] J. P. Farler to Bishop Edward Steere, Magila, Tanga, 10 October 1876, A1 (6) A, 387, UMArch.

[43] 'A Typical Day at Mbweni', *African Tidings*, June 1911.

[44] Rev. F. R. Hodgson to R. M. Heanley, 'A Journey from Zanzibar to Magila', 16 May 1871, 18, A1 (4) A, 7, UMArch.

[45] R. Webb, *A Visit to Africa, 1896* (London: Universities' Mission to Central Africa, 1897), 67.

[46] 'Our African Mail', *African Tidings*, April 1909.

[47] Emmanuel Ngoma, interview by Zuhura Mohammed, Korogwe, 2 October 2014; William Kamna, interview by Michelle Liebst, Kisarawe, Pwani, Dar es Salaam, 23 September 2014; Gerrard Michael Francis Kiongoa Yambi, interview.

Freund argued that domestic labour became less kinship-based and more 'systematic' because of the presence of settlers and colonialism.[48] European employment practices brought in a new type of domestic service. Indeed, domestic service became more professional in three ways. First, it was a move away from a kinship-based 'economy of affection', dominated by exchange of non-monetary goods and services.[49] Second, it commanded a wage. Third, it became essential for servants to provide proof of their suitability, training and previous work experience. Fourth, it gave birth to a new vocabulary of worker identities.[50] However, this is not an account of a transition from 'informal' to 'formal' domestic labour. The binary distinction is too simplistic. Accordingly, Maxim Bolt urged economic historians to ask instead, 'How [...] do workforces shape not only income flows, but also notions of moral regulation, kinship, space, and time?'[51] Thus, domestic labour should be set within a context of diverse labour practices with which it was entangled.

Clearly, domestic service for Europeans grew over time, and that this had great social implications that reflect servant–employer and colonised–coloniser relationships. Nancy Rose Hunt's work on domestic service showed that, usually, it was not race, but slave status, at stake. Hunt demonstrated that in the early twentieth century the employment of students in the mission household was prestigious, at least prior to the 1940s. This prestige was relative because they were ex-slaves and therefore 'honoured to locate new patrons'. This troubled parishioners at home, but the missionaries insisted that these ex-slaves were not servants and that domestic service was part of the educational scheme.[52] Indeed, Hunt showed that domesticity conditioned the way in which knowledge was spread to these students, though not always in the way missionaries intended. For example, in 1928 one student wrote in a class composition: 'white people are people who sit at a table to

[48] Bill Freund, *The African Worker* (Cambridge: Cambridge University Press, 1988), 89.
[49] Goran Hyden, *No Shortcuts to Progress: African Development Management in Perspective* (Berkeley; Los Angeles: University of California Press, 1983).
[50] Iliffe noted a comparable development in professional medical labour. John Iliffe, *East African Doctors: A History of the Modern Profession*, vol. 95 (Cambridge: Cambridge University Press, 1998).
[51] Maxim Bolt, 'Transcending the Economic', *Africa*, 84, no. 01 (February 2014): 142–45. doi.org/10.1017/S0001972013000594.
[52] The prestige of being a 'house boy' diminished by the 1950s partly because the punishments for work-related failures were so severe. The 1954 laws about schooling meant that these men referred to as "boys" had to leave school at a certain age so it was no longer possible to keep them on past a certain age and therefore support the mission with cheap labour. Hunt, *Colonial Lexicon of Birth Ritual, Medicalization, and Mobility in the Congo*, 136.

eat food [...] and they are constantly saying to their boy "never bring us dirty plates and spoons"'.[53]

Africans could be very receptive to European domesticity.[54] Michael West argued that, 'the cult of domesticity was not [...] simply a missionary or government imposition on Africans. Both female and male members of the emerging middle class voluntarily subscribed to it.'[55] Still, though, 'domesticating' Africans was a way of attempting to colonise them. As Jean and John Comaroff argued, in Western Europe domesticity was closely aligned with a 'civilising' mission to eradicate what was perceived as poor housekeeping practices and the immorality and backwardness that were considered characteristic of poor urban households.[56] Robyn Pariser, too, made a strong case that Tanzanian men shaped domesticity in colonial households, which in turn helped create the categories 'colonizer' and 'colonized'.[57] However, the drawback of considering domesticity as a tool of colonialism is that we might obscure the role of domesticity in relationships between Africans. Domesticity was also supposed to have been an important feature of Christian marriages. Wives of the elite Christian teachers and clergy members were ideally expected to act much like middle-class women and tried to generate interest in needlework and other respectable occupations.

Karen Hansen's work on domesticity demonstrates how 'modern' Western ideas of gendered division of labour did not translate so easily in domestic life in Africa. For example, she notes that many African men were first incorporated into wage labour through their work in domestic service, a domain supposedly meant for females according to British norms.[58] The acquisition of knowledge was an activity almost completely reserved for male students. Female students would face a more practical education. As one missionary in

---

[53] Hunt, 121.
[54] Pariser, 'The Servant Problem: African Servants and the Making of European Domesticity in Colonial Tanganyika'; Hunt, *Colonial Lexicon of Birth Ritual, Medicalization, and Mobility in the Congo*.
[55] Michael O. West, 'African Middle Class Formation in Colonial Zimbabwe, 1890–1965' (1990), 2, 3, 102. Cited, David Maxwell, *African Gifts of the Spirit: Pentecostalism and the Rise of a Zimbabwean Transnational Religious Movement* (Oxford: James Currey; Weaver Press, 2006), 92.
[56] Jean Comaroff and John L. Comaroff, 'Home-Made Hegemony: Modernity, Domesticity, and Colonialism in South Africa', in *African Encounters with Domesticity*, ed. Karen Tranberg Hansen (New Brunswick, NJ: Rutgers University Press, 1992), 37.
[57] Pariser, 'The Servant Problem: African Servants and the Making of European Domesticity in Colonial Tanganyika', 273.
[58] Karen Tranberg Hansen, ed., 'Introduction: Domesticity in Africa', in *African Encounters with Domesticity*, 17.

Uganda put it, 'Our aim is not so much to fill the girls' heads with knowledge, as to develop their character and make them good sensible women who are not afraid to work.'[59] Indeed, the missionaries' insistence on teaching women how to work must have seemed strange to societies in which it was not only expected but essential for women to perform manual labour.

New working cultures and masculinity were tightly connected, as has been well documented in the Southern and West African literature. For example, T. Dunbar Moodie revealed mine labour's function was a kind of initiation ritual into manhood.[60] Carolyn Brown's work on the Nigerian coal industry in the early twentieth century showed that these emasculating, racial, colonial, workplaces, in which men were referred to as 'boys', had the paradoxical effect of allowing these men to affirm their masculinity at home. The 'boys' who were in the most marginal positions as local slaves, unmarried men or poor, challenged the hegemony of powerful elites and claimed their position in a rural patriarchy. They did this by revolting against the coercion with which men were recruited to the mines, the conditions in the mines and the wages. All this gave them a stronger standing in their communities.[61] These mineworkers challenged both the authoritarian positions of colonial chiefs and village elites, and the racist and emasculating treatment on the mines, by drawing on their connections with 'modern' industry and their position as self-improving rural men.

Though Brown's research is not about domestic service, this study poses similar questions. The awkward femininity of male domestic work reveals the limits of modernisation: the introduction of 'Western' domesticity is supposed to be an aspect of modernisation. However, domesticity is neither straightforwardly 'Western' nor straightforwardly feminine. Unlike in Brown's study, there is no evidence to suggest that young *boi* in Tanzania could transcend the generational boundary by becoming 'big men' before reaching a certain age and establishing a family. In the context of this study, being a 'boy' was part of a longer game to attain social status. Even so, Brown

---

[59] Nakanyike B. Musisi, 'Colonial and Missionary Education: Women and Domesticity in Uganda, 1900–1945', in *African Encounters with Domesticity*, ed. Karen Tranberg Hansen, 17. Similarly, Strayer notes that in Kenya, women's education had a much higher proportion of practical work (particularly sewing and cultivation) than schoolwork. Robert W. Strayer, *Making of Mission Communities in East Africa: Anglicans and Africans in Colonial Kenya, 1875–1935* (London: Heinemann, 1978), 21.

[60] T. Dunbar Moodie and Vivienne Ndatshe, *Going for Gold: Men, Mines, and Migration* (Berkeley: University of California Press, 1994), 131–2.

[61] Brown, 'A History of the Development of Workers' Consciousness of the Coal Miners at Enugu Government Colliery, Nigeria, 1914–1950'.

usefully conceptualised how knowledge and new labour categories prompted opportunities to claim social status in new ways, which is precisely what this chapter hopes to investigate.

Uboi in the nineteenth-century mission

Missionaries were simultaneously employers with far-reaching entitlements, and educators. However, they were also generally ignorant about household management, often unable to even warm up food, having depended on domestic servants while living in England.[62] This was especially the case for UMCA missionaries of the 1860s up until the 1880s who were not used to manual labour and tended to have upper-class social backgrounds.[63] Indeed, domestic life was one major way in which missionaries faced a steep learning curve in Africa. Some missionaries took to it more easily than others. Bishop Steere, who was celebrated for being humble enough to perform any chore, gave the following advice to a young Herbert Willoughby Woodward in 1880: 'Don't be content with bad food or allow Eustace not to do what he is told – possibly Lourdes' Swahili is bad and his ideas of cooking vague so that he puzzles a native more than he instructs him.'[64]

Thus, missionaries learned about domestic chores through a combination of necessity and their missionary principles, but it rarely came easily. This is why Gertrude Ward, a missionary who was at the UMCA in the 1890s, suggested that the UMCA organise a teaching session in London so that new missionaries could learn about the domestic challenges they were bound to face including laundry, making soda water, cooking, opening tins, and popping champagne bottles.[65] Crucially, missionaries, male ones in particular, lacked experience managing domestic servants.[66] In England, interactions between

---

[62] J. E. Griffin, 'A Journey to Kologwe'; Scholars have frequently noted how Europeans were very dependent on male domestic servants. Pariser, 'The Servant Problem: African Servants and the Making of European Domesticity in Colonial Tanganyika'.

[63] Helen Tozer, bishop Tozer's sister, was a key example of a missionary lacking domestic knowledge. Helen Tozer to Mary Steere, Zanzibar, 1865, A1 (3) A, 28, UMArch; Helen Tozer to Mary Steere, Zanzibar, September 1865, A1 (3) A, 44, UMArch.

[64] Eustace was an African convert and Lourdes was a missionary. Steere acquired extensive knowledge about cooking and gave Woodward additional advice on cooking with local produce. Edward Steere to H. W. Woodward, Zanzibar, December 1880, A1 (3) A, 308, UMArch.

[65] Gertrude Ward, *Letters from East Africa, 1895–1897* (Universities' Mission to Central Africa, 1899), 87.

[66] Edward Steere to Mary Steere, Zanzibar, December 1873, A1 (3) A, 147, UMArch;

domestic servants and their masters were typically kept to a minimum because domestic servants were trained by other more senior domestic servants who in turn were far more engaged with their employers, who were usually female. This distance was impossible to uphold in the African context, which made missionaries miserable. For example, May Allen grumbled that: 'It is a hard life superintending a household of these natives'.[67]

These challenges were intensified by the fact that the African environment was alien to them and not suited to European domesticity. At times, male missionaries complained of being at the mercy of their African domestic servants and desperately wrote home asking for female missionaries to come and fill the role of 'housekeeper'.[68] This was a long time before advice manuals (usually aimed at women) about how to manage settler households came to be printed, but there are some examples of travel or settler accounts that give advice on how to run a household in colonial Tanzania.[69] Thus, the peculiarity of missionary (and other European) demands for domestic service was that, as employers, they struggled to train domestic servants to meet their demands.

Whatever the extent of a missionary's domestic knowledge, they were both teachers and employers (as they put it, 'masters') of these mission students. Strict discipline characterised the missionaries' style of education. In a mission periodical, Dora Mills[70] narrated a story about how she found out about the theft of a pumpkin and how she proceeded to punish the students for the theft. The story went that one evening she walked into the room in which the pumpkin was being boiled:

> Inwardly choking with laughter, but outwardly stern and displeased I walked up to the cooking pot, amid dead silence, and kicked it over into the fire, and then severely ordered each boy to take up a stick of firewood, and the stones, and the pieces of the cooking-pot – which was broken, of course – and the pumpkin, and carry them all solemnly the whole length of the playground, and pitch them into the sea as far as they could throw.[71]

Edward Steere to Polly, Zanzibar, July 1865, A1 (3) A, 34, UMArch.
[67] May Allen to Rev. Edward S. L. Randolph, Mkunazini, Zanzibar, March 1877, A1 (4) A, 128, UMArch.
[68] J. P. Farler to Rev. W. H. Penney, Kiungani, Zanzibar, 28 July 1885, A1 (6) A, 478, UMArch.
[69] Younghusband, *Glimpses of East Africa and Zanzibar*; Gerald Fleming Sayers, ed., *The Handbook of Tanganyika* (London: Macmillan & Co, 1930).
[70] Mills was nicknamed, 'she who must be obeyed' and *'mama wa zamani'* ('mother of the old days'). P. M. W., 'A Joyful Reunion', *Central Africa*, July 1921.
[71] D. Y. Mills, 'The Pumpkin That Was Cooked but Never Eaten', *African Tidings*, April 1904.

One of the students tried to throw the pumpkin near enough so they could collect it in the morning but she noticed and insisted that another 'boy' should throw it even further out to sea.

Many years later, Mills invited many of her 'boys' – who had by this time become either teachers or deacons – to tea for a reunion. They were finally able to laugh about the story. As they reminisced, one of her former students enquired, 'But, Bibi,[72] when you kicked over that cooking-pot full of boiling water, didn't it hurt?' She admitted that it did, adding she intentionally hid her physical pain from them. Interestingly, Mills had not noticed at the time that her students were aware of her pain. The 'boys' noticed that Mills 'went about in an old shoe', presumably a more comfortable one, but were too afraid to mention the pumpkin incident. One 'boy' said, 'we thought you were very brave not to cry out, but that you had no sense, and we were sorry for you'. [73]

This anecdote demonstrates how many missionaries – along with other Europeans – believed dramatic performance was necessary to instil discipline, perhaps partly as a consequence of not being comfortable with the language. It also suggests that Mills shared with her old students a nostalgia for 'days gone by'. Equally, the anecdote reveals how Africans closely involved with the mission kept an observant, critical distance from missionaries.

Mission schoolboys' role as domestic servants in the nineteenth century was distinct from the profession of *uboi* in the twentieth century. It was also different from the compulsory labour of boarding school students in England at the time. Schoolboys were domestic servants because the missionaries wanted and needed (preferably free) domestic servants, but they also wanted to teach discipline and humility.[74] In Zanzibar the maintenance of the mission school was left almost entirely to its students, with a greater share for the 'industrial students', who specialised in skilled manual labour rather than academic work. There also existed – as in an English boarding school – systems of superintendence among them as 'head boys' were responsible for ensuring the work was done.[75] Some children became full-time domestic servants, rather than proceeding with their studies, sometimes because they were thought to lack 'talent for learning' and other times because they were particularly good at domestic work.[76] Schoolboys' role as domestic servants was equally institutionalised in Magila. They even had uniforms. In the late 1870s and early

---

[72] Literally meaning 'grandmother' but in this case '*bibi*' was a term like 'Miss' that was used to refer to female missionaries.
[73] D. Y. Mills, 'The Pumpkin That Was Cooked but Never Eaten'.
[74] 'How the Boys Spend Their Evenings at Mkunazini', *African Tidings*, 1886.
[75] J. S. Wimbush, 'My Impressions of Zanzibar Today', *African Tidings*, October 1895.
[76] 'Our African Postbag', *Central Africa*, October 1884.

1880s the increasing band of 'houseboys' wore *visibau* (waistcoats), which was, incidentally, the same attire allocated to prize-winning 'native school boys'. This, again, emphasises the blurred boundaries between domestic workers and students.[77]

The work of schoolboys in this period was extremely varied. It included nursing other children, accompanying missionaries on journeys, laying the table, overseeing the cleanliness of dormitories, etc.[78] A student 'boy' might be a personal servant or simply contribute to the general domestic labour of the mission household. At Mkuzi, on the mainland, in 1895: 'A certain portion of the work of the station is done by paid servants, but also a certain part by our boys. They clean up the courtyards and the rooms of the Europeans and the schoolrooms, and help to sweep out the church. We teach them to do this as some kind of return for what they receive. [...] They are perfectly willing.'[79] The missionaries did not recognise these children as economic actors even if they were performing the same tasks as paid adult domestic servants. Even so, schoolboys often acquired a liking for 'boy' work. There was, at any rate, no clear distinction between schoolboys who worked for free and those who were paid, partly because the payment itself was unregulated and informal. For the schoolboys who did receive a wage in some shape or form, the ability to buy things was, unsurprisingly, highly prized.[80]

In addition to material benefits, domestic service was also about pride and perfectionism. When the Kilimani head waiter (a paid position) was ill, two small boys were enlisted to take his place (Josefu Dona, an academic student, and Juma, who was a 'work boy'). Josefu became very enthusiastic about his newly appointed role: 'It annoys him much to see a knife or a fork the least crooked on the table, and he bustles round to put things straight. The other day, when he was wiping the breakfast things which Miss Stevens was washing up, he twice handed her back a plate gently remarking "this is not clean".'[81] Michael was another young boy who replaced a paid domestic worker. He took pride in the fact that he decorated a pastry with a figure of a man, saying, 'you make them without any decoration'.[82]

---

[77] J. P. Farler to Rev. W. H. Penney, Magila, Tanga, 2 November 1881, A1 (6) A, 345, UMArch.
[78] Mr. Geldart, 'Boys at Umba'; 'Letters from Children', *African Tidings*, 1886; Nicholas Kusi to Mrs Mallender, 10 September 1890.
[79] Rev. Godfrey Dale, 'Stories Illustrating African Life', *African Tidings*, 1895.
[80] 'Letters from Children'.
[81] 'Our African Mail', *African Tidings*, February 1906; 'Our African Mail', *African Tidings*, September 1906.
[82] Josefu Dona first took up this position as a temporary worker in February 1906

The distinctive qualities of schoolboys' domestic service provide texture to the linguistic history of 'boyness' and the part servile, part privileged status that came with it. The use of the term 'boy' to allude to domestic servants emerged as early as the 1870s both in Zanzibar and the mainland, and Kiungani missionaries would customarily refer to all Kiungani students as boys, 'both young and old'.[83] A similar explanation of the connection between age and the term 'boy' was found on the mainland. As one missionary put it, '[a] "boy" in Africa need not mean a young person', and may well have been, 'quite grown up, and a most solemn and responsible man'.[84] This was because men who could not establish their own households could not achieve elder status, whatever their age. The term 'boy' seems also to have been part of the language, even among African students. For example, in 1890 some Mkuzi students signed their letters to patrons in England, 'I am your boy'.[85] This is all the more interesting because it suggests that being a 'boy' was a social condition as well as a labour category. In Zanzibar the term also had currency. For instance, there was a seven-year-old student named Herbert Frank Mrashi, nicknamed 'Boy' because he was happy to do chores for the missionaries. His parents lived on Mbweni *shamba* and were almost certainly ex-slaves.[86]

Students in Zanzibar and the mainland were often displaced children and thus had marginal social status in the nineteenth century, which was compounded by the fact that they acted as domestic servants for the missionaries.[87] This provided ammunition for Muslims competing with the missionaries for followers. Even on the mainland, Muslims referred to students of the mission as 'slaves of the European teachers'.[88] In one of Godfrey Dale's missionary anecdotes from 1894, one day a student refused to sweep the floors in response to such invective from Muslim observers. The 'boy' was given an ultimatum to keep sweeping or to leave the school. He ended up going to Msalabani instead, where Herbert W. Woodward, who was more permissive than other missionaries, was principal. However, when Woodward found out why the 'boy' had

but was still working there in August 1907. 'Our African Mail (Kilimani)', *African Tidings*, August 1907.
[83] 'Kiungani Boys', *African Tidings*, July 1893; Rev. F. R. Hodgson to R. M. Heanley, 'A Journey from Zanzibar to Magila', 16 May 1871, 18.
[84] M. W. B., 'A Town without a Toy-Shop', *African Tidings*, January 1904.
[85] 'Letters from Children'; Nicholas Kusi to Mrs Mallender, 10 September 1890.
[86] *African Tidings*, 1910, 22.
[87] Still, missionaries generally took all mainland children as 'free' by defitinition. Bishop Charles Alan Smythies, 'Our Schools', *Central Africa*, June 1885.
[88] C. C. C., 'Our Free Native Scholars', *African Tidings*, June 1893; a similar observation is made by Rev. Godfrey Dale, 'Stories Illustrating African Life', *African Tidings*, January 1894.

left, he told him he had to go to Mkuzi and apologise. After some time, he finally came back to Mkuzi, accompanied by friends for support. They had a meeting and for a long time the ex-student was silent. Then he broke down into tears, reportedly blurting out, 'Sir! Why should I perish?'[89] It is unclear whether he feared the consequences of being expelled, eternal damnation, or both. This anecdote, problematic and partial though it is, not to mention its agenda to tell a story of salvation, demonstrates how young people often had to make anguished decisions about going to school. Though this was surely the case also in the twentieth century, it was particularly true of the 1890s, as this was a decade of particularly bad famine.

It is possible that students were seemingly happy to work without wages for Europeans because they had few other options open to them. This was almost certainly the case for the ex-slave children of Zanzibar. In the nineteenth century the 'boys' in mission schools were from marginal social and economic backgrounds. Archdeacon John Prediger Farler had two 'boys' on a particular safari, working as cook and attendant. The one who served as Farler's attendant was a young Hugh Peter Kayamba, who later became one of the first African civil servants. He was one of the sons of Chief Mwelekwanyuma of Kilole, son of Kimweri Za Nyumbai, King of the Kilindi.[90] Though this sounds like a socially elite background, Justin Willis has shown that these 'sons' of chiefs were part of a distinctly marginal social group and their transition to mission life was in fact part of an exchange that reflected local human pawning practices. As Willis put it, '[Hugh Kayamba's] position as a trusted member of the mission marked his lack of choice'.[91] The marginal social backgrounds, domestic service, and corporal punishment in the mission all reinforced the association of these pupils with slave status.[92] Whether or not Christians believed or accepted

---

[89] Rev. Godfrey Dale, 'Stories Illustrating African Life', January 1894.

[90] He was probably only six years old at this time if the estimation of Martin Kayamba is correct. Martin Kayamba, 'The Story of Martin Kayamba Mdumi, MBE, of the Bondei Tribe', in *Ten Africans*, ed. Margery Perham, 2nd edn. (London: Faber, 1963); Rev. F. R. Hodgson to R. M. Heanley, 'A Journey from Zanzibar to Magila', 16 May 1871; Hugh was born a Muslim but after converting to Christianity he received an education in England and taught at Kiungani. He died an untimely death in 1882. J. P. Farler to Rev. W. H. Penney, Magila, Tanga (private), 17 March 1882, A1 (6) A, 428, UMArch.

[91] Justin Willis, 'The Nature of a Mission Community: The Universities' Mission to Central Africa in Bonde', *Past & Present*, no. 140 (1 August 1993): 127–54.

[92] Some evidence of the missionaries' corporal punishment of students: Dora S. Yarnton Mills to R. M. Heanley, Mbweni, Zanzibar (private), July 1881, A1 (4) A, 604, UMArch; H. W. Woodward, 'Difficulties of School Work', *Central Africa*, April 1892; Alice Foxley, 'Panya', *Stories of Africa*, 1902; These are a few examples of evidence staggered over the period of corporal punishment of school

this social categorisation is less clear. The ambiguities of status are palpable in this odd mixture of servility, dependence, hierarchy, domestic intimacy, and the self-assertive impulse that comes with acquiring skills.

In 1895 the only paid servant in the school was a 'Goan cook' and so the maintenance of the school was left almost entirely to its students, with a greater share for the industrial students. The use of child and adolescent labour was common amongst Christian missions in Africa and the UMCA-taught mission 'boys' were considered good servants.[93] From the students' perspective their role as servants meant that many felt exploited and rumour spread that the missionaries saw them only as a means of producing financial profit.[94] The students' resistance included refusal to attend classes and complete chores. Students also ran away. In order to ensure that this work was done, missionaries set out systems of superintendence amongst them, as the head boys' main responsibility was to ensure the work was done. This sense of self-regulation was particularly strong in the industrial school, apparently making the missionary a mere 'figurehead' within this 'self-governing body'.[95]

The narratives of social mobility are closely tied to the history of slavery, but in ways that are difficult to read. John Mhina, a historian of the UMCA in Magila, cited Booker Washington's book *Up From Slavery* when discussing domestic service in mission schools.[96] Mhina suggested his elders were in quite a similar situation to the upwardly mobile ex-slaves of the Americas, though he did not identify his ancestors as slaves. In the book, the young boy protagonist desperately wanted to go to school so proved himself by working as a cleaner for the missionary teacher. His zeal for cleaning impressed the missionary so much that he was allowed to come to school.[97] Mhina's view of domestic service as a test of early converts' commitment is not representative; most respondents did not remember or were not aware of this phase of

---

children. Frank Weston to H. M., Kiungani, Zanzibar, 8 March 1902, A1 (17) A, 114, UMArch; Frank Weston to H. M., Kiungani, Zanzibar, 1904, A1 (17) A, 175, UMArch; D. C. A., 'Tommy the Waif', *African Tidings*, August 1915.

[93] H.S. Newman, *Banani*, 1898, 154.

[94] Farler to Penney, 12 September 1884, TC C1 UMArch. Erasto Mangénya, a UMCA mission-educated Tanzanian civil servant, writes about missionary brutality and prejudice in *Discipline and Tears: Reminiscences of an African Civil Servant on Colonial Tanganyika* (Dar es Salaam: Dar es Salaam University Press, 1984), 29–30.

[95] J. S. Wimbush, 'My Impressions of Zanzibar Today', 99.

[96] John Mhina, *Historia ya Magila Msalabani 1848–2012: Mlango wa Kuingia Kanisa la Anglikana Tanzania Bara*, 2012.

[97] John Geldart Mhina, interview by Zuhura Mohammed, Magila, 15 October 2014, 7.

the mission's history. Even so, as a historian, it is possible that Mhina's ideas express what many in the area took for granted.

The general decline of domestic service indicates two important changes. First, the mission was getting more students coming to the mission of their own volition, and fewer displaced children. These 'voluntary' students had parents who did not wish for their male children to carry out chores that were considered feminine. Out of the respondents, Josephine Thomas Mungayao explained it best: 'The customs didn't allow boys to sweep the floor, to do the dishes or to fetch water. These were considered girls' tasks.'[98] Preventing boys or young men from performing what was perceived to be girlish chores was a way of introducing them to manhood. The phrase in Swahili that people would use was '*kumkuza mtoto wa kiume*', which literally translates as 'to make a boy grow', which denotes, 'to cultivate a boy's masculinity'.[99] Second, mission schools were becoming more academically inclined. The number of students considered to be destined for manual labour, who were generally given the largest share of the household chores, was in decline. Moreover, missionaries' demands increased and they found it more efficient to employ people who had taken the initiative, to varying degrees, to fashion themselves as domestic servants.

Given the abolitionist movement and its emphasis on the plight of children, one might have expected to find that one reason for the declining importance of domestic service in schools was that employing students for menial tasks became too controversial and the UMCA risked losing the support of English donors. During the early phase, educated protégés and children alike often performed the labour of a *boi* without receiving regular wages.[100] Missionaries did not see this as contentious. Rather, they saw it as problematic that they were paying wages to dependents because they believed it risked making them adopt a culture of 'materialism' and gave them a sense of entitlement. For some, the solution was to simply stop paying these educated students for their work. For instance, Bishop Smythies tried to put a stop to the payments Caroline Thackeray made to the girls at Mbweni because he believed their work should be 'voluntary'.[101] Moreover, ensuring the students did the domes-

---

[98] '*Mila za huku watoto wa kiume walikuwa hawahusiki kufanya kazi za nyumbani kufagia, kuosha vyombo, kuteka maji zile zilikuwa ni kazi za watoto wa kike.*' Josephine Thomas Mungayao, interview by Zuhura Mohammed, Mkuzi, Tanga, 21 October 2014.

[99] Josephine Thomas Mungayao, interview by Zuhura Mohammed, Mkuzi, Tanga, 21 October 2014.

[100] Rev. F. R. Hodgson to R. M. Heanley, 'A Journey from Zanzibar to Magila', 16 May 1871.

[101] Bishop Charles Alan Smythies, 'A Letter from the Bishop', *Central Africa*, September 1885.

tic chores of course meant the mission could save their funds, an advantage missionaries were not ashamed to have benefitted from in the 1880s. In fact, quite the opposite, it was positive evidence of their frugality.[102]

Colonial employers

Being a missionary's 'boy' or domestic servant generally implied a fairly vague job description.[103] There is a case to be made for a distinction between personal domestic servants on the one hand and people who were paid to do domestic chores of one kind or another on the other. Indeed, missions needed far more workers to perform demanding piecemeal duties such as collecting water or firewood, sweeping, and lighting lamps, than they needed personal domestic servants to wait on them. Thus, most of the domestic service in the mission was routinized. In contrast, domestic servants who had specific duties were less likely to struggle for respect. As Hansen has argued, a lack of specialisation was likely to lead to a decline in prestige.[104]

But having a specific domestic role did not automatically lead to enhanced respect. Domestic chores were varied and some involved greater interdependence than others. In 1900 Herbert Woodward, a relatively benign missionary in terms of discipline, found that there was a huge amount of theft of the oil needed to light lamps. Woodward explained that the stealing was finally stopped when one of the schoolboys took it up on himself to watch over the 'lamp-man':

> At last one of the school boys (who had been helping me by writing in the calendar all tins given out and the date), Stefano Mkacha, took it in hand of his own accord, and watched over the unfortunate Hugh till his life became a burden. He stood over him when he filled the lamps, he took charge in every way, with the result that in one month instead of twelve tins we only used 8 tins – less than ever before![105]

Thus, this anecdote shows that a schoolboy could transcend the relations of authority that one would expect to exist and preside over the labour of an older wage-earner.

Mission 'boys' were similar to domestic servants of other Europeans in that they were dependent on their employers for more than their wages. In particular, they were dependent on their missionary employers for paying

---

[102] 'How the Boys Spend Their Evenings at Mkunazini'.
[103] H. A. M. Cox, 'My Boy, and What He Does'.
[104] Hansen, *Distant Companions*, 245.
[105] H. W. W., 'Lamps!', *Central Africa*, April 1900.

bridewealth.[106] This was the state of things right into the twentieth century and was part of a long tradition.[107] For example, Woodward paid for his domestic servant, Peter Lukindo's, bridewealth. This is an extract from one of Lukindo's letters from 1887:

> My work here is to cook the food. My mother is alive at this day, but my father died a long time ago when I was quite small, so I have never seen him. [...] Now I am growing up, I have sought a sweetheart, and Mr Woodward helped me to give the 'turban' (*kilemba*, that is, the payment or price required by the parents). And now I have paid everything to her father so she is my sweetheart, and perhaps by and by when I am grown up, you may hear further news. My elder brother, whose name is George Sungimo, does the same work that I do; he cooks at Magila, and I cook here [Misozwe]. He has just gone to Zanzibar with the bishop.[108]

There was another domestic worker, a 'young man', Christopher Hiza, who was not deemed suitable for the teaching profession. He worked as 'a kind of steward or butler, or rather general servant to the establishment'. Woodward was clearly very close with Hiza, who had been his employee for eight months:

> A more generally useful boy I could hardly have, or one more trustworthy and upright in his general character. He has charge of the stores of maize, rice, and all in the commissariat line; attends to the table and washing up; trims and lights the lamps; washes the clothes and irons very well, besides looking after the place as a whole; also he can do a little carpentering as occasion may require.[109]

Woodward was also overseeing Hiza's marriage to his non-Christian 'sweetheart' who was under instruction to be baptised. In this letter, Woodward was asking the patrons to donate some money or useful items to help Hiza start married life.[110] 'Boys' like Hiza, then, were valued, and to some extent skilled dependents, even if they did not receive wages. Increasingly, this kind of relationship contrasted with more formalised and routinised employment in other European households.

---

[106] Similarly, it was customary for slave masters to pay the bridewealth of their slaves. Captain H. A. Fraser, William Tozer, and James Christie, *The East African Slave Trade, and the Measures Proposed for Its Extinction as Viewed by Residents in Zanzibar*, ed. Edward Steere (London: Harrison, 1871), 33.
[107] Emmanuel Ngoma, interview.
[108] Peter Lukindo, 'Letter from a Misozswe Boy to the Children of St Peter's, Dublin, Who Support Him (Translated)', *African Tidings*, 1887.
[109] H. W. Woodward, 'Extracts from Letters', *African Tidings*, 1887.
[110] H. W. Woodward.

There was, unsurprisingly, greater demand for mission-educated domestic servants for Europeans – both male and female – in urban Zanzibar than in places like Magila.[111] But that is not to say that mission-educated domestic servants flooded the domestic service labour market. According to a census from Percy L. Jones-Bateman in 1890, 65 per cent of Kiungani's students (who did not pass away by the time they collected the results) had gone on to work as servants or porters.[112] The fact that this census combined servants and porters in the same category indicates that the system of domestic service developed out of the history of portage and personal service, just as van Onselen suggests in the case of South Africa.[113] But there was also much greater demand for porters who could double up as servants. Bearing in mind the lack of roads at this point, it may well have been necessary for aspiring domestic servants to take up porterage until they managed to secure their desired employment.[114] However, while employers seemed to perceive similarities between domestic service and porterage, there is evidence to suggest domestic servants actively distanced themselves from porters. For instance, *boi* did not like to share their knowledge with socially mobile porters looking to climb the employment ladder.[115] All this being said, there were social and economic advantages to being a porter, which were obscured by European writings that overemphasised the overlap between slavery and porterage.[116]

Still, Europeans looked to missions on the mainland to provide domestic servants and guides. However, as early as 1887, the reputation of mission-educated domestic servants among settlers was very poor. Farler's retort to a criticism of this kind from Dr Oskar Lentz (who directed the Austro-Hungarian Congo Expedition, 1885-7) was that:

> [Missionaries] do not consider it their duty to train up a lot of servants for European travellers; they consider that their work is a far higher one than this – namely, to restore to the poor, degraded African savage the image of God which he has lost, and generally they would prefer that their converts should do

---

[111] M. A. Cameron, 'Round about the Cathedral', *African Tidings*, April 1896.

[112] My percentage calculation excludes the number of Kiungani students who died. Percy L. Jones-Bateman, 'What Becomes of Your Mission Boys When They Leave You?', *Central Africa*, 1890; Percy L. Jones-Bateman, '"What Becomes of Your Mission Boys When They Leave You?"', *African Tidings*, October 1890.

[113] Charles Van Onselen, *Studies in the Social and Economic History of the Witwatersrand, 1886–1914* (Johannesburg: Ravan Press, 1982), 1–2.

[114] Stephen J. Rockel, *Carriers of Culture: Labor on the Road in Nineteenth-Century East Africa* (Portsmouth, NH: Heinemann, 2006), 3.

[115] Ferdinand Stephen Joelson, *The Tanganyika Territory, Formerly German East Africa: Characteristics and Potentialities* (London: T. Fisher Unwin, 1920).

[116] Rockel, *Carriers of Culture*, 16–17.

any other work rather than act as servants for Europeans, who sometimes have been known to live and act in Central Africa so as to destroy in the native all the good effects of the teaching of the missionaries. [117]

Even if mission 'boys' had a bad reputation as 'boys', they still very often went on to become domestic servants for non-missionary settlers. There was increased demand from colonial agents and settlers for mission-educated domestic servants, particularly in the British colonial period. For example, a missionary from Mkuzi noted in 1928 that: 'Our settlers in the neighbourhoods seem to look to us to supply them with all their boys. We have lately sent off two Mission cooks from here at the urgent request of settlers.' [118] It was not that missionaries wanted to recruit domestic servants; rather, they were responding to the wishes of the African Christians who saw missionaries as recruiters. However, British settlers complained that mission 'boys' were lazy, manipulative and untrustworthy, with an air of superiority despite their superficial knowledge of elementary education.[119] Settlers believed that the missionaries' reforming mission was failing, largely because they wanted Africans to 'know their place' and believed missionaries tended to 'indulge' Africans.

There were tensions between European employers about the best way to train Africans in domestic service. Missionaries argued that these 'black sheep', meaning the poor-quality domestic servants, were not strictly products of the mission. According to the settlers, these semi-educated men from the mission went to work for Europeans, trading upon what they learnt from missionaries.[120] Indeed, there was some debate among missionaries, colonial agents, and settlers about whether it was better to hire trained or untrained domestic servants. Some believed mission domestic servants who had encountered Europeans and had been minimally trained were a good option because at least they could produce references and demonstrated some knowledge of European domesticity. Others believed it was best to hire 'raw' 'boys' and teach them from scratch, on the basis that it was easier to learn than to unlearn.[121]

[117] J. P. Farler, 'Mission Work in Africa' (July 1887).
[118] Cyril S. S. M., 'A Letter from Mkuzi', *Central Africa*, January 1928. This missionary author proudly added that the Mkuzi mission 'boys' had a better reputation than those from other mission stations, suggesting there was some inter-UMCA competition.
[119] Joelson, *The Tanganyika Territory, Formerly German East Africa: Characteristics and Potentialities*, 89; William Harold Ingrams, *Zanzibar: Its History and Its People* (London: Stacey International, 2007), 223.
[120] Cyril S. S. M., 'A Letter from Mkuzi'; Farler, 'Mission Work in Africa'.
[121] H. A. M. Cox, 'My Boy, and What He Does'; Joelson, *The Tanganyika Territory, Formerly German East Africa: Characteristics and Potentialities*; Cyril S. S. M.,

For the aspiring domestic servant, the challenge was to respond to all sorts of European demands without seeming too 'Europeanised', as Europeans were often suspicious of Africans who appeared to be accustomed to European cultures. There is also evidence to suggest that Africans recognised that European employers – particularly settlers – feared educated workers. Thus, some African workers feigned ignorance before their European masters. In fact, in one instance a European settler complained about a domestic servant who pretended to be illiterate and then used his employer's signature to sign off on cases of whiskey. Missionaries retorted that it was the settlers' own fault for failing to investigate their prospective workers' character and not taking an interest in their morality, as the next section will show.[122]

At the turn of the century, 'boy' work was becoming increasingly clearly defined but this was a process of change confined largely to the *boi* of settlers in Zanzibar and Mombasa, rather than the missionaries in more rural locations. Outside of the frugal mission, 'boys' tended to have clearly defined roles and higher wages.[123] In much the same way, a government official would usually take a band of different kinds of servants on safari, including a cook, who – in a missionaries' words intended to mark the contrast with the frugal mission – could 'turn out a four or five course meal just as if he were in his own kitchen'. Conversely, mission journeys tended to demand far fewer servants who would each be expected to fulfil a more varied job description.[124]

Being a cook by profession was quite another matter. Professional cooks were rarely employed in nineteenth-century Magila and Zanzibar mission stations though the UMCA records demonstrate that professional cooks could be employed as early as the 1870s. They were usually described as 'Goanese cooks' and considered a luxury. It was the students who did the greater part of the cooking. However, professional cooks – usually of Asian origin – would be specially outsourced to prepare the missionaries' food, the justification being that this was an essential precaution against missionary illness.[125]

At the beginning of the twentieth century, there were frequent complaints from Europeans that Africans did not have to be well qualified to get a position

---

'A Letter from Mkuzi'. Similar ideas were put forward in this advice manual on European domesticity in Northern Rhodesia: Emily G. Bradley, *Dearest Priscilla: Letters to the Wife of a Colonial Civil Servant* (London: Max Parrish & Co., 1950), 49, 123.

[122] Cyril S. S. M., 'A Letter from Mkuzi'.
[123] Younghusband, *Glimpses of East Africa and Zanzibar*, 28.
[124] Mary Wallace, 'Safari Cook', *African Tidings*, September 1924.
[125] J. P. Farler to Chauncy Maples, Magila, Tanga, 27 April 1877, A1 (6) A, 421, UMArch; A. C. Madan, 'The Zanzibar Treasurer's Order Book', *Central Africa*, February 1887; J. S. Wimbush, 'My Impressions of Zanzibar Today'.

as a 'boy'. For example, in 1913 this British army officer in Zanzibar protested: 'Wages, especially of servants, are high in the Protectorate, a boy who has an elementary idea of the relative positions a knife and fork should occupy when laid on the dinner table and a hazy idea that he must not finger the food until his master's back is turned, demands and obtains about twice the pay of an Indian bearer who will attend to all one's wants.'[126] Over the next few decades, domestic servants became more familiar with European demands and expectations, and they used their enhanced knowledge to their advantage.

But more than this, domestic servants were people who had access to rare knowledge. As Amin bin Said, a domestic servant, whose memoirs were recorded in the early 1960s, put it:

> I think that it is well for Africans to be taught and to try to learn all that the Europeans have to teach. For if we were left in ignorance we would suffer many hardships, but a man who has brains and works hard may make a name even when everyone is civilized. Our old people who have not learned anything or worked even now they are only fools. But when a man has learned a lot, let him not think he can learn no more, for anyone can go on learning till he dies, and even then a fool is buried.[127]

The reason why Said was saying this is that he had had multiple employers, including settlers and missionaries, and each had their own preferences. Thus, he learned to be flexible and to unlearn for some employers in order to meet their expectations. As we can see from Said's testimony, his appreciation for knowledge, and ability to accumulate it, formed part of his identity and his observations appear to confirm the extent of European hegemony at this time.

By 1930 each household servant customarily performed specific duties and refused to extend past their original job description. Thus, Gerald Sayers, a British colonial official, explained in his 1930 handbook that, 'a normal household', which could have consisted of just one European or a small European family, required 'a kitchen-boy, head-boy and assistant, and a "*dhobi*" or washerman'.[128] Sayers also noted that a 'Goan cook' (where they were obtainable) could demand at least double the wages of a good 'African cook', and triple that of a 'fair plain cook' (see Table 7).[129] 'Kitchen-boys', who were subordinate

---

[126] Captain Chauncey H. Stigand, *The Land of Zinj: Being an Account of British East Africa, Its Ancient History and Present Inhabitants* (London: Constable & Co, 1913), 308.

[127] Margery Perham and Malcolm, eds., 'The Story of Amini Bin Saidi', in *Ten Africans*, 2nd edn. (London: Faber, 1963), 139–58.

[128] Sayers, *The Handbook of Tanganyika*.

[129] Sayers, 470.

to cooks, were the lowest paid household servants, receiving shillings (Shs) 8–20 per month. Meanwhile, wages for 'house-boys' ranged significantly but could go up to Shs 70 per month in towns.[130] In contrast, missionaries paid Shs 5–20 per month for most of their domestic servants and also did not tend to hire highly skilled servants, partly to reduce their costs but also because most mission stations were remote and highly skilled domestic servants were less plentiful.

Table 7 Wages for cooks, c.1930

Description	Wages per month (Shs)
'Fair plain cook'	< 40–50
'Good cook'	60–80
'Goan cook'	150–200

Source: Gerald Fleming Sayers, ed., *The Handbook of Tanganyika* (London: Macmillan & Co, 1930)

Cooking for Europeans was a different world to that of cooking in an African household. Edith Yambi told us:

> Being a cook was a special job and it was a job of respect. Even my paternal uncle who was a cook told me that in those days if you were known to be a cook, you were seen to be important and that's why they learnt how to do it. I mean it was a like learning a special task; like teaching, nursing, and so cooking was known to be a special job. [...] Becoming a cook didn't mean that you had to stop your studies.[131]

Much as Edith Yambi suggested, in the 1910s and 1920s well-trained domestic servants could command high wages and specify their role. This was largely because there were so few domestic servants of this kind and they had skills that were difficult to master. 'Boys' and cooks– from a domestic servants' perspective – ideally did different kinds of work. Settlers also struggled to find

[130] Sayers, 470.
[131] 'Ninavyojua mimi, ilikuwa ni kazi maalum tena ilikuwa ni kazi ya sifa hii ya upishi. Hata baba yangu mdogo alikuwa mpishi alinieleza zamani ukionekana mpishi, unaonekana mtu wa maana na walisomea yaani ile ni somo kama kazi maalum, ualimu kama hivi unesi na nini na upishi ilikuwa ni kazi maalum ambazo zilikuwa zinajulikana. [...] Na kwa watu jinsi walivyokuwa wanasome sasa, ilikuwa si sababu hakuendelea.' Edith Yambi, interview by Zuhura Mohammed, Tanga, 25 October 2014.

'good servants' and complained this was why they were able to demand high wages in the Tanganyika Territory in the twentieth century. The incentives for taking up domestic service outside the mission were again a mixture of financial and status considerations that were very much tied up with European cultural hegemony at this moment.

Settlers' domestic servants were often mission-educated. However, they were rarely the missionaries' favourite students. The mission's favoured students – who were more interested in theology – were retained in the mission or encouraged to acquire agricultural livelihoods. This is partly because missionaries feared that employment under a settler would lead to moral degradation. This opprobrium was also an expression of missionary frustration with their inability to keep trained labour because of the low wages they paid. Though missionaries were pioneer employers of a particular culture of domestic service that occurred in schools, the *boi* of the twentieth century were not dissimilar to the upwardly mobile slave of the nineteenth century, who combined servitude and social mobility, as we shall see in the next section of this chapter.

UMCA missionaries generally discouraged their students from working for other Europeans. The career of Robert Ngoma demonstrates the missionaries' concerns and how they impacted upon Ngoma, so it is worth considering it in detail. As a student at the school Ngoma was given leave in 1885 by Rev. Samuel Sehoza to go and find work so he could feed his mother and younger siblings during a time of famine. Ngoma initially worked in an Indian's shop but was not satisfied with the pay so he went on to work for a European as a 'house-boy'. Ngoma worked there until the European died, which seems to have been only a few years later, and Ngoma then returned to his Indian employer. After some time, famine subsided and Ngoma returned to Magila. However, he was no longer a child and could not resume his studies. Even so, Ngoma was qualified enough to take up a teaching post at an out-school in 1894.[132]

At least for Ngoma, the opportunities domestic service offered were more tempting and pressing than the opportunities of furthering his education. Another way of looking at it is that Ngoma's work experience as a European's 'boy' may have added to his qualifications to be a teacher. Indeed, it is possible that he continued to learn about Christianity and literacy while he was a domestic servant. This story is narrated in an article by Samuel Sehoza that celebrated how Ngoma heroically returned to the mission in the end, despite what the missionaries saw as the corrupting temptations that the earning

---

[132] Samwil Sehoza, 'Robert Ngoma, an African Teacher', *African Tidings*, May 1910.

potential of *uboi* inspired. The notion that receiving a mission education rendered people indebted to the mission carried on in the twentieth century, as the oral history interviews suggest.[133]

According to the missionaries, the 'temptations' of life working as a settler's 'boy' included drinking alcohol, becoming vain, and paying for sex. They were also less likely to live with their families than mission 'boys', which missionaries feared would lead to broken homes and sexual deviance.[134] This demonstrated the recurring theme of moral mistrust but also indicates that missionary concerns over morality blurred with their concerns over their lack of control over these young men. Missionaries were also unconvinced that wage-earning Africans were capable of managing their finances by saving their wages. Indeed, it was said that many were in debt to Asian money-lenders.[135] This, the missionaries reasoned, was a world away from agricultural livelihoods that usually depended upon an agriculturalist's ability to prepare for the future many months or years in advance.[136] As Cyril Frewer, a missionary based in Zanzibar and Pemba, put it, 'boys [...] are not a power for good in the community. They too often follow the vices of their masters without assimilating their virtues'.[137] In a similar vein, Frank Weston, the Bishop of Zanzibar, objected to the way in which Africans were left with little choice but to 'learn to be worth a regular monthly wage, and to avoid nakedness like the plague'.[138] Most missionaries shared Weston's doubts that wages had a positive reforming capacity. Missionaries were not interested in training Africans in domestic service unless they were training their own employees. The moral objection to competitive wages was accompanied by a pragmatic concern. Due to the missionaries' financial constraints, they could only offer very low wages, which may partly explain their frustration when their domestic servants searched for jobs elsewhere.

---

[133] Gerrard Michael Francis Kiongoa Yambi, interview; Anthony Christopher Mabundo, interview by Zuhura Mohammed, Handeni, 8 October 2014.

[134] Bishop Richardson, 'Letter to Members of UMCA', 1897, A1 (7), UMArch; T., 'Bare Feet', *Central Africa: A Monthly Record of the Universities' Mission to Central Africa*, January 1920; 'Intercessions and Thanksgivings' (Mkusi, 16 October 1922), A1 (22), 182, UMArch.

[135] C. C. Frewer, 'Industrial Work in Zanzibar and Pemba', *Central Africa*, April 1905.

[136] Frank Weston, 'Africa: And the Blight of Commercialism', *The Nineteenth Century and After*, June 1920, 1082.

[137] C. C. Frewer, 'The Native of Zanzibar and Pemba'.

[138] Frank Zanzibar, 'If the Salt Have Lost Its Savour?', *The Church Socialist*, November 1920, A1 (18) B, 132, UMArch.

Meanwhile, for settlers and colonial officials, wages were a way of introducing ideas of an African subject's duty to colonial government and to reinforce the hierarchy of colonial society. Thus, in Tanganyika's British colonial period, Lord Milner reasoned that: 'As their knowledge and their wants increase, they will appreciate the need for more employment and more wages to satisfy those wants, so that the supply of labour should become continuous, while the condition of the native himself will inevitably improve at the same time.'[139] The government official's approach to reforming African workers, then, was to expose them to new material cultures, which would make them hunger for wages and thus become more ambitious.[140] Needless to say, the importance of wages increased from the time of German colonialism as taxes were enforced.

Appearances and the ambiguities of status

As Eastman has shown, the status struggles that *boi* faced in the early twentieth century were rooted in nineteenth-century slave identity. Related to that, the importance of dress to post-slavery status struggles at this time is well documented.[141] As such, *boi* were trying to assert status in the terms of coastal society, and simultaneously needed to placate Europeans who mistrusted them. Their sartorial compromise was creative, but it also reflected the precariousness of their position and internal status struggles of (mission) dependants. Accordingly, contemporary observers noted that *boi* were anxious to perform their social status and wealth. This is evidenced by UMCA literature. For example, in the 1870s Steere hired a Muslim domestic servant in Zanzibar:

> We have in the employ of the mission a certain Mohammedan servant, who on state occasions, such as a visit to the Seyed, etc., used to walk in front of the Bishop with an air and manner so completely in contrast to the bearing of his master that one was always greatly amused at seeing the two together. I said so

---

[139] Lord Milner, 'No. 1 Despatch to the Governor of the East Africa Protectorate', Parliamentary paper, Despatch to the Governor of the East Africa Protectorate Relating to Native Labour, and Papers Connected Therewith (Downing Place, London, 22 July 1920).

[140] Missionaries had used the same reasoning when arguing for abolition in Jamaica. Thomas C. Holt, *Problem of Freedom: Race, Labor, and Politics in Jamaica and Britain, 1832–1938* (Baltimore, MD: Johns Hopkins University Press, 1992).

[141] Laura Fair, 'Dressing up: Clothing, Class and Gender in Post-Abolition Zanzibar', *The Journal of African History*, 39, no. 1 (1 January 1998): 63–94; Laura Fair, *Pastimes and Politics: Culture, Community, and Identity in Post-Abolition Urban Zanzibar, 1890–1945*, Eastern African Studies (Athens, OH; Oxford: Ohio University Press; James Currey, 2001).

to the Bishop one day, and he laughed and said, 'Yes, I think it is very fortunate I can get the swagger done for me, I think it is cheap at 8 [MTD] a month, I am sure I couldn't do it for the money'.[142]

Early twentieth century accounts also describe how *boi* were developing a complex professional identity that was materialised in their attire and comportment. A mixture of pity and mild irritation characterises European accounts of the fashion and public performance of 'boys'. For example, the missionary Cyril Frewer complained in 1907 that wage-earning ex-slaves were guilty of spending money thoughtlessly, buying 'a new cap and *kanzu* and becoming what they call malidadi (i.e. a dandy) and spending the rest of their earnings in debauchery'. [143]

Likewise, Ethel Younghusband, writing in 1910, like many British travellers and settlers in East Africa, recorded her amusement at the public performance, 'strong penetrating scent', and attire of her 'boy':

> Baruku appeared fearfully hot, but quite a swell in appearance, in his travelling costume of white cap, white coat and trousers, stick (silver-topped) and cigarette. Boys like to travel in their best clothes, then they walk about at each station with an air of great importance, and talk to friends, and feel they are being gazed at with envy by their lesser dressed comrades.[144]

But not all *boi* were the same. The connected but contrasting case of *uboi* in settler households here is relevant because the mission trained servants for this milieu. Settlers distinguished between new *boi* and the *boi* who no longer felt the need to indulge in performance.[145]

Stephen Joelson, a settler writing in 1920, approvingly observed that a *boi* who had 'realised the dignity of his position' – as he put it – would wear a fez-shaped linen cap, *kanzu*, and Arab sandals:

> A light cane is carried in the hand, more often swung gently to and fro than used as an aid in walking; and as a rule a watch ranks as an indispensable article of adornment. Nowadays a silver wrist-watch with luminous dial is the hallmark of the aristocrat, but until the last few years a huge pocket watch with massive silver chain was the envy of less fortunate mortals.[146]

---

[142] Robert Heanley, *A Memoir of Edward Steere: Third Missionary Bishop in Central Africa* (London: Office of the Universities' Mission to Central Africa, 1898), 290.
[143] C. C. Frewer, 'The Native of Zanzibar and Pemba'.
[144] Younghusband, *Glimpses of East Africa and Zanzibar*, 29, 35.
[145] Joelson, *The Tanganyika Territory, Formerly German East Africa: Characteristics and Potentialities*.
[146] Joelson.

European accounts suggest that it took time for a 'boy' to settle into his new attire. Europeans preferred to hire domestic servants who appeared humble. Even if ideas of *uungwana* were contested in the specific environments domestic servants operated, and even if young men tended to be more boisterous in the way they expressed their status as I have already suggested, humility was also valued in coastal society. Indeed, there is a Swahili proverb that goes, 'Arrogance does not make a gentleman'.[147] Nevertheless, the calm self-possession expected of a *mwungwana* was different from the humility expected of a servant and herein lies the contradictory status of *boi* identity.[148] Both missionaries and settler employers pushed 'coastal' dress styles for African dependants (albeit, I take it, for different reasons: presumably the missionaries endorsed them as 'traditional', whereas the settlers liked them for being decorous, but non-European); they find themselves, unusually, on the same side of this particular debate on how to treat (i.e. dress) 'natives'.

Domestic servants, then, took enjoyment in the performance that European civility entailed but walked a tight line between sophistication and servitude.[149] An anecdote that encapsulates this dilemma is told in Joelson's memoir. The story went that a settler, returning to his house from a safari earlier than planned, caught his *boi* entertaining two African ladies at table with tea and cakes, dressed in the finest attire the settler kept in his trunk. Joelson suggests that the settler-employer was more amused than he was angry.[150] Settlers enjoyed telling stories like this because, though they were exasperated with how they saw African work ethic, they believed they had at least succeeded in transforming Africans as consumers.

Notions of sophistication and propriety remained indebted to precolonial ideas of *uungwana* even for mission-trained *boi* – partly because their European employers preferred them exoticised in Swahili garb. Like all other European observers in Tanganyika, missionaries feared they would help produce a 'bad version' of the European in the form of an 'imitating' African. However, employers' preferences did not stop domestic servants from wearing what they wanted and shaping domestic service fashion. One missionary wrote

---

[147] '*Kiburi si mwungwana.*' See the University of Illinois Swahili Proverbs Collection, http://swahiliproverbs.afrst.illinois.edu/pride.html, accessed 3 November 2020.

[148] Glassman highlights the importance of humility to the village teacher in Zanzibar, though also shows that not all teachers followed this principle. Jonathon Glassman, *War of Words, War of Stones: Racial Thought and Violence in Colonial Zanzibar* (Bloomington, IN: Indiana University Press, 2011), 83.

[149] Joelson, *The Tanganyika Territory, Formerly German East Africa: Characteristics and Potentialities*, 153.

[150] Joelson, 153.

in 1906 regretfully of one of her old students, Giles Kushelwa, who became a cook in Zanzibar town and dressed in a European fashion.[151]

There were nuances to how Europeans presented and offered or denied Europeanness to Africans through access to clothing. Apparently without difficulty, missionaries praised coastal dress while avoiding praising Islam. Young men from the mission were more likely to be required to wear semi-European clothing or less ornate versions of 'Arab' dress. For example, Charles Nasibu was a messenger for the mission and one missionary described his dress as that of a 'dignified old gentleman'. This entailed 'a shooting coat and a Terai hat[152] with a red ribbon round it'.[153] However, mission *boi* did not tend to be so finely dressed. In general, it was settlers' *boi* who boasted resplendent garments. There were two reasons for the difference between the attire of domestic servants for settlers and for missionaries. One was that missionaries preferred simple dress. As far as the missionaries were concerned, European dress was demoralising and they admired the dignity that came with coastal fashions, which shows how they operated under the long shadow of Muslim cultural hegemony. Missionaries were even more perturbed by Africans in European dress than settlers. However, unlike settlers, in principle missionaries had an ambition to remake Africans in their own image and they saw that dressing in coastal fashions would not set Christians apart from Muslims. The other reason was simpler. Settlers tended to procure their domestic servants on arrival at the coast. In contrast, missionaries tended to find their domestic servants in the rural locations of their mission stations, further from coastal cultures and fashions.

The clothing fashions of *boi*, combined with their flamboyant performance, suggest that *boi* were making claims to belonging to a coastal sphere of civilisation that, European rule notwithstanding, continued to be Arabocentric (Glassman's term).[154] *Boi* identified themselves as 'Swahili' in the 1910s and 1920s, which is a sign of their aspiration to civility and elite status. According to mission sources, domestic servants on safari and in the town would parade themselves around to admiring women in their *kanzu* and fez. For example,

---

[151] 'Old Boys', *African Tidings*, March 1906.
[152] Also known as a 'slouch hat'. It is wide-brimmed and associated with military uniform in the nineteenth century.
[153] Strangely, in 1887 Nasibu was working as a teacher and describes himself as an evangelist. However, in the 1927 obituary he was described as a messenger for the mission. Henry Nasibu, 'News from Misozwe by a Native Evangelist', *Central Africa*, July 1887; 'Charles Nasibu, a Faithful Servant', *African Tidings*, 1910; O. D., 'Henry Nasibu', *Central Africa*, March 1927.
[154] Glassman, *War of Words, War of Stones: Racial Thought and Violence in Colonial Zanzibar*, 38.

George William Mallender made this observation of the behaviour of wage-earners (including hire slaves) in Zanzibar in 1896:

> There is no idea of saving, when a workman in Zanzibar town, a Mohammedan, has worked for, say three months and has saved a little money, he will put on his best clothes and strut about the street just like the Arabs do, and this will go on until his money has all gone when he will go to work again and repeat the same over again. This is their idea of enjoyment, to be a swell about the streets if only for a few weeks at a time.[155]

Joelson made similar observations but noted a disjuncture, or a sudden fall from grandeur, because, 'an hour later he is once more content to peel potatoes or to make the master's bed'. Joelson also noted that although *boi* would wear 'handsome Arab sandals', they would have to remove them before entering the presence of their master.[156]

There is tension here between the social respect and servile status that *uboi* conjures up. Domestic servants had to counter their servility, which could undermine their claims to respectability. *Boi* were often young men notorious among settlers and missionaries for enjoying an independent income and the 'moral dangers' that came with it.[157] This latter interpretation belongs to Europeans of the time, who believed they were, like slaves, incapable of saving money and thinking about the future. From the perspective of these domestic servants, the fact that they may have been spending their wages on women, rather than their kin, tells a story of a departure from communal and kinship obligations. All this being said, the sources I draw upon probably exaggerated the extent to which male wage-earners sought to escape kin-based responsibilities. Indeed, if they did fail to save, this may have been precisely because they spent money on kin, in addition to other forms of generosity.

The ostentation and public performance were to some extent a compensation for the fact that they were unable to establish and control households, given their travelling lifestyle and need to constantly be available in a European household. Servility characterised *uboi* and at times this posed a contradiction to the perks of the job and the status it entailed. Domestic servants' way of life was fractured and so they routinely compartmentalised different aspects of

---

[155] George William Mallender, 'Missionary life in Central Africa' (Journal, 1896), A1 (4) B, UMArch.

[156] Joelson, *The Tanganyika Territory, Formerly German East Africa: Characteristics and Potentialities*, 157.

[157] Missionaries frequently complained that *boi* and teachers alike spent their wages on themselves, leaving their wives and families to fend for themselves. E.g. J. Zanzibar to Duncan Travers, Mkunazini, 2 March 1904, A1 (13), 200, UMArch.

their lives. At work they had to serve their employers, but in public they sought to project a very opulent persona.

Conclusion

Evidently, the meaning of *uboi* changed dramatically over the period discussed here, and between different contexts. Within the mission, initially children, who were usually displaced and kinless in one way or another, worked as domestic servants. In some ways, this hardly differed from child slavery. However, the patronage, pursuit of knowledge, and, if lucky, the winning of cash currency and gifts, were important benefits that may have aided an individual in their search for a better life. There is little evidence of the incorporation of these children into mission households as fictive kin, which sets this labour style apart from an 'economy of affection', to use Goran Hayden's turn of phrase.[158] The European-dominated and culturally exceptional nature of mission households meant that despite their domestic responsibilities, these young workers had no chance of being absorbed in the manner of junior dependants elsewhere.

Instead, over time domestic service became at least a potential gateway into a variety of wage-earning professions, both in the mission and beyond it. Male domestic servants in the mission moved on from their original roles to become teachers, medical assistants and priests. Others remained domestic servants, but changed employers, thus leaving the mission. The mission was a crucial space in which knowledge of European domesticity and domestic service was shared at an early date, enabling domestic servants to enter a labour market beyond it.

Nevertheless, the mission-trained domestic servants of the early twentieth century drew upon coastal cultures as much as they did mission cultures. They were, after all, aspiring to become a version of *waungwana*, coastal freemen. Within their own households, missionaries tried to control what their servants wore, and demonstrated that they were at variance with coastal culture outside of the mission. But the possibility of moving on from the mission to the wider labour market undermined their efforts and ultimately reflects the missionaries' lack of control. In conclusion, the emergence of a professional *uboi* identity from the unpaid student-servants of the nineteenth century reflects both missionaries' changing strategies and requirements, and employees' struggles for status.

---

[158] Hyden, *No Shortcuts to Progress*.

Conclusion

This study has explored the livelihood struggles of the African workers at the UMCA mission, many of whom had recently emerged from a background of slavery. For the period that this study covers, the mission offered livelihood opportunities that did not just serve as vocational training, but as survival for many African children, women and men. As we have seen, during most of the 1864–1926 period, the formal education that the mission offered was not necessarily seen as the primary tool that it would later become for overcoming livelihood and status struggles. Often, markers of coastal sophistication, such as clothing or knowledge of Swahili, had greater social currency, while the coast remained a prime source of paid employment, often preferable to conditions offered by the mission. The focus in the scholarly literature on the central role of missions in fostering the emergence of an educated African elite that would, over time, challenge colonialism and inherit the colonial state, has however tended to overshadow the fact that in 1900 it was not clear that formal mission education would become so widespread and desirable and could be crucial to securing a good livelihood.[1] In short, from the 1860s to the 1910s, the mission was initially a space in which people could – often inventively – make a living through employment and patronage. Although not all African workers in the mission were Christian, most Christians were mission employees (usually teachers) and their families. For those who were both workers and Christians, being Christian was, in important ways, a livelihood.

---

[1] John Iliffe, *A Modern History of Tanganyika* (Cambridge: Cambridge University Press, 1979); Derek R. Peterson, *Creative Writing: Translation, Bookkeeping, and the Work of Imagination in Colonial Kenya* (Portsmouth, NH: Heinemann, 2004). Frederick Cooper and Geiger are examples of authors who acknowledge that decolonisation was not only driven by educated elites' activity but also by uneducated subalterns: Frederick Cooper, *Colonialism in Question: Theory, Knowledge, History* (Berkeley, CA: University of California Press, 2005); Susan Geiger, *TANU Women: Gender and Culture in the Making of Tanganyikan Nationalism, 1955–1965* (Portsmouth, NH; Oxford: Heinemann; James Currey, 1997).

Concomitantly, mission stations were continually sites of contestation that served changing purposes. During the 1870s, the mission station in Magila was focused on surviving physically and politically, as the region was politically unstable and prone to slave-raiding and violence. Several chiefs converted to Christianity and in doing so, claimed mission allegiance, though their impact on mission development was short-lived as most of them died or lost power under German rule in the 1890s. A more enduring impact was made by child-pawns who were traded to the mission by chiefs. Notably, Rev. Samuel Sehoza and Rev. Petro Limo – who were both child dependants (probably slaves) gifted to the mission by a chief (Semnkai) in the early stages of conversion – became some of the leading agents of UMCA's history in Magila. Although their transition to the mission severed the ties they had to Semnkai, they went on to create their own social networks as Christian priests who held social authority. At this time, then, education was important to only a small number of dependents bereft of alternatives to allegiance to the mission, while the mission itself was an involuntary participant in densely networked, fractious politics that involved guns, rituals, slavery and relations to the coast.

Meanwhile, in the 1860s and 1870s in Zanzibar, the first cohorts of ex-slaves were being brought to the mission. At this early stage, most ex-slaves remained in the mission rather than venturing to live and work among the townspeople, partly for fear of re-enslavement. Some ex-slaves were sent to mission stations on the mainland, either to supplement the mission's labour force (as in Magila) or to populate ex-slave settlements (as in Masasi). Selected young female ex-slaves, in whom female missionaries saw potential, were thoroughly trained in English domesticity. Missionaries selected young male ex-slaves to be educated and eventually become teachers and priests. The mission, then, faced struggles also in Zanzibar and, as on the mainland, its support base was limited to the displaced people who lacked alternatives. Nevertheless, this was a time of missionary optimism as they hoped to have established a cohort of educated ex-slave followers who would one day be ready to take up the missionaries' project. Compared to the mainland, the political and security context in Zanzibar was much less volatile, with British influence on the Sultans securing a fairly safe, if not exactly hospitable, climate for the mission.

It is worth considering this phase, before the emergence of education as the defining benefit of interaction with the mission, a bit further. In both Zanzibar and Magila, then, the missionaries found themselves playing the role of patron, and competing with many other potential patrons. There were changes as colonialism encroached: in Magila in the 1880s and 1890s, settled children, ones who had parents living locally and were not displaced, were coming to the mission school. The anxieties among parents about their children's involvement with the mission conveys how missionaries must have seemed quite similar to local power brokers as they were both interested in acquiring children as followers. Missionaries even gave these students items, particularly clothes, such as *kanzu* and *visibau*, which were markers of coastal respectability. This caused parents and children much concern as they suspected missionaries would expect to keep the children as hostages or slaves.[2] This concern was compounded by the fact that mission students were also the missionaries' domestic servants. The blurred lines between servitude and education in the mission were the beginning of a complex social history of domestic service, in which the mission became a reluctant and poorly reputed contributor to a labour market beyond its control.

Education and the Mission

From the late 1920s, it had become a well-worn colonial trope across Sub-Saharan Africa that, '[t]he African is everywhere more and more awaking to the advantages of education and beginning to desire to have it.'[3] In an English writing practice essay from 1932, a student in a Magila mission school declared that he was going to be a teacher because he wanted, 'to have a splendid life'.[4] Of course, people were always in search of a better life, but by the late 1920s, formal education was considered the fundamental building block to securing one. The importance of education, then, emerged soon after the transition to British rule in Tanganyika.

In the late colonial period, after the years covered here, oral history evidence makes it clear that of all the themes that emerged during interviews, education – for both men and women – was the most obviously important. For instance, Canon Samuel Sepeku recalled his father telling him that: 'Education was the only important inheritance from our parents; not money or other kinds of wealth. Our father valued education more than riches. He promised to educate us to highest possible level. He pressed that notion upon us and we repeated same message to our children.'[5]

Likewise, John Raymond Ngovi echoed what many of my respondents had noted, that in his parents' generation, a considerable number of people joined the church with hopes of receiving education, believing it would offer them

---

[2] 'Post Bag', *Central Africa*, October 1897.
[3] Rev. G. N. Bacon, 'The High Leigh Conference', *Central Africa*, November 1924.
[4] H. Hay Wilson, 'About Kiwanda', *Central Africa*, January 1932.
[5] '*Elimu ilikuwa ndio kitu pekee cha muhimu tulichorithi kutoka kwa wazazi wetu sio pesa au mali nyingine. Baba yetu alithamini elimu kuliko utajiri. Alituahidi kutusomesha hadi kiwango cha juu tutakachoweza kufikia. Daima alisisitiza wazo hilo, na sisi tumerudia wazo hilo kwa watoto wetu.*' Canon Sepeku, interview by Zuhura Mohammed, Dar es Salaam, 29 October 2014.

socio-economic opportunity.[6] Respondents wholeheartedly emphasised how central education was as part of the mission's gift to the people and the basis for *'maendeleo'* ('progress' or 'development'). Not only was education presented as something essential to personal success, it was a way of establishing personhood. In fact, respondents mentioning members of their families would summarise who they were according to what level of education they received.

The meanings of mission education for its recipients during the period covered by this book were also gendered in complicated ways. At this time, young female children rarely interacted with the mission in Magila on the mainland, except during times of famine. In contrast, the girls' school in Mbweni, Zanzibar, was growing. However, it was also clear that the girls of Mbweni faced future marriages and livelihoods that posed significant potential dangers at worst and compromised their autonomy at best, because these young women lacked the security of kinship. Equally, missionaries increasingly sidelined the educated male ex-slaves in Zanzibar in favour of the freeborn 'voluntary' students of the mission stations on the mainland, especially by the 1890s. Yet, ironically, greater numbers of male students from the mainland travelling to Zanzibar for an education reinforced the association between the education they provided and coastal culture, with its standards of sophistication quite alien to the missionaries. Even so, as I have shown, people were circumspect about these Zanzibar-educated individuals and what many viewed as their tendency towards arrogant behaviour.

Arguably, with missionaries increasingly frustrated by their attempts to provide vocational training to ex-slaves or re-socialise them into their notion of 'yeomen', education emerged as the mission's main attraction and the project to Christiainise freed slaves was no longer spoken of. For the adult ex-slaves who did not receive a mission education, the opportunities the mission offered them for social mobility were increasingly limited to no more than a basic livelihood. Thus, the more enterprising among them endeavoured to centre their lives in the town. The result was that, by the early 1900s, the Mbweni *shamba* was a home to elderly and sick ex-slaves who made a living as best they could. For more educated ex-slaves, by contrast, networks created with fellow students in the mission helped them as they moved outside it.

After the First World War and with British colonialism, the mission rose to prominence as a place of education. From this point, people carried knowledge and experience away with them from the mission to make a living elsewhere, in keeping with the well-known narrative of mission and 'modernity'. Throughout this period, the mission did not create unified progressive

---

[6] John Raymond Ngovi, interview by Zuhura Mohammed, Kisiwani, 23 October 2014.

communities. Instead, the mission provided resources for status struggles. The definitions of high status in these struggles continued to draw on a variety of sources, not all of them European or Christian.

The Mission, livelihoods and social identity

The embattled, far from hegemonic status of the cultural markers the mission represented during this period challenges the notion of 'colonisation of consciousness' and forces us to rethink what belonging and authority meant to those interacting with the mission.[7] In Magila and Zanzibar up to 1926, the mission was a place where one could develop social identities, livelihoods and obtain certain types of knowledge. However, it was not self-contained and neither did it sufficiently fulfil all a person's social and economic needs. Everybody had to interact with people, spaces and ideas that were not defined by the mission. This was not only on social grounds, but also simply to make ends meet. UMCA teachers and priests, who were those most likely to depend upon the mission for the means to support themselves, had to engage in subsistence agriculture as the payments they received from missionaries and congregations were not enough to establish a livelihood.

Moreover, most Christians took part in practices and livelihoods that the missionaries did not condone. Livelihoods, after all, were not solely about survival and economic opportunity. They also reflected personhood; the way people saw their individual selves in relation to others. They represented aspirations publicly and created social distinctions.[8] Making a living was closely connected to decisions people made about interacting with and being part of various kinds of social networks. Indeed, well-developed social networks helped a person make a living and provided opportunities to pursue different kinds of livelihoods. It worked the other way around, too, that changes in livelihoods could prompt changes in the way people went about making, maintaining and losing their part in social networks.

Neither Christianity, nor the mission as a space, offered anyone a complete identity. That missionaries struggled to impose their standards of behaviour and that African converts refashioned missionary influence in multiple ways, has often been recognised in the scholarship.[9] Nonetheless, it is useful to con-

---

[7] 'Colonisation of consciousness' as in Jean Comaroff and John L. Comaroff, *Of Revelation and Revolution: The Dialectics of Modernity on a South African Frontier*, vol. 2 (Chicago; London: University of Chicago Press, 1997).

[8] Just as Guyer suggested: Jane I. Guyer, 'Wealth in People and Self-Realization in Equatorial Africa', *Man*, 28, no. 2 (1 June 1993): 256.

[9] E.g. Nancy Rose Hunt, *Colonial Lexicon of Birth Ritual, Medicalization, and*

sider this not only as a reflection of divergent aims and expectations among missionaries and the people interacting with them, but also as the reflection of a layered, diverse and ever-shifting cultural context.[10] Like Christian education, so European styles of dress and comportment were not yet clearly hegemonic during the period considered here. The choice of cultural reference points and elaboration of cultural allegiances among the mission's dependants and interlocutors was a fluid process, anxiously perched between economic needs and social aspirations.

As discussed in the Introduction, the scholarship published to date on the mission has rarely focused on the economic circumstances and livelihoods of Africans involved with the mission. In rectifying this inattention, it is clear that economic needs and aims were inseparable from social and cultural ones. For the often marginal, displaced people discussed here, livelihoods, status struggles and personhood could be pursued through the elaboration of varied cultural allegiances. What I have attempted to do is to explore how Africans utilised the mission in pursuit of a variety of aims, not all of them 'modern', and how they created networks in the mission in their pursuit of security, livelihood and social status. In this process, it has become evident that the history of the UMCA in Magila and Zanzibar also forms part of the history of cosmopolitanism in the Western Indian Ocean, which has been much discussed in recent years.[11] During the period discussed here, the mission was in effect another actor among many peddling their cultural wares.

By the end of the period discussed here, the ascendancy of Christian, European-infused cultural forms was just becoming discernible, in connection with the emerging importance of mission education. One cause of this change is evident from the transformation colonisation wrought on the political context of the mission in Magila. The relations to the coast and the Sultan, which had been so important in the late precolonial period, fade from sight entirely when German control was established. Yet in other ways, both coastal culture

---

Mobility in the Congo (Durham, NC: Duke University Press, 1999); Peterson, *Creative Writing: Translation, Bookkeeping, and the Work of Imagination in Colonial Kenya*.

[10] Taking inspiration from John D. Y. Peel, *Religious Encounter and the Making of the Yoruba* (Bloomington, IN: Indiana University Press, 2000).

[11] Matthew S. Hopper, *Slaves of One Master: Globalization and Slavery in Arabia in the Age of Empire* (New Haven, CT: Yale University Press, 2015); Kai Kresse, *Struggling with History: Islam and Cosmopolitanism in the Western Indian Ocean* (New York: Columbia University Press, 2008); Felicitas Becker and Joel Cabrita, 'Introduction: Performing Citizenship and Enacting Exclusion on Africa's Indian Ocean Littoral', *The Journal of African History*, 55, no. 02 (2014): 161–71 (and remainder of this issue).

and indigenous ritual showed enormous staying power. Moreover, at times these reference points co-existed with little conflict, at least when European missionaries were not paying attention. African Christians compartmentalised their social lives and ritual expressions. Inasmuch as the mission was a harbinger of modernity, then, it was a very composite modernity. Rather than being broken, the former cultural hegemony of the Zanzibar Sultanate was compartmentalised into particular niches.

In this early period, there were different, sometimes competing or co-existing modernities. The mission itself at times reinforced notions of sophistication derived from coastal influences and more typically associated with Islam, as with the dress styles it encouraged in African dependents. Missionaries were awkwardly inserted into coastal cultures and sought to draw leverage from association with both European-derived notions of modernity and Arabocentric ones. Often, they found the latter more influential. In fact, missionaries had limited control and had to defer to coastal hegemony politically and culturally. The mission was not culturally hegemonic, and it was often peripheral to the Africans who crossed its paths, and there was a spectrum of identities that accompanied the relative states of dependence and independence that Africans developed in relation to the mission.

This early period of mission history was different from the later periods scholars usually focus upon because formal institutional education only became widely important by the 1920s. The fact that education came to be seen as arguably the most positive and important output of mission work obscures the central role of labour, especially domestic service in schools, in mission stations. Struggles for livelihood and status were not only managed with education but through employment, patronage and political alliances. In other words, the mission could be creatively drawn upon for livelihood and status not only through formal institutional education but through many other forms of association. Of course, with figures like Sehoza and Limo in the mission elite, the significance of education did exist long before the 1920s, just very minimally. For these kinds of mission affiliates, schools were major sources of personal networks in a diverse and disunited mission community. For the Africans who worked as builders and domestic servants, life trajectories were more varied, difficult to trace, and their networks tended to spread much further beyond the mission boundaries as they pieced together various forms of livelihood.

Appendices

1 Chronology of UMCA founding

1857	David Livingstone's speech in Senate House, Cambridge
1858	'Oxford and Cambridge Mission to Central Africa' established
1861	First bishop Charles MacKenzie, consecrated in Cape Town
1862	Death of bishop Charles MacKenzie near Shire River
1863	Second bishop, William Tozer, consecrated in London
1864	Mission headquarters moved to Zanzibar from the Shire River region
1866	Kiungani school founded
1867	The first UMCA visit to the Bondei region
1868	Charles Argentine Alington established a base in Bondei
1870	John Swedi and George Farajallah made subdeacons
1871	Mbweni land purchased
1875	First permanent mission in Bondei region (Magila)
1876	UMCA station established in Rovuma region, southeast Tanzania
1885	First permanent mission in Lake Nyasa
1864	Bishop Tozer arrived in Zanzibar and formed the diocese of Zanzibar
1874	Freed slave settlement established in Mbweni
1895	Diocese of Nyasaland formed out of the Diocese of Zanzibar
1910	Diocese of Northern Rhodesia formed
1926	Diocese of Masasi formed out of the Diocese of Zanzibar

2 General chronology for Zanzibar and Magila

1877	Famine in Magila
1884–85	Famine in Magila
1888	German occupation of the coast and Arab rising
1889	German protectorate proclaimed
1890	Heligoland–Zanzibar treaty between Germany and England
1891	First German governor appointed
1892	Famine in Magila, Masaai suffering in particular
1893	Usambara Railway opened to Pongwe
1894–96	Famine in Magila
1896	First African UMCA conference without Europeans
1897	Hut-tax introduced
1899–1901	Famine in Magila
1902	Usambara Railway opened to Korogwe
1910–11	Famine in Magila
1916	General Smuts defeated Germans at Moshi, occupation begins
1920	Smallpox in Magila
1920	Second Kikuyu conference
1934	Famine in Magila

3 African power-brokers and the mission elite

Austini Sipindu	From Umba. Converted to Christianity, d. 1883
Barghash bin Said	Sultan of Zanzibar, 1870–88
Cecil Majaliwa	Ex-slave, ordained 1886
Henry Semnkai	Chief from Umba. Baptised 1884
Hugh Peter Kayamba	Paramount chief, 1931
John Kirk	Consul General at Zanzibar, 1873–87
John Swedi	Ex-slave, ordained 1870
Kibanga	Muslim Kilindi chief based in Bulwa
Kimweri ya Nyumbai	Kilindi-Shambaai leader

Majid bin Said   Sultan of Zanzibar, 1856–70
Manfred Mabundo   Ordained c.1904, d. 1926
Martin Kayamba   Colonial civil servant, 1891–1940
Michael Kifungiwe   Kilindi chief. Baptised 1881
Peter Sudi   Ex-slave, mission employee
Petro Limo   Ex-slave, ordained 1893
Samuel Sehoza   Ordained 1894
Segao   Power-broker, Umba
Semboja   Power-broker, Usambara

4 Bishops of the UMCA

1861–62	Charles MacKenzie	Died in office	Diocese of Zanzibar
1863–73	William Tozer	Resigned	
1874–82	Edward Steere	Died in office	
1883–94	Charles Smythies	Died in office	
1895–1900	William Richardson	Resigned	
1901–08	John Hine	Resigned	
1908–24	Frank Weston	Died in office	
1925–43	Thomas Birley	Resigned	
1926–44	Vincent Lucas	Resigned, died soon after	Diocese of Masasi

5 Other significant UMCA missionaries

Caroline D. M. Thackeray   Arrived 1877, d. 1926
Christopher Fixsen   Arrived 1911, d. 1915
Cyril C. Frewer   Active as missionary 1904–10
Dora S. Yarnton Mills   Arrived 1879
Godfrey Dale   Arrived 1889
Herbert A. B. Wilson   d. 1882
Herbert W. Woodward   Arrived 1875
John Farler   Active as missionary 1875–94

Bibliography

Interviews

Nasoro Ali. Interview by Irene Mashasi. Zanzibar, 12 September 2014.
George Chambai. Interview by Elias Mutani. Mkuzi, 22 April 2016.
Ernest Chambo. Interview by Zuhura Mohammed. Muheza, 19 October 2014.
Durham Kaleza. Interview by Irene Mashasi. Zanzibar, 10 September 2014.
William Kamna. Interview by Michelle Liebst. Dar es Salaam, 23 September 2014.
Anthony Mabundo. Interview by Zuhura Mohammed. Handeni, 8 October 2014.
John Makange (pseudonym). Interview by Zuhura Mohammed. Magila, 23 October 2014.
John Geldart Mhina. Interview by Zuhura Mohammed. Magila, 15 October 2014.
———. Interview by Zuhura Mohammed. Magila, 17 October 2014.
Tereza Mwakanjuki. Interview by Irene Mashasi. Zanzibar, 19 September 2014.
Canon Mwamazi. Interview by Zuhura Mohammed. Dar es Salaam, 29 October 2014.
Josephine Mungayao. Interview by Zuhura Mohammed. Tanga, 21 October 2014.
Esther Musa. Interview by Irene Mashasi. Zanzibar, 10 November 2014.
Emmanuel Ngoma. Interview by Zuhura Mohammed. Korogwe, 2 October 2014.
John Raymond Ngovi. Interview by Zuhura Mohammed. Kisiwani, 23 October 2014.
George Salim. Interview by Zuhura Mohammed. Dar es Salaam, 3 November 2014.
Vincent Semkuruto. Interview by Zuhura Mohammed. Dar es Salaam, 30 October 2014.
Canon Sepeku. Interview by Zuhura Mohammed. Dar es Salaam, 29 October 2014.
Bibi Shishi. Interview by Irene Mashasi. Zanzibar, 17 September 2014.
Margaret Sudi. Interview by Irene Mashasi. Zanzibar, 12 September 2014.
Sylvester Tayari. Interview by Irene Mashasi. Zanzibar, 16 September 2014.

Gerrard Yambi. Interview by Zuhura Mohammed. Tanga, 25 October 2014.
Edith Yambi. Interview by Zuhura Mohammed. Tanga, 25 October 2014.

Primary sources

Manuscripts

USPG archives, Bodleian Library, Oxford
A1 (3) A, Bishop Steere, 1863–82.
A1 (3) B, Bishop Steere; newspaper cuttings, 1865–92.
A1 (3) C, Bishop Steere printed leaflets etc., 1859–94.
A1 (4) A-B letters, misc., 1870–88.
A1 (5) A Bishop Smythies, 1883–94.
A1 (6) A-B, Letters, misc., 1876–1926.
A1 (7) Bishop Richardson and letters misc. (Zanzibar) c.1895–1910.
A1 (8) Bishop Richardson and letters misc. (Zanzibar).
A1 (13), Bishop Hine (Zanzibar), 1901–25.
A1 (17) A, Revd. Weston, 1898–1934.
A1 (17) B, Bishop Weston, 1908–24.
A1 (18) A, Bishop Weston-printed pamphlets etc. 1908–24.
A1 (18) B, Bishop Weston-printed pamphlets etc. 1908–24.
A1 (21) Letters, misc. (Zanzibar), 1908–24.
A1 (22) Letters, misc. (Zanzibar), 1908–24.
C2, UMCA newspaper cuttings, pamphlets, etc. c.1873–1958.
D4, Polygamy, Slavery and Islam, c.1871–1910.
TC C1, Reverend W Forbes Capel Correspondence with UMCA committee regarding mission work in Zanzibar, 1884.
TC E30, Report to parliament on slavery with related correspondence, 1870.

East Africana Library, University of Dar es Salaam
UMCA Masasi Logbook, 149.

Zanzibar National Archives (ZNA). CB1/5-9.
CB 1-1 Bishop Tozer's Journals and letters: hand written, with annex volumes, 1863–65.
CB 1-2. Island Out-stations logbook, 1915–21.
CB 1-3. Deeds of Freedom, 1874-96.

CB 1-4. Bishop Tozer and Steere: documents, letters, memorandum to and from various people, includes plan of the Christian burial cemetery, 1866–87
CB 1-5. Central African Mission Diary: includes the arrival of Bishop Tozer and Bishop Steere in Zanzibar, 1863–88.
CB 1-6. Central African mission diary, 1888–1908.
CB 1-7. Central African Mission diary: includes information on the Boys industrial House, Ziwani, 1901–10.
CB 1-8. Central African Mission diary: includes info on Mbweni Mkunazini Girls Schools. 1919– 46.
CB 1-9. Central African Mission Diary, 1922–32.

Periodicals

Mambo Leo (Dar es Salaam: Tanganyika National Newspapers, 1927–62).
African Tidings (London: 1892–).
Central Africa: A Monthly Record of the Universities' Mission to Central Africa (London: 1883–1964).
The Church Socialist (London: 1912–).
Habari za Mwezi: Bonde na Zigua (Magila: Kanisa la Msalaba Mtakatifu, 1895–1907).
The Nineteenth Century and After (London: Marston & Co., 1901–50).
Mission Life (London: 1866–85).
Tanganyika Notes and Records (Dar es Salaam: Tanzania Society, 1936–82).

Published texts

Anderson-Morshead, A. E. M. *The History of the Universities' Mission to Central Africa 1859–1896*. London: Universities Mission to Central Africa, 1897.
———. *The History of the Universities' Mission to Central Africa, 1859–1909*. London: Universities' Mission to Central Africa, 1909.
Burton, Sir Richard Francis. *Zanzibar; city, island and coast*. Vol. 2. 2 vols. London: Tinsley Brothers, 1872.
Cave, Basil S. 'The End of Slavery in Zanzibar and British East Africa', *African Affairs*, 9, no. 33 (1909): 24
Christie, James. 'Slavery in Zanzibar as It Is'. In *The East African Slave Trade, and the Measures Proposed for Its Extinction as Viewed by Residents in Zanzibar*, edited by Edward Steere. London: Harrison, 1871.
———. *Cholera Epidemics in East Africa, from 1821 till 1872*. London, 1876.
Colomb, Captain Philip Howard. *Slave-Catching in the Indian Ocean: A Record of Naval Experiences*. London: Longmans Green and Co., 1873.

Farler, J. P. 'The Usambara Country in East Africa'. *Proceedings of the Royal Geographical Society and Monthly Record of Geography* 1, no. 2 (1 February 1879): 81–97.

Farler, Ven. J. P. 'Native Routes in East Africa from Pangani to the Masai Country and the Victoria Nyanza'. *Proceedings of the Royal Geographical Society and Monthly Record of Geography* 4, no. 12 (1 December 1882): 730–42. doi:10.2307/1800695.

Fraser, Captain H. A., William Tozer, and James Christie. *The East African Slave Trade, and the Measures Proposed for Its Extinction as Viewed by Residents in Zanzibar*. Edited by Edward Steere. London: Harrison, 1871.

Frere, Henry Bartle Edward. *Eastern Africa as a Field for Missionary Labour. Four Letters to the Archbishop of Canterbury, Etc.* London, 1874.

Gregory, Reverend Francis Ambrose. 'Madagascar'. *The Mission Field*. 2 December 1879.

Heanley, R. M. *A Memoir of Edward Steere: Third Missionary Bishop in Central Africa*. London: Office of the Universities' Mission to Central Africa, 1898.

Ingrams, William Harold. *Zanzibar: Its History and Its People*. London: H. F. & G. Witherby, 1931. New edition, London: Stacey International, 2007.

Joelson, Ferdinand Stephen. *The Tanganyika Territory, Formerly German East Africa: Characteristics and Potentialities*. London: T. Fisher Unwin, 1920.

Johnson, William Percival. *My African Reminiscences, 1875–1895*. London: Universities' Mission to Central Africa, 1926.

Johnston, Keith. 'Notes of a Trip from Zanzibar to Usambara, in February and March, 1879'. *Proceedings of the Royal Geographical Society and Monthly Record of Geography* 1, no. 9 (1 September 1879): 545–58.

Jones-Bateman, Percy L. 'What Becomes of Your Mission Boys When They Leave You?' *Central Africa*, 1890.

Kitabu cha Ibada za Kanuni na kuhudumu sakramenti pamoja na kawaida za kanisa ilivyo desturi ya kanisa la unguja [The Book of Principle Services and Ministering the Sacraments of the Zanzibar Church]. Society of SS Peter & Paul, 1928.

Krapf, Johann Ludwig. *A Dictionary of the Swahili Language*. London: Trübner and Co., 1882.

———, and Ernst Georg Ravenstein. *Travels, Researches, and Missionary Labours, during an Eighteen Years' Residence in Eastern Africa*. London: Trübner and Co., 1860.

Lanchester, Henry Vaughan. *Zanzibar: A Study in Tropical Town Planning*. Cheltenham: Ed. J. Burrow, 1923.

Livingstone, David and Charles Livingstone. *Narrative of an Expedition to the Zambesi and Its Tributaries; and of the Discovery of the Lakes Shirwa and Nyassa. 1858–1864. With Map and Illustrations.* London: John Murray, Albemarle Street, 1865.

Lyne, Robert Nunez. *Zanzibar in Contemporary Times: a short history of the southern east in the nineteenth century.* London: Hurst and Blackett, Ltd., 1905.

Mabundo, Manfred. *An African David and Jonathan. The Autobiography of Padre Manfred Mabundo.* London: Universities' Mission to Central Africa, 1927.

Madan, A. C., ed. *English-Swahili Vocabulary. Compiled from the works of the late Bishop Steere and from other sources.* London: Christian Knowledge Society, 1884.

———. *Kiungani, Or, Story and History from Central Africa.* London: G. Bell and Sons, 1887.

Maples, Chauncy, and Ellen Gilbert Maples Cook. *Journals and Papers of Chauncy Maples: Late Bishop of Likoma, Lake Nyasa, Africa.* Lond. &c., 1899.

Mhina, John. *Historia ya Magila Msalabani 1848–2012: Mlango wa Kuingia Kanisa la Anglikana Tanzania Bara*, 2012.

Milner, Lord. 'No. 1 Despatch to the Governor of the East Africa Protectorate'. Parliamentary paper. Despatch to the Governor of the East Africa Protectorate Relating to Native Labour, and Papers Connected Therewith. Downing Place, London, 22 July 1920.

Pearse, Francis Eling. *Africa on the Hilltops.* London: Universities' Mission to Central Africa, 1926.

'Report of Education Conference 1925, Together with the Report of the Committee for the Standardisation of the Swahili Language'. Tanganyika Territory. Dar es Salaam: Government printer, 1926.

Rowley, Henry. *Twenty Years in Central Africa: Being the Story of the Universities' Mission to Central Africa, from Its Commencement under Bishop Mackenzie to the Present Time.* London: W. Gardner, Darton, 1881.

Sayers, Gerald Fleming, ed. *The Handbook of Tanganyika.* London: Macmillan & Co, 1930.

Schapera, Isaac. *The Khoisan Peoples of South Africa.* London: George Routledge & Sons, 1934.

Smith, H. Maynard. *Frank, Bishop of Zanzibar: Life of Frank Weston, 1871–1924.* London: Society for Promoting Christian Knowledge, 1926.

Speke, John Hanning. *Journal of the Discovery of the Source of the Nile.* Second Edition. Edinburgh; London: W. Blackwood and sons, 1864.

Steere, Edward. *Some Account of the Town of Zanzibar* (London: Charles Cull, Houghton Street, Strand, 1869), 11.Steere, Bishop Edward. *Central African Mission, Its Present State and Prospects*. London: Rivingtons, 1873.

———. *The Free Village in Yao Land*. London: Universities' Mission to Central Africa, 1879.

———. *Collections for a Handbook of the Nyamwezi Language: As Spoken at Unyanyembe*. London: Society for Promoting Christian Knowledge, 1885.

———, and Arthur Cornwallis Madan. *A handbook of the Swahili language, as spoken at Zanzibar*. London Society for promoting Christian knowledge, 1894.

Stigand, Captain Chauncey H. *The Land of Zinj: Being an Account of British East Africa, Its Ancient History and Present Inhabitants*. London: Constable & Co, 1913.

Tanganyika Territory Blue Book for the year ended 31st December 1921. Dar es Salaam: The Government Printer, 1922.

Tanganyika Territory Blue Book for the year ended 31st December 1922. Dar es Salaam: The Government Printer, 1923.

Tanganyika Territory Blue Book for the year ended 31st December 1923. Dar es Salaam: The Government Printer, 1926.

Tanganyika Territory Blue Book for the year ended 31st December 1924. Dar es Salaam: The Government Printer, 1926.

Tanganyika Territory Blue Book for the year ended 31st December 1925. Dar es Salaam: The Government Printer, 1926.

Tanganyika Territory Blue Book for the year ended 31st December 1926. Dar es Salaam: The Government Printer, 1930.

Tanganyika Territory Blue Book for the year ended 31st December 1927. Dar es Salaam: The Government Printer, 1930.

Thomson, Joseph. *To the Central African Lakes and Back*. London: Sampson, Low, Marston, Searle & Rivington, 1881.

Waller, Horace. *Heligoland for Zanzibar, Or, One Island Full of Free Men for Two Full of Slaves*. London: Edward Stanford, 1893.

Ward, Gertrude. *Letters from East Africa: 1895–1897*. London: Office of the Universities' Mission to Central Africa, 1899.

———. *Father Woodward of UMCA: A Memoir*. London: Universities' Mission to Central Africa, 1927.

Webb, R. *A Visit to Africa, 1896*. London: Universities' Mission to Central Africa, 1897.

Weston, Frank. *The Black Slaves of Prussia: An Open Letter to General Smuts*. London: Universities' Mission to Central Africa, 1917.

———. 'Africa: And the Blight of Commercialism'. *The Nineteenth Century and After*, 87, June 1920.

———. *The Serfs of Great Britain: Being a Sequel to The Black Slaves of Prussia*. London, 1920.
William Carmichael Porter: Missionary. Westminster: Universities' Mission to Central Africa, 1910.
Younghusband, Ethel. *Glimpses of East Africa and Zanzibar*. London: J. Long, 1910.

Secondary sources

Published books and chapters

Abrahams, R. G. *The Nyamwezi Today: A Tanzanian People in the 1970s*. Cambridge: Cambridge University Press, 1981.
Agyemang, Fred M. *A Century with Boys: The Story of Middle Boarding Schools in Ghana, 1867–1967*. Accra: Waterville Pub. House, 1967.
Ally, Shireen. 'Slavery, Servility, Service: The Cape of Good Hope, the Natal Colony and Witwatersrand, 1652–1914'. In *Towards a Global History of Domestic and Caregiving Workers*, edited by Dirk Hoerder, Elise van Nederveen Meerkerk, and Silke Neunsinger, 254–70. Leiden; Boston: Brill, 2015.
Askew, Kelly. *Performing the Nation: Swahili Music and Cultural Politics in Tanzania*. PAP/COM edition. Chicago: University of Chicago Press, 2002.
Austin, Gareth. *Labour, Land and Capital in Ghana: From Slavery to Free Labour in Asante, 1807–1956*. Cambridge: Cambridge University Press, 2012.
Ballantyne, Tony. *Entanglements of Empire: Missionaries, Maori, and the Question of the Body*. Auckland, New Zealand: Auckland University Press, 2015.
Bang, Anne K. *Islamic Sufi Networks in the Western Indian Ocean (c.1880–1940)*. Leiden: Brill, 2014.
Barnes, Bertram Herbert, and Janice Stein. 'Introduction: The Secularisation and Sanctification of Humanitarianism'. In *Sacred Aid: Faith and Humanitarianism*, edited by Michael Barnett and Janice Stein, 3–36. Oxford: Oxford University Press, 2012.
Bayly, C. A. *The Birth of the Modern World, 1780–1914*. Oxford: Blackwell, 2004.
Becker, Felicitas. *Becoming Muslim in Mainland Tanzania 189–-2000*. Oxford: Oxford University Press, 2008.
———. *The Politics of Poverty in Africa: Policy-Making and Development in Tanzania*. Cambridge: Cambridge University Press, 2019.

———, and P. Wenzel Geissler, eds. *Aids and Religious Practice in Africa*. Leiden: Brill, 2009.

Beidelman, Thomas O. *Colonial Evangelism: A Socio-Historical Study of an East African Mission at the Grassroots*. Bloomington, IN: Indiana University Press, 1982.

Bennett, Norman R. 'The Church Missionary Society at Mombasa'. In *Boston University Papers in African History*, edited by Jeffrey Butler, 157–94. Boston: Boston University Press, 1964.

Berg, Lawrence D., and Jani Vuolteenaho. *Critical Toponymies: The Contested Politics of Place Naming*. Farnham, Surrey: Ashgate Publishing, Ltd., 2009.

Bissell, William Cunningham. *Urban Design, Chaos, and Colonial Power in Zanzibar*. Bloomington, IN: Indiana University Press, 2011.

Bourdieu, Pierre. *Outline of a Theory of Practice*. Cambridge: Cambridge University Press, 1977.

Bradley, Emily G. *Dearest Priscilla: Letters to the Wife of a Colonial Civil Servant*. London: Max Parrish & Co., 1950.

Bravman, Bill. *Making Ethnic Ways: Communities and Their Transformations in Taita, Kenya, 1800–1950*. Oxford: James Currey, 1999.

Brennan, James R. *Taifa: Making Nation and Race in Urban Tanzania*. Athens, OH: Ohio University Press, 2012.

Bujra, Janet M. *Serving Class: Masculinity and the Feminisation of Domestic Service in Tanzania*. Edinburgh: Edinburgh University Press for the International African Institute, 2000.

Campbell, Gwyn. *An Economic History of Imperial Madagascar, 1750–1895: The Rise and Fall of an Island Empire*. Cambridge: Cambridge University Press, 2005.

Chanock, Martin. *Law, Custom, and Social Order: The Colonial Experience in Malawi and Zambia*. Portsmouth, NH: Heinemann, 1998.

Cohen, David William, Luise White, and Stephan F. Miescher. 'Introduction: Voices, Words, and African History'. In *African Words, African Voices: Critical Practices in Oral History*, edited by Luise White, Stephan F. Miescher, and David William Cohen, 1–27. Bloomington, IN: Indiana University Press, 2001.

Coldicott, Diana K. *Two Zanzibar Missionaries: Canon and Mrs A.B. Hellier of the Universities' Mission to Central Africa*. Abingdon: Anton, Hearn & Scott, 2008.

Comaroff, Jean. *Body of Power, Spirit of Resistance: The Culture and History of a South African People*. Chicago: University of Chicago Press, 2013.

Comaroff, Jean, and John L. Comaroff. *Of Revelation and Revolution: Christianity, Colonialism, and Consciousness in South Africa*. Vol. 1. Chicago, IL: University of Chicago Press, 1991.

———. 'Home-Made Hegemony: Modernity, Domesticity, and Colonialism in South Africa'. In *African Encounters with Domesticity*, edited by Karen Tranberg Hansen. New Brunswick, NJ: Rutgers University Press, 1992.

———. *Modernity and Its Malcontents: Ritual and Power in Postcolonial Africa*. Chicago, IL: University of Chicago Press, 1993.

———. *Of Revelation and Revolution: The Dialectics of Modernity on a South African Frontier*. Vol. 2. Chicago, IL; London: University of Chicago Press, 1997.

Cooper, Barbara MacGowan. *Evangelical Christians in the Muslim Sahel*. Bloomington, IN: Indiana University Press, 2006.

Cooper, Frederick. *Plantation Slavery on the East Coast of Africa*. New Haven, CT: Yale University Press, 1977.

———. *From Slaves to Squatters: Plantation Labor and Agriculture in Zanzibar and Coastal Kenya, 1890–1925*. New Haven, CT: Yale University Press, 1980.

———. *Africa since 1940: The Past of the Present*. Cambridge: Cambridge University Press, 2002.

———. *Colonialism in Question: Theory, Knowledge, History*. Berkeley, CA: University of California Press, 2005.

Coupland, Sir Reginald. *Exploitation of East Africa, 1856–1890: The Slave Trade and the Scramble; with an Introduction by Jack Simmons*, 2nd ed (London: Faber, 1968).

Daneel, M. L. *Old and New in Southern Shona Independent Churches: Church Growth-Causative Factors and Recruitment Techniques*. The Hague; Paris: Mouton De Gruyter, 1974.

Deutsch, Jan-Georg. *Emancipation without Abolition in German East Africa, c.1884–1914*. Oxford; Athens, OH: James Currey; Ohio University Press, 2006.

Dirks, Nicholas B. *Colonialism and Culture*. Ann Arbor, MI: University of Michigan Press, 1992.

Englund, Harri. 'Rethinking African Christianities: Beyond the Religion-Politics Conundrum'. In *Christianity and Public Culture in Africa*, edited by Harri Englund. Athens, OH: Ohio University Press, 2011.

Fabian, Johannes. *Language and Colonial Power: The Appropriation of Swahili in the Former Belgian Congo, 1880–1938*. Cambridge: Cambridge University Press, 1986.

Fair, Laura. *Pastimes and Politics: Culture, Community, and Identity in Post-Abolition Urban Zanzibar, 1890–1945*. Eastern African Studies. Athens, OH; Oxford: Ohio University Press; James Currey, 2001.

Fazan, S. H. *Colonial Kenya Observed: British Rule, Mau Mau and the Wind of Change*. Edited by John Lonsdale. London: I.B. Tauris, 2015.

Feierman, Steven. *Peasant Intellectuals: Anthropology and History in Tanzania*. Madison, WI: University of Wisconsin Press, 1990.
Ferguson, James. *Give a Man a Fish: Reflections on the New Politics of Distribution*. Durham, NC; London: Duke University Press, 2015.
Fields, Karen Elise. *Revival and Rebellion in Colonial Central Africa*. Portsmouth, NH: Heinemann, 1997.
Foucault, Michel. *Discipline and Punish: The Birth of the Prison*. New York: Pantheon Books, c. 1977.
Freund, Bill. *The African Worker*. Cambridge: Cambridge University Press, 1988.
———. *The Making of Contemporary Africa: The Development of African Society Since 1800*. Basingstoke: Macmillan Press, 1998.
Gaitskell, Deborah 'At Home with Hegemony? Coercion and Consent in the Education of African Girls for Domesticity in South Africa before 1910'. In *Contesting Colonial Hegemony: State and Society in Africa and India*, edited by Shula Marks and Dagmar Engels. London: British Academic Press, 1994.
Geiger, Susan. *TANU Women: Gender and Culture in the Making of Tanganyikan Nationalism, 1955–1965*. Greenwood Publishing Group, Incorporated, 1997.
Giblin, James L. *A History of the Excluded: Making Family a Refuge from State in Twentieth-Century Tanzania*. Eastern African Studies. Athens, OH: James Currey, 2005.
Glassman, Jonathon. *Feasts and Riot: Revelry, Rebellion, and Popular Consciousness on the Swahili Coast, 1856–1888*. Social History of Africa. Portsmouth, NH; London; Nairobi; Dar es Salaam: Heinemann; James Currey; EAEP; Mkuki Na Nyota, 1995.
———. 'Racial Violence, Universal History, and Echoes of Abolition in Twentieth-Century Zanzibar'. In *Abolitionism and Imperialism in Britain, Africa, and the Atlantic*, edited by Derek R. Peterson, African Studies from Cambridge, 176–80. Athens, OH: Ohio University Press, 2010.
———. *War of Words, War of Stones: Racial Thought and Violence in Colonial Zanzibar*. Bloomington, IN: Indiana University Press, 2011.
Good, Charles M. *Steamer Parish: The Rise and Fall of Missionary Medicine on an African Frontier*. Chicago, IL; London: University of Chicago Press, 2004.
Goody, Jack. 'Slavery in Time and Space'. In *Asian and African Systems of Slavery*, edited by James L. Watson. Berkeley, CA: University of California Press, 1980.
Gray, Richard. *Black Christians and White Missionaries*. New Haven, CT: Yale University Press, 1959.

Hansen, Karen Tranberg. *Distant Companions: Servants and Employers in Zambia, 1900–1985*. Ithaca, NY: Cornell University Press, 1989.

———, ed. 'Introduction: Domesticity in Africa'. In *African Encounters with Domesticity*. New Brunswick, NJ: Rutgers University Press, 1992.

Harris, Joseph E. *Repatriates and Refugees in Colonial Society: The Case of Kenya*. Washington DC: Howard University Press, 1987.

Hastings, Adrian. *The Church in Africa, 1450–1950*. Oxford: Oxford University Press, 1996.

Hine, J. E. *Days Gone by: Being Some Account of Past Years Chiefly in Central Africa*. London: J. Murray, 1924.

Hodgson, Dorothy L. *The Church of Women: Gendered Encounters between Maasai and Missionaries*. Bloomington, IN: Indiana University Press, 2005.

Holt, Thomas C. *Problem of Freedom: Race, Labor, and Politics in Jamaica and Britain, 1832–1938*. Baltimore, MD: Johns Hopkins University Press, 1992.

Hopper, Matthew S. *Slaves of One Master: Globalization and Slavery in Arabia in the Age of Empire*. New Haven, CT: Yale University Press, 2015.

Hunt, Nancy Rose. *Colonial Lexicon of Birth Ritual, Medicalization, and Mobility in the Congo*. Durham, NC: Duke University Press, 1999.

Hyden, Goran. *No Shortcuts to Progress: African Development Management in Perspective*. Berkeley; Los Angeles, CA: University of California Press, 1983.

Ibrahim, Abdullahi. 'The Birth of the Interview: The Thin and the Fat of It'. In *African Words, African Voices: Critical Practices in Oral History*, edited by Luise White, Stephan Miescher, and David William Cohen, 103–26. Bloomington, IN: Indiana University Press, 2001.

Iliffe, John. *A Modern History of Tanganyika*. Cambridge: Cambridge University Press, 1979.

———. *East African Doctors: A History of the Modern Profession*. Vol. 95. Cambridge: Cambridge University Press, 1998.

———. *Honour in African History*. Cambridge: Cambridge University Press, 2005.

———. *Tanganyika Under German Rule 1905–1912*. Cambridge: Cambridge University Press, 2009.

Kayamba, Martin. 'The Story of Martin Kayamba Mdumi, MBE, of the Bondei Tribe'. In *Ten Africans*, edited by Margery Perham, 2nd edn. London: Faber, 1963.

Kimambo, Isaria N. 'Environmental Control and Hunger: In the Mountains and Plains of Nineteenth-Century Northeastern Tanzania'. In *Custodians of the Land: Ecology & Culture in the History of Tanzania*, edited by G.

Maddox, James L. Giblin, and Isaria N. Kimambo, 71–95. Eastern African Studies. Athens, OH: James Currey, 1996.

Kollman, Paul V. *The Evangelization of Slaves and Catholic Origins in Eastern Africa*. Maryknoll, NY: Orbis Books, 2005.

Koponen, Juhani. *People and Production in Late Precolonial Tanzania: History and Structures*. Helsinki: Finnish Society of Development Studies, 1988.

Kresse, Kai. *Struggling with History: Islam and Cosmopolitanism in the Western Indian Ocean*. New York, NY: Columbia University Press, 2008.

Landau, Paul Stuart. *The Realm of the Word: Language, Gender, and Christianity in a Southern African Kingdom*. Portsmouth, NH; Cape Town; London: Heinemann; D. Philip; James Currey, 1995.

Larsson, Birgitta. 'Haya Women's Response to Revival'. In *The East African Revival: History and Legacies*, edited by Kevin Ward and Emma Wild-Wood, 119–28. Farnham: Ashgate Publishing Limited, 2016.

Lewis, Arthur Roland. *Twilight over Mlinga*. London: Universities' Mission to Central Africa, 1956.

Linden, Marcel van der. *Workers of the World: Essays toward a Global Labor History*. Leiden, Netherlands; Boston, MA: Brill, 2008.

———, and Magaly Rodríguez García. 'Introduction'. In *On Coerced Labor: Work and Compulsion after Chattel Slavery*, edited by Marcel van der Linden and Magaly Rodríguez García, 1–7. Studies in Global Social History. Leiden, Netherlands; Boston, MA: Brill, 2016.

Lindsay, Lisa A., and Stephan F. Miescher, eds. 'A "Man" in the Village Is a "Boy" in the Workplace: Colonial Racism, Worker Militance and Igbo Notions of Masculinity in the Nigerian Coal Industry, 1930–1945'. In *Men and Masculinities in Modern Africa*. Portsmouth, NH: Heinemann, 2003.

Lipschutz, Mark R., and R. Kent Rasmussen. *Dictionary of African Historical Biography*. Berkeley, CA: University of California Press, 1989.

Livingston, Julie. *Debility and the Moral Imagination in Botswana*. Bloomington, IN: Indiana University Press, 2005.

Lockwood, Matthew. *Fertility and Household Labour in Tanzania: Demography, Economy, and Society in Rufiji District, c.1870–1986*. Oxford: Clarendon Press, 1998.

Lonsdale, John. '"Listen While I Read": The Orality of Christian Literacy in the Young Kenyatta's Making of the Kikuyu'. In *Ethnicity in Africa: Roots, Meanings and Implications*, edited by Louise De La Gorgendière, Kenneth King, and Sarah Vaughan, 17–53. Edinburgh: Centre of African Studies, University of Edinburgh, 1996.

Lovejoy, Paul E. *Transformations in Slavery: A History of Slavery in Africa*. Cambridge: Cambridge University Press, 2011.

Mangényà, Erasto A. M. *Discipline and Tears: Reminiscences of an African Civil Servant on Colonial Tanganyika*. Dar es Salaam: Dar es Salaam University Press, 1984.

Maughan, Steven. 'Missionaries, Science and the Environment in Nineteenth-Century Africa'. In *The Imperial Horizons of British Protestant Missions, 1880-1914*, edited by Andrew N. Porter, 32–57. Michigan and Cambridge: Wm. B. Eerdmans Publishing, 2003.

Maughan, Steven S. *Mighty England Do Good: Culture, Faith, Empire, and World in the Foreign Missions of the Church of England, 1850-1915*. Cambridge: Wm. B. Eerdmans Publishing, 2014.

Maxwell, David. *Christians and Chiefs in Zimbabwe: A Social History of the Hwesa People c. 1870s–1990s*. Edinburgh: Edinburgh University Press, 1999.

———. *African Gifts of the Spirit: Pentecostalism and the Rise of a Zimbabwean Transnational Religious Movement*. Oxford: James Currey; Weaver Press, 2006.

McCracken, John. *Politics and Christianity in Malawi, 1875–1940: The Impact of the Livingstonia Mission in the Northern Province*. Cambridge: Cambridge University Press, 1977.

McMahon, Elisabeth 'Trafficking and Reenslavement: The Social Vulnerability of Women and Children in Nineteenth-Century East Africa'. In *Trafficking in Slavery's Wake: Law and the Experience of Women and Children in Africa*, edited by Benjamin N. Lawrance and Richard L. Roberts, 29–41. Athens, OH: Ohio University Press, 2012.

———. *Slavery and Emancipation in Islamic East Africa: From Honor to Respectability*. African Studies. Cambridge: Cambridge University Press, 2013.

Meillassoux, Claude. *Maidens, Meal and Money: Capitalism and the Domestic Community*. Cambridge: Cambridge University Press, 1981.

Meyer, Birgit. *Translating the Devil: Religion and Modernity among the Ewe in Ghana*. Edinburgh: Edinburgh University Press, 2000.

Middleton, John. *World Monarchies and Dynasties*. London; New York: Routledge, 2015.

Miers, Suzanne. *Britain and the Ending of the Slave Trade*. New York, NY: Africana Publishing Corporation, 1975.

Miers, Suzanne, and Igor Kopytoff, eds. *Slavery in Africa: Historical and Anthropological Perspectives*. Madison, WI: University of Wisconsin Press, 1977.

Molnos, Angéla. *Cultural Source Materials for Population Planning in East Africa: Innovations and Communication*. Nairobi: East African Publishing House, 1972.

Moodie, T. Dunbar, and Vivienne Ndatshe. *Going for Gold: Men, Mines, and Migration*. Berkeley, CA: University of California Press, 1994.

Moorhouse, Geoffrey. *The Missionaries*. London: Eyre Methuen, 1973.

Morton, Fred. *Children Of Ham: Freed Slaves And Fugitive Slaves On The Kenya Coast, 1873 To 1907*. New York: Routledge, 1990.

Musisi, Nakanyike B. 'Colonial and Missionary Education: Women and Domesticity in Uganda, 1900–1945'. In *African Encounters with Domesticity*, edited by Karen Tranberg Hansen, 172–94. New Brunswick, N.J: Rutgers University Press, 1992.

Nwulia, Moses D. E. *Britain and Slavery in East Africa*. Washington DC: Three Continents Press, 1975.

Palmer, Robin H., and Neil Parsons. *The Roots of Rural Poverty in Central and Southern Africa*. Berkeley, CA: University of California Press, 1977.

Pariser, Robyn Allyce. 'The Servant Problem: African Servants and the Making of European Domesticity in Colonial Tanganyika'. In *Towards a Global History of Domestic and Caregiving Workers*, 271–95. Leiden; Boston, MA: Brill, 2015.

Peel, John D. Y. *Aladura: A Religious Movement among the Yoruba*. London: Oxford University Press, 1968.

———. *Religious Encounter and the Making of the Yoruba*. Bloomington, IN: Indiana University Press, 2000.

———. 'Problems and Opportunities in an Anthropologist's Use of a Missionary Archive'. In *Missionary Encounters*, edited by Robert A. Bickers and Rosemary Seton. London: Routledge, 2013.

Pels, Peter. *A Politics of Presence: Contacts between Missionaries and Waluguru in Late Colonial Tanganyika*. Amsterdam, Netherlands: Harwood Academic Publishers, 1999.

Perham, Margery, ed. 'The Story of Amini Bin Saidi'. In *Ten Africans*, 2nd edn., 139–58. London: Faber, 1963.

Peterson, Derek R. *Creative Writing: Translation, Bookkeeping, and the Work of Imagination in Colonial Kenya*. Portsmouth, NH: Heinemann, 2004.

———. *Ethnic Patriotism and the East African Revival: A History of Dissent, c.1935–1972*. Cambridge: Cambridge University Press, 2012.

Porter, Andrew. *Religion Versus Empire? British Protestant Missionaries and Overseas Expansion, 1700–1914*. Manchester: Manchester University Press, 2004.

Porter, Andrew N. 'The Universities' Mission to Central Africa'. In *Missions, Nationalism and the End of Empire*, edited by Brian Stanley, 79–100. Michigan; Cambridge: Wm. B. Eerdmans Publishing, 2003.

Pouwels, Randall L. *Horn and Crescent: Cultural Change and Traditional Islam on the East African Coast, 800–1900*. Cambridge: Cambridge University Press, 2002.

Prestholdt, Jeremy. *Domesticating the World: African Consumerism and the Genealogies of Globalization*. Berkeley, CA: University of California Press, 2008.

Prichard, Andreana C. *Sisters in Spirit: Christianity, Affect, and Community Building in East Africa, 1860–1970*. East Lansing, MI: Michigan State University Press, 2017.

Ranger, T. O. 'Missionary Adaptation of African Religious Institutions: The Masasi Case'. In *The Historical Study of African Religion : With Special Reference to East and Central Africa*, edited by Isaria N. Kimambo and T. O. Ranger, 221–51, 1972.

———. 'The Mwana Lesa Movement of 1925'. In *Themes in the Christian History of Central Africa*, edited by Terence O. Ranger and John Weller. London: Heinemann, 1975.

Reed, Colin. *Pastors, Partners, and Paternalists: African Church Leaders and Western Missionaries in the Anglican Church in Kenya, 1850–1900*. Leiden: Brill, 1997.

Robbins, Joel. *Becoming Sinners: Christianity and Moral Torment in a Papua New Guinea Society*. Berkeley, CA; London: University of California Press, 2004.

Robinson, David. *Paths of Accommodation: Muslim Societies and French Colonial Authorities in Senegal and Mauritania, 1880–1920*. Athens, OH: Ohio University Press, 2000.

Robinson, Morgan. 'Binding Words: Student Biographical Narratives and Religious Conversion'. In *The Individual in African History: The Importance of Biography in African Historical Studies*, edited by Klaas van Walraven, 197–218. Leiden: Brill, 2020.

Rockel, Stephen J. *Carriers of Culture: Labor on the Road in Nineteenth-Century East Africa*. Portsmouth, NH: Heinemann, 2006.

Rossi, Benedetta. 'Introduction'. In *Reconfiguring Slavery: West African Trajectories*, edited by Benedetta Rossi, 1–18. Liverpool: Liverpool University Press, 2009.

———. *From Slavery to Aid*. Cambridge: Cambridge University Press, 2015.

———. 'What "Development" Does to Work'. *International Labor and Working-Class History* 92 (ed 2017): 7–23.

———. 'From Unfree Work to Working for Free: Labor, Aid, and Gender in the Nigerien Sahel, 1930–2000'. *International Labor and Working-Class History* 92 (ed 2017): 155–82.

Sandbrook, Richard, and Robin Cohen. *The Development of an African Working Class: Studies in Class Formation and Action*. Toronto: University of Toronto Press, 1975.

Sheriff, Abdul. *Slaves, Spices, & Ivory in Zanzibar: Integration of an East African Commercial Empire Into the World Economy, 1770–1873*. London: James Currey, 1987.

Smythe, Kathleen R. 'The Creation of a Catholic Fipa Society: Conversion in Nkonsi District, Ufipa'. In *East African Expressions of Christianity*, edited by Isaria N. Kimambo and T. Spear. Athens: James Currey, 1999.

Spear, T. 'Toward the History of African Christianity'. In *East African Expressions of Christianity*, edited by Isaria N. Kimambo and T. Spear. Oxford: James Currey Publishers, 1999.

Stilwell, Sean. *Slavery and Slaving in African History*. Cambridge: Cambridge University Press, 2014.

Strayer, Robert W. *Making of Mission Communities in East Africa: Anglicans and Africans in Colonial Kenya, 1875–1935*. London: Heinemann, 1978.

Sundkler, Bengt. *Christian Ministry in Africa*. London: S. C. M. Press, 1960.

———, and Christopher Steed. *A History of the Church in Africa*. Cambridge: Cambridge University Press, 2000.

Sunseri, Thaddeus Raymond. *Vilimani: Labor Migration and Rural Change in Early Colonial Tanzania*. Portsmouth, NH: Heinemann, 2002.

Temu, A. J. *British Protestant Missions*. London: Longman, 1972.

Thompson, T. Jack. *Light on Darkness? Missionary Photography of Africa in the Nineteenth and Early Twentieth Centuries*. Grand Rapids, MI.: Wm. B. Eerdmans Publishing, 2012.

Van Onselen, Charles. *Studies in the Social and Economic History of the Witwatersrand, 1886–1914*. Johannesburg: Ravan Press, 1982.

Vansina, Jan. *Oral Tradition as History*. London: James Currey, 1985.

Vansina, J.M. *Paths in the Rainforests: Toward a History of Political Tradition in Equatorial Africa*. Madison, WI: University of Wisconsin Press, 1990.

Waller, Richard. 'They Do the Dictating and We Must Submit: The Africa Inland Mission in Maasailand'. In *East African Expressions of Christianity*, edited by Isaria N. Kimambo and T. Spear. Oxford: James Currey Publishers, 1999.

Walls, Andrew F. *Missionary Movement in Christian History: Studies in the Transmission of Faith*. Maryknoll, NY: Orbis; T&T Clark, 1996.

Ward, Kevin. *A History of Global Anglicanism*. Cambridge: Cambridge University Press, 2006.

West, Michael O. *African Middle-Class Formation in Colonial Zimbabwe, 1890–1965*, 1990.

White, Landeg. *Magomero: Portrait of an African Village*. Cambridge: Cambridge University Press, 1987.
White, Luise. *Speaking with Vampires: Rumor and History in Colonial Africa*. Berkeley, CA: University of California Press, 2008.
———, S. Miescher, and D. W. Cohen, eds. *African Words, African Voices: Critical Practices in Oral History*. Bloomington, IN: Indiana University Press, 2001.
Wilson, George Herbert. *The History of the Universities' Mission to Central Africa*. London: Universities' Mission to Central Africa, 1936.
Wilson, Godfrey. *An Essay on the Economics of Detribalisation in Nothern Rhodesia*. Livingstone, Northern Rhodesia: Rhodes Livingstone Institute, 1942.
Wilson, Godfrey, and Monica Hunter Wilson. *The Analysis of Social Change: Based on Observations in Central Africa*. Cambridge: CUP Archive, 1945.
Zabus, Chantal. *Out in Africa: Same-Sex Desire in Sub-Saharan Literatures & Cultures*. Oxford: James Currey, 2013.
Zürcher, Erik-Jan, ed. *Fighting for a Living: A Comparative History of Military Labour 1500–2000*. Amsterdam: Amsterdam University Press, 2015.

Published articles

Allen, James de Vere. 'Swahili Culture and the Nature of East Coast Settlement'. *The International Journal of African Historical Studies*, 14, no. 2 (1981): 306–34. doi:10.2307/218047.
Allen, Julia. 'Slavery, Colonialism and the Pursuit of Community Life: Anglican Mission Education in Zanzibar and Northern Rhodesia 1864–1940'. *History of Education*, 37, no. 2 (1 March 2008): 207–26. doi:10.1080/00467600701585682.
Atkins, Keletso E. 'Origins of the Amawasha: The Zulu Washermen's Guild in Natal, 1850–1910'. *The Journal of African History*, 27, no. 1 (1 January 1986): 41–57.
Austin, Gareth. 'Cash Crops and Freedom: Export Agriculture and the Decline of Slavery in Colonial West Africa'. *International Review of Social History*, 54, no. 1 (April 2009): 1–37.
Bayart, Jean-Francois. 'African in the World: A History of Extraversion'. *African Affairs*, 99, no. 395 (2000): 217.
Becker, Felicitas. 'Obscuring and Revealing: Muslim Engagement with Volunteering and the Aid Sector in Tanzania'. *African Studies Review*. 58, no. 02 (September 2015): 111–33.

Becker, Felicitas and Joel Cabrita. 'Introduction: Performing Citizenship and Enacting Exclusion on Africa's Indian Ocean Littoral'. *The Journal of African History*, 55, no. 02 (2014): 161–71.

Beech, Mervyn W. H. 'Slavery on the East Coast of Africa'. *African Affairs*, 15, no. LVIII (1916): 145–49.

Beidelman, Thomas O. 'Social Theory and the Study of Christian Missions in Africa'. *Africa: Journal of the International African Institute*. 44, no. 3 (1974): 235–49. doi:10.2307/1158391.

Bolt, Maxim. 'Transcending the Economic'. *Africa*. 84, no. 01 (February 2014): 142–45.

Cooper, Frederick. 'The Problem of Slavery in African Studies'. *The Journal of African History*, 20, no. 1 (1 January 1979): 103–25.

Cory, H. 'Jando. Part I: The Constitution and Organization of the Jando'. *The Journal of the Royal Anthropological Institute of Great Britain and Ireland*, 77, no. 2 (1947): 159–68. doi:10.2307/2844480.

Dale, Godfrey. 'An Account of the Principal Customs and Habits of the Natives Inhabiting the Bondei Country, Compiled Mainly for the Use of European Missionaries in the Country'. *The Journal of the Anthropological Institute of Great Britain and Ireland*, 25 (1 January 1896): 181–239.

Decker, Corrie R. 'Biology, Islam and The Science of Sex Education in Colonial Zanzibar'. *Past & Present*, 222, no. 1 (13 December 2013): 215–47.

Eastman, Carol. 'Service, "Slavery" (Utumwa) and Swahili Social Reality'. *AAP*, no. 37 (1994): 87–107.

Elbourne, Elizabeth. 'Word Made Flesh: Christianity, Modernity, and Cultural Colonialism in the Work of Jean and John Comaroff'. *The American Historical Review*, 108, no. 2 (2003): 435–59.

Etherington, Norman. 'Missionaries and the Intellectual History of Africa: A Historical Survey'. *Itinerario*, 7, no. 02 (July 1983): 116–143. doi:10.1017/S0165115300024256.

Fair, Laura. 'Dressing up: Clothing, Class and Gender in Post-Abolition Zanzibar'. *The Journal of African History*, 39, no. 1 (1 January 1998): 63–94.

Ferguson, James. 'Declarations of Dependence: Labour, Personhood, and Welfare in Southern Africa'. *The Journal of the Royal Anthropological Institute*, 19, no. 2 (1 June 2013): 223–42.

Githige, R. M. 'The Issue of Slavery: Relations between the CMS and the State on the East African Coast Prior to 1895'. *Journal of Religion in Africa*, 16, no. 3 (1986): 209–25.

Glassman, Jonathon. 'The Bondsman's New Clothes: The Contradictory Consciousness of Slave Resistance on the Swahili Coast'. *The Journal of African History*, 32, no. 2 (1 January 1991): 277–312.

Guyer, Jane I. 'Wealth in People and Self-Realization in Equatorial Africa'. *Man*, 28, no. 2 (1 June 1993): 243–65. doi:10.2307/2803412.

Horton, Robin. 'Ritual Man in Africa'. *Africa*, 34, no. 02 (April 1964): 85–104. doi:10.2307/1157900.

Hunter, Emma. 'Voluntarism, Virtuous Citizenship, and Nation-Building in Late Colonial and Early Postcolonial Tanzania'. *African Studies Review*, 58, no. 02 (September 2015): 43–61. doi:10.1017/asr.2015.37.

Leonardi, Cherry. 'Laying the First Course of Stones: Building the London Missionary Society Church in Madagascar, 1862–1895'. *The International Journal of African Historical Studies*, 36, no. 3 (2003): 607–33. doi:10.2307/3559436.

Liebst, Michelle. 'African Workers and the Universities' Mission to Central Africa in Zanzibar, 1864–1900'. *Journal of Eastern African Studies*, 8, no. 3 (3 July 2014): 366–81. doi:10.1080/17531055.2014.922279.

Lonsdale, John. 'Agency in Tight Corners: Narrative and Initiative in African History'. *Journal of African Cultural Studies*,13, no. 1 (1 June 2000): 5. doi:10.1080/713674303.

Lord, Jack. 'Child Labor in the Gold Coast: The Economics of Work, Education, and the Family in Late-Colonial African Childhoods, C. 1940-57'. *Journal of the History of Childhood and Youth*, 4, no. 1 (2011): 86.

Manji, Firoze, and Carl O'Coill. 'The Missionary Position: NGOs and Development in Africa'. *International Affairs (Royal Institute of International Affairs 1944–)* 78, no. 3 (2002): 567–83.

Maxwell, David. 'Writing the History of African Christianity: Reflections of an Editor'. *Journal of Religion in Africa* 36, no. 3/4 (2006): 379–99.

———. 'Photography and the Religious Encounter: Ambiguity and Aesthetics in Missionary Representations of the Luba of South East Belgian Congo'. *Comparative Studies in Society and History*, 53, no. 1 (January 2011): 38–74.

———. 'Freed Slaves, Missionaries, and Respectability: The Expansion of the Christian Frontier from Angola to Belgian Congo'. *Journal of African History*, 54, no. 1 (2013): 79–102.

McCracken, John. 'Underdevelopment in Malawi: The Missionary Contribution'. *African Affairs*, 76, no. 303 (1977): 195–209.

McMahon, Elisabeth. '"A Solitary Tree Builds Not": Heshima, Community, and Shifting Identity in Postemancipation Pemba Island'. *The International Journal of African Historical Studies*, 39, no. 2 (1 January 2006): 197–219.

Merry, Sally Engle. 'Hegemony and Culture in Historical Anthropology: A Review Essay on Jean and John L. Comaroff's Of Revelation and Revolution'. *The American Historical Review*, 108, no. 2 (1 April 2003): 460–70.

Okia, Opolot. 'The Windmill of Slavery: The British and Foreign Antislavery Society and Bonded Labor in East Africa'. *The Middle Ground Journal*, 3 (2011): 1–35.

Ott, Alice T. 'The "Faithful Deacon" and the "Good Layman": The First Converts of the UMCA and Their Responses to Mission Christianity'. *Studies in World Christianity*, 24, no. 2 (6 July 2018): 140. doi.org/10.3366/swc.2018.0217.

Peel, John D. Y. '"For Who Hath Despised the Day of Small Things?" Missionary Narratives and Historical Anthropology'. *Comparative Studies in Society and History*, 37, no. 3 (1995): 581–607.

———. 'Morality Plays: Marriage, Church Courts, and Colonial Agency in Central Tanganyika, Ca. 1876–1928'. *The American Historical Review*. 111, no. 4 (1 October 2006): 983–1010.

Porter, Andrew. '"Cultural Imperialism" and Protestant Missionary Enterprise, 1780–1914'. *The Journal of Imperial and Commonwealth History*, 25, no. 3 (1 September 1997): 367.

Ranger, Terence O. 'Godly Medicine: The Ambiguities of Medical Mission in Southeast Tanzania, 1900–1945'. *Social Science & Medicine. Part B: Medical Anthropology*, Special Issue: Causality and Classification in African Medicine and Health, 15, no. 3 (July 1981): 261–77. doi.org/10.1016/0160-7987(81)90052-1.

Ranger, Terence. 'Myth and Legend in Urban Oral Memory: Bulawayo, 1930–60'. *Journal of Postcolonial Writing*, 44, no. 1 (1 March 2008): 77–88.

Robinson, Morgan. 'Cutting Pice and Running Away: Discipline, Education and Choice at the UMCA Boys' Industrial House, Zanzibar, 1901–1905'. *Southern African Review of Education with Education with Production*, 19, no. 2 (2013): 9–24.

Rockel, Stephen. 'Wage Labor and the Culture of Porterage in Nineteenth Century Tanzania: The Central Caravan Routes'. *Comparative Studies of South Asia, Africa and the Middle East*, 15, no. 2 (1 August 1995): 14–24.

Rockel, Stephen J. 'Slavery and Freedom in Nineteenth Century East Africa: The Case of Waungwana Caravan Porters'. *African Studies*, 68, no. 1 (1 April 2009): 87–109. doi:10.1080/00020180902827464.

Rossi, Benedetta. 'African Post-Slavery: A History of the Future'. *The International Journal of African Historical Studies*, 48, no. 2 (1 May 2015): 303.

———. 'Dependence, Unfreedom and Slavery in Africa: Towards an Integrated Analysis'. *Africa: The Journal of the International African Institute*, 86, no. 3 (2016): 571–90.

———. 'From Unfree Work to Working for Free: Labor, Aid, and Gender in the Nigerien Sahel, 1930–2000'. *International Labor and Working-Class History*, 92 (ed 2017): 155–82.

———. 'What "Development" Does to Work'. *International Labor and Working-Class History* 92 (ed 2017): 7–23.

Schildkrout, Enid. 'Recommended Readings Age and Gender in Hausa Society Socio-Economic Roles of Children in Urban Kano'. *Childhood*, 9, no. 3 (1 August 2002): 342–68. doi:10.1177/0907568202009003605.

Shane Doyle. '"The Child of Death": Personal Names and Parental Attitudes towards Mortality in Nuyoro, Western Uganda, 1900–2005'. *The Journal of African History*, 49, no. 3 (2008): 361–82.

Stambach, Amy. 'Education, Religion, and Anthropology in Africa'. *Annual Review of Anthropology*, 39, no. 1 (2010): 361–79. doi:10.1146/annurev.anthro.012809.105002.

———, and Aikande C. Kwayu. 'Take the Gift of My Child and Return Something to Me: On Children, Chagga Trust, and a New American Evangelical Orphanage on Mount Kilimanjaro'. *Journal of Religion in Africa*, 43, no. 4 (1 January 2013): 379–95. doi:10.1163/15700666-12341263.

Stoner-Eby, Anne Marie. 'African Clergy, Bishop Lucas and the Christianizing of Local Initiation Rites: Revisiting "The Masasi Case"'. *Journal of Religion in Africa*, 38, no. 2 (1 January 2008): 171–208. doi:10.2307/27594460.

White, Bob W. 'Talk about School: Education and the Colonial Project in French and British Africa, (1860–1960)'. *Comparative Education*, 32, no. 1 (1996): 9–25.

Willis, Justin. '"And So They Called a Kiva": Histories of a War'. *Azania: Journal of the British Institute in Eastern Africa*, 25, no. 1 (1990): 79–85.

———. 'The Makings of a Tribe: Bondei Identities and Histories'. *The Journal of African History*, 33, no. 2 (1 January 1992): 191–208. doi:10.2307/182998.

———. 'The Administration of Bonde, 1920–60: A Study of the Implementation of Indirect Rule in Tanganyika'. *African Affairs*, 92, no. 366 (1 January 1993): 53–67. doi:10.2307/723096.

———. 'The Nature of a Mission Community: The Universities' Mission to Central Africa in Bonde'. *Past & Present*, no. 140 (1 August 1993): 127–54.

———, and Suzanne Miers. 'Becoming a Child of the House: Incorporation, Authority and Resistance in Giryama Society'. *The Journal of African History*, 38, no. 3 (1997): 479–95.

Unpublished dissertations

Brown, Carolyn A. 'A History of the Development of Workers' Consciousness of the Coal Miners at Enugu Government Colliery, Nigeria, 1914–1950'. PhD, Columbia University, 1985.

Cadogan, Thomas Edward. 'Students and Schools in the Southern Highlands: Education in Tanzania, 1890s to the Present'. PhD, School of Oriental and African Studies, 2006.

Christiansen, Catrine. 'Development by Churches, Development of Churches: Institutional Trajectories in Rural Uganda'. PhD, Faculty of Social Sciences, University of Copenhagen, 2010.

Longair, Sarah. '"A Gracious Temple of Learning": The Museum and Colonial Culture in Zanzibar, 1900–1945'. PhD, Department of History, Classics and Archaeology, Birkbeck College, University of London, 2012.

Mndolwa, William Fabian. 'From Anglicanism To African Socialism: The Anglican Church And Ujamaa In Tanzania 1955–2005'. PhD, School of Religion, Philosophy & Classics, Kwa Zulu-Natal, n.d.

Prichard, Andreana. 'African Christian Women and the Emergence of Nationalist Subjectivities in Tanzania, 1860–1960s'. PhD, Northwestern University, 2011.

Stoner-Eby, Anne-Marie. 'African Leaders Engage Mission Christianity: Anglicans in Tanzania, 1876–1926'. PhD, University of Pennsylvania, 2003.

Conference and workshop papers

Becker, Felicitas. 'Transformations of Inequality in a Former Slave Plantation Settlement: Mingoyo, Tanzania'. In *Islam and Memories of Slavery*. New College, University of Toronto, 2009.

Brennan, James R. 'First-Comers, Chiefs and Republicans: Political Legitimacy and the Shadow of Servitude among the "Indigenous" People of Dar Es Salaam, 1890–1968'. In *Post-Slavery Societies in East Africa*. Cambridge, 2014.

Deslaurier, Christine. '"Boys" in Bujumbura (Burundi), or How to Domesticate Politics'. In *Domestic Workers in Africa (19th–21th Centuries). Historical and Socio-Anthropological Perspectives*. Paris, 2015.

Hepburn, Sacha. 'Making Class at Home: Domestic Service and Class Formation in Postcolonial Zambia'. At Domestic Workers in Africa (19th-21th Centuries). Historical and Socio-Anthropo logical Perspectives. European Conference for African Studies. La Sorbonne, Paris, 2015.

Jedwab, Remi, Felix Meier zu Selhausen and Alexander Moradi. 'The Economics of Missionary Expansion: Evidence from Africa and Implications for Development'. Working Paper Series 1019, Department of Economics, University of Sussex Business School, 5 July 2018

Stoner-Eby, Anne-Marie. 'Not Merely Cooks: The Missionary Wives of the African Leadership of the Universities' Mission to Central Africa, 1880–1940'. London: Institute of Commonwealth Studies, University of London, 1999.

Zöller, Katharina. '"Manyema Hatutoki Boi": Manyema Group Identification and the Issue of Slavery in Urban Tanganyika'. In *Post-Slavery Societies in East Africa*. University of Cambridge, 2014.

Unpublished notes

Sehoza, Joel. 'Samuel Sehoza'. Notes. Magila, 2012.

Websites

'Terence Ranger: Life as Historiography'. *History Workshop Online*, 16 July 2011. http://www.historyworkshop.org.uk/terence-ranger-life-as-historiography/, accessed 1 April 2019.

Index

abolition (of slavery)   77, 79, 86, 167
African Christians   1, 2, 9, 10, 22, 30, 120, 122, 125, 137, 171, 189
African missionaries   80, 137
Africans   1, 2, 7, 20, 21, 48, 67, 107, 179, 189
  and colonialism   24, 90, 158
  and Europeans   15, 18, 171, 172
  ex-slaves   87, 102, 105, 106
  and missionaries   9, 12, 22, 23, 31, 34, 56, 103, 156, 176, 180
  and missions   6, 25, 69, 77, 162, 188, 189
African Tidings   156
agriculture   2, 20, 21, 79, 95, 96, 97, 99, 119, 128, 133, 137, 175, 176, 187 *see also* plantations
Ajawa people   38
Alington, Charles Argentine   36
Allen, James de Vere   25
Allen, May   127, 161
Amwitamno, Aaron   153
Arabocentric   27, 180, 189
Arabs   25, 75, 181
Austin, Gareth   2

Bagamoyo, Tanzania   4, 81
Bang, Anne   26
baptism   120
Basil, Fundi   96
Becker, Felicitas   143
Beidelman, Thomas   6
Bissell, William   90, 124
boi (boy)   7, 151, 153, 155, 159, 167, 170, 172, 175, 177, 178, 180, 181

Bolt, Maxim   157
Bonde nation   40, 43, 49
Bondei people   13, 14, 35, 36, 40–43, 46, 47, 48, 50, 55, 58, 60, 61, 63 72, 117
British Baptist Missionary Society   7, 148
British colonial rule   2, 10, 11, 12, 18, 24, 31, 84, 123, 171, 177, 185, 186
British government   79, 86, 93
British influence   46, 90, 158, 184
British missionaries   20
British navy   76, 92, 97, 118, 128
Brown, Carolyn   150, 159
Burundi   150

Capel, Forbes   127, 132
capitalism   23
Catholic   19, 20, 81
Central Africa   17
child labour   14, 148
Christianisation   19
Christian labour   76, 78, 92, 93
Christians   47, 48, 53, 77, 89, 103, 113, 117, 118, 120, 122–5, 131, 139, 141, 165, 180, 183, 187
Christian slaves   79
Church Missionary Society (CMS)   4, 6, 20, 77
clergy   6, 8, 10, 17, 18, 19, 20, 81, 91, 92, 94, 96, 112, 136, 158
colonial period   2, 16, 171, 177, 185 *see also* pre-colonial period
colonialism   1, 10, 12, 18, 23, 24, 31, 34, 157, 158, 177, 183, 184, 186, 187, 188
Comaroff, Jean   22, 158

Comaroff, John   22, 158
commoners   37, 44, 48, 49, 54, 55, 57, 58, 63, 64, 73
Congo   129, 148
cooking   143, 155, 156, 172, 174
Cooper, Barbara   6, 148
Cooper, Frederick   2, 11
Cust, Robert Needham   80, 81, 82

Dale, Godfrey   17, 95, 112, 113, 116, 123, 164
Deslaurier, Christine   150
developmentalism   2, 3
Digo people   61, 63, 68, 69
discipline   39, 41, 52, 81, 82, 88, 93, 94, 102, 106, 130, 161, 162, 168
domesticity   30, 150, 154, 157, 158, 159, 161, 171, 182, 184
domestic labour   6, 7, 132, 134, 141, 152, 156, 157, 163
domestic servants   83, 132, 161, 168, 174, 181, 189
    boys   147, 154, 155, 162
    and Europeans   173, 179, 180
    female   129, 133, 141, 142
    and missionaries   160, 163, 164, 167, 185
    mission-educated   148, 170, 171, 175, 182
domestic service   30, 132, 133, 134, 141, 142, 185, 189

East Africa   1, 27, 31, 76, 137, 150, 178
Eastman, Carol   153, 154, 177
economic depression   10
emancipation   4, 19, 30, 99, 100, 108, 123
England   20, 162
English   19, 20, 22, 130, 142, 162, 184
    language   5, 129, 147, 150, 185
    people   31, 45, 78, 84, 119, 167
Europe   137, 150, 158
European missionaries   31, 189
Europeans   20, 23, 28, 75, 91, 147, 162, 172, 177, 180, 181
    and domestic service   152, 157, 170, 171, 179
    and female workers   141, 142, 144
    and missionaries   1, 21, 48
    and students   163, 165, 168
    working for   76, 83, 95, 99, 175
ex-slaves   1, 4, 10, 12, 86, 99, 102, 104, 112, 117, 123, 129, 132, 136, 157, 166, 178
    and Christianity   87, 92, 115, 120, 122
    education of   29, 119, 186
    of Mbweni shamba   88, 89, 91, 94, 95, 98, 100
    and missionaries   8, 28, 103, 105, 106, 108, 109, 124, 125
    of Pemba   96, 97, 111
    see also freed slaves

Fair, Laura   90, 106, 116, 123, 124
famine   47, 49, 62, 165
Farler, John Prediger   36, 37, 40, 41–6, 56, 57, 60, 61, 66, 83, 127, 165, 170
    and Bondei people   47, 48, 49, 50
    and chiefs   51, 54, 55, 58, 62, 63, 72
    and lime burning   59, 67, 68
    and Umba people   64, 65, 69, 70, 71
Feierman, Steven   35, 71, 73
female missionaries   129, 138, 144, 161, 184
firearms   35, 43, 44, 45, 46, 55, 58 *see also* guns
First World War   18, 31, 186
Fixsen, Christopher   16, 17
freed slaves   75, 77, 79, 81, 82, 91–4, 103, 186
free wage labour   3, 8, 78, 79
free wage workers   10, 104
Frere, Bartle   20
Freund, Bill   157
Frewer, Cyril C.   87, 92, 95, 96, 97, 103, 105, 108, 119, 176, 178

Geldart, Herbert   41, 53, 112, 147

German colonial rule 10, 15, 16, 18, 24, 34, 177, 184, 188
Germans 18, 19
Ghana 2
Gikuyu people 4, 5
Glassman, Jonathon 12, 18, 28, 107, 152
God 9, 55, 78, 79
government schools 1, 16
Gray, Sir John Milner 24, 177
Gregory, Reverend Francis Ambrose 80
Guild of All Saints 141
gunpowder 33, 45, 46, 50, 63, 69, 72
guns 43, 46, 184

Hansen, Karen 158, 168
Hardinge, Sir Arthur Henry 120
heshima (respectability) 105, 106 125, 155
Hine, John 77, 127
Holy Ghost Fathers 4
humanitarianism 3
Hunter, Emma 3
Hunt, Nancy Rose 7, 148, 151, 157

Iliffe, John 43, 48, 109, 150
Imperial British East Africa Company 76
Indian Ocean 14, 188
industrialization 20, 78
Islam 6, 12, 15, 18, 26, 43, 115, 122, 180, 189 *see also* Muslims

Joelson, Stephen 178, 179, 181
Johnson, William 104, 130
Johnston, Keith 45
Jones-Bateman, Percy L. 120, 122, 170

Kalulu 150
Kayamba, Hugh Peter 165
Key, Canon Sir John 46
Kibanga (son of King Kimweri) 36, 45, 49, 50, 52, 55, 60, 61, 67, 69
Kifungiwe, Michael 50, 51, 52, 53, 61
Kilindi clan 35, 36, 40, 43, 48, 49, 50, 51, 55, 165

Kinyashi 49 n.84
Kirk, John 46, 47, 55, 80, 108
Kiungani Boys' School 19, 29, 97, 101, 104, 109, 111–7, 119, 120, 132, 155, 164, 170
Kiva Rebellion 13, 35, 51, 72
Kopytoff, Igor 107
Koran 123
Korogwe village 156

Lentz, Oskar 170
lime-burning 29, 33, 34, 41, 56–61, 63, 67, 68, 69, 70–3
Limo, Blandina (wife of Rev. Limo) 140
Limo, Rev. Petro 40, 112, 113, 184, 189
Livingstone, David 83, 85, 150
Lockwood, Matthew 152

Mabruki, Francis (husband of Kate) 137
Mabruki, Kate 137, 138, 139, 144 n.88
Mabruki, Sheldon 117
MacKenzie, Charles Frederick (bishop of Central Africa) 38
Madan, Arthur 115
Magila Central School 117
Magila chiefs 57, 58, 59, 64, 65, 72
Magila diocese 13, 18
Magila mission 34, 42, 43, 48, 69, 74, 134, 153, 184–7
Magila people 60, 71
Magila region 11, 12, 15, 19, 33, 36, 60, 137
Magomero village 38
Majaliwa, Rev. Cecil 102, 118
maliwali (governors) 11
Mallender, George William 138, 181
Mambo Sasa market 37
Manyema people 17, 155
mapepo (spirits) 63, 114
Maples, Chauncy 81, 82
Maria Theresa Dollar (MTD) 12
Masasi diocese 18
Masasi mission 34, 38, 81, 82, 184
Maxwell, David 129
'Mbweni girls' 30, 89, 127

Mbweni Girls' School   128, 129, 130, 132, 133, 186
Mbweni mission   86, 128
Mbweni shamba   75, 86, 88, 92, 96, 100, 112, 113, 118, 127, 164
  ex-slaves of   91, 94, 95, 97, 111, 117, 186
  and 'Mbweni girls'   129, 131, 135
  and missionaries   87, 98, 99
Mbweni, Zanzibar   69, 81, 167
McCracken, John   5
McMahon, Elizabeth   97, 105, 116
Mfunte village   61, 70
Miers, Suzanne   107
migrant labour   20, 21, 97
migrants   15, 17, 153
Mills, Dora   139, 161, 162
Mission Life   80
mission schools   2, 16, 23, 30, 34, 40, 101, 132, 165, 166, 167
Mkunazini mission station   89, 90, 111, 138, 145
Mkuzi village   33, 61, 130, 163
Modern History of Tanganyika (Iliffe)   43
modernity   4, 23, 25, 27, 30, 78, 115, 189
modernization   159
Mombasa, Kenya   4, 172
Moodie, T. Dunbar   159
Moses (prophet)   79
Mrs. Beeton's Cookery-book   156
Msalabani village   12, 17, 33, 57, 70, 139
mshenzi (uncivilised)   28
mtumwa (slave)   108, 153
Muslims   6, 11, 20, 25, 26, 30, 56, 77, 79, 108, 109, 118, 122–4, 137, 140, 141, 144, 164, 180, 181
Muslim Sahel   148
Mwelekwanyuma (chief of Kilole)   165
mwungwana (urban)   25, 26, 27, 28, 56, 154, 179

Ndume village   62
Ng'ambo mission station   89, 90, 120, 122
Niger   3

nyika (land)   17, 33, 47, 59, 63, 64, 67, 69, 70, 71
Nyumbai, Kimweri ya (king of Kilindi clan)   35, 36, 51, 165

Oman   11
Omani Sultanate   11, 19
Ott, Alice   117
Oxford and Cambridge Universities' Mission to Central Africa   19

Pangani district   15, 18, 46, 47, 48, 61, 62
Pariser, Robyn   158
Paul, Saint (the apostle)   78, 79
Pearse, Francis Eling   28
Peel, John   4, 23, 24
Pels, Peter   23
Pemba Island   66, 96, 97, 105, 111
Peterson, Derek   4
plantations   11, 14, 15, 16, 25, 90, 94, 96, 97, 105, 108, 141
polygamy   51, 52, 54
Pouwels, Randall   152
power-brokers   26, 29, 36, 40, 43–5, 48, 50, 52, 53, 55, 56, 58, 59, 67, 71–3
precolonial period   10, 21, 39, 40, 42, 44, 74, 188
Prestholdt, Jeremy   108
Prichard, Andreana   5, 104 n.14, 128
priests   2, 8, 10, 20, 40, 91, 94, 104, 112, 117, 156, 182, 184, 187
prostitution   *see* sex work

Ramadhani, John (bishop of Zanzibar)   117
Rockel, Stephen   84, 99
Rossi, Benedetta   3, 107, 108

Saad, Siti Binti   106
Said, Amin bin   173
Said, Sultan Barghash bin   11, 46, 47, 60
Sayers, Gerald   173
Segao (slave dealer)   57, 58, 63, 66, 69
Sehiza (Umba chief)   62, 63
Sekehufya (Umba chief)   50, 51

Semboja (Kilindi chief)   35, 36, 43, 49, 50
Semnkai, Henry   40, 50, 53, 54, 57, 61, 63, 67, 184
sex work   100, 144, 176
Shafi sect   25
Shambaai civil war   15
Shambaai kingdom   13, 16, 35, 37, 48, 50, 73
shamba (farm)   93, 94
shenzi (rebuke)   27, 28, 138
Sipindu, Austini   50, 54, 57, 63
Siyenu, Hilda   135, 136
slave dealers   47, 66
slave labour   29, 76, 77, 105
Slave Market Memorial Church   29, 75
slave owners   11, 76, 84, 85, 108
slavery   2, 3, 4, 10, 26, 29, 78, 85, 86, 153, 170, 177
    anti-   8, 51, 75, 76, 83, 84, 104, 105, 125
    and missionaries   82, 93, 100
    morality of   29, 80, 82, 100
    and UMCA   77, 79, 80
slaves   1, 9, 11, 35, 40, 41, 47, 79, 93, 107, 138, 152, 159, 181
    and chiefs   51–4
    employment of   76, 77, 80–5, 100
    and missionaries   10, 38, 68, 185
slave trade   11, 36, 46, 76, 80
slave-traders   33, 36, 47
Smythies, Charles Alan (bishop of Central Africa)   8, 52, 66, 127, 144, 167
social mobility   7, 22, 23, 28, 29, 30, 98, 118, 125, 143, 166, 175, 186
Society for the Propagation of the Gospel (SPG)   80, 81
South Africa   170
Stanley, Henry Morton   150
Steere, Edward (bishop of Central Africa)   20, 22, 25, 27, 39, 45, 46, 62, 67, 77, 80, 109, 119, 136, 160, 177
    and John Farler   41, 42, 57, 60, 65
    and slaves   75, 76, 79, 81, 82

St. Katherine's Home for Women   141, 142
St. Mary's Girls School   128 *see also* Mbweni Girls' School
St. Monica school   130
Stoner-Eby, Anne Marie   34, 74
Sub-Saharan Africa   185
Sudan Interior Mission   6
Swahili   17, 18, 25–8, 48, 98, 106, 153, 154, 156, 167, 180, 183
Swedi, Rev. John   113, 118
synod   91

Tanganyika   1, 4, 10, 12, 15, 18, 175, 177, 179, 185
Tanganyikans   28, 48
Tanga, Tanzania   13, 15, 17, 18
Tanzanian Christians   26
teachers   2, 6, 8, 16–9, 27, 31, 91, 94, 102, 104, 112, 117, 136, 151, 155, 158, 161–4, 182–4, 187
Thackeray, Caroline   92, 129, 130–3, 136, 138, 139, 140, 143, 145, 167
Tozer, Helen (sister of Bishop Tozer)   129
Tozer, William George (bishop of Central Africa)   112, 117

uboi (domestic service)   151–5, 162, 176, 178, 181, 182
Ukaguru, Tanzania   6
Umba people   57, 58, 59, 61–5, 67–71
Umba village   53, 54, 57, 63, 147
Universities' Mission to Central Africa (UMCA)   2, 11, 18, 22, 24, 31, 39, 44, 57, 67, 72, 78, 83, 92, 116, 123, 167
    and ex-slaves   75, 93, 143
    and John Farler   41, 43, 54
    in Magila   29, 33, 34, 184, 188
    missionaries   8, 20, 21, 23, 37, 38, 85, 94, 108, 117, 160, 175
    schools   30, 109, 132
    and slaves   62, 77, 80
    studies of   4, 5, 10
    in Zanzibar   12, 55, 86, 188
unyago (female initiation)   140

Up From Slavery (Washington)   166
urban   20, 26, 90, 102, 103, 114, 119, 123, 154, 158
   life   30, 77, 88, 111, 124
   Zanzibar   83, 96, 106, 170
urbanisation   78
Usambara mountains   15, 17, 49
ustaarabu (Arabness)   25, 26, 153
utumwa (slavery)   152, 153, 154, 155
uungwana (civilization)   25, 26, 179

van Onselen, Charles   170
vibarua (day labourer)   84, 85
vitumbua (fried rice cake)   134
Vuga kingdom   35, 36, 37, 45

Wabondei people   36, 65
Wadigo (slave traders)   33, 36, 37, 46
wage labour   2, 6, 15, 22, 44, 70, 76, 78, 84, 95, 143, 154, 158
Wakilindi (slave traders)   37
Wakumba   57 *see also* Umba people
wali (governor)   37, 46, 47, 48, 62
Waller, Horace   84
Ward, Gertrude   160
Washington, Booker T.   166

Waswahili (Swahili person)   26, 89
watumwa (released slaves)   111, 152, 153
wazungu (European)   46, 65, 67, 152
Webb, R.   156
wenyeji (indiginous)   104, 111
West, Michael   158
Weston, Frank   22, 23, 24, 101, 102, 103, 120, 131, 176
Willis, Justin   41, 40, 44, 48, 58, 165
Wilson, George Herbert   41, 54, 64
Wilson, H. A. B.   53
Woodward, Herbert Willoughby   40, 53, 54, 61, 62, 70, 71, 115, 160, 164, 168, 169

Yao people   61, 104
Yoruba people   4, 5
Younghusband, Ethel   178

Zanzibar   2, 10, 11, 12, 19, 123
Zanzibar missions   30, 79, 111, 139, 153, 172
Zanzibar Town   11, 89, 130, 142, 180, 181
Zigua people   13, 14, 15

Previously published titles in the series

Violent Conversion: Brazilian Pentecostalism and Urban Women in Mozambique, Linda Van de Kamp (2016)

Beyond Religious Tolerance: Muslim, Christian & Traditionalist Encounters in an African Town, edited by Insa Nolte, Olukoya Ogen and Rebecca Jones (2017)

Faith, Power and Family: Christianity and Social Change in French Cameroon, Charlotte Walker-Said (2018)

Contesting Catholics: Benedicto Kiwanuka and the Birth of Postcolonial Uganda, Jonathon L. Earle and J. J. Carney (2021)

Islamic Scholarship in Africa: New Directions and Global Contexts, edited by Ousmane Oumar Kane (2021)

From Rebels to Rulers: Writing Legitimacy in the Early Sokoto State, Paul Naylor (2021)

Sacred Queer Stories: Ugandan LGBTQ+ Refugee Lives and the Bible, Adriaan Van Klinken and Johanna Stiebert, with Sebyala Brian and Fredrick Hudson (2021)

Labour & Christianity in the Mission: African Workers in Tanganyika and Zanzibar, 1864–1926, Michelle Liebst (2021)

The Genocide against the Tutsi, and the Rwandan Churches: Between Grief and Denial, Philippe Denis (2022)

Competing Catholicisms: The Jesuits, the Vatican & the Making of Postcolonial French Africa, Jean Luc Enyegue, SJ (2022)

Islam in Uganda: The Muslim Minority, Nationalism & Political Power, Joseph Kasule (2022)

Spiritual Contestations – The Violence of Peace in South Sudan, Naomi Ruth Pendle (2023)

www.ingramcontent.com/pod-product-compliance
Lightning Source LLC
Chambersburg PA
CBHW070801230426
43665CB00017B/2452